Two Centuries of Overseas Trading

Two Centuries of Overseas Trading

The Origins and Growth of the Inchcape Group

Stephanie Jones

Foreword by Sir David Orr

Published by
PALGRAVE MACMILLAN
Houndmills, Basingstoke, Hampshire RG21 6XS and
175 Fifth Avenue, New York, N. Y. 10010
Companies and representatives throughout the world

PALGRAVE MACMILLAN is the global academic imprint of the Palgrave
Macmillan division of St. Martin's Press, LLC and of Palgrave Macmillan Ltd.
Macmillan® is a registered trademark in the United States, United Kingdom
and other countries. Palgrave is a registered trademark in the European
Union and other countries.

ISBN 0–333–37172–0

This book is printed on paper suitable for recycling and made from fully
managed and sustained forest sources.

A catalogue record for this book is available from the British Library.

Printed and bound in Great Britain by
Antony Rowe Ltd, Chippenham and Eastbourne

To my parents, Alan and Decima Jones, with love

Contents

List of Maps

List of Tables

List of Figures

List of Line-drawings at the Beginning of Each Chapter

List of Photographs

NOTE All the photographs are taken from the *Inchcape Archives*.

List of Appendices

List of Abbreviations

AUSN	Australasian United Steam Navigation Co.
BEWAC	British West Africa Corporation
BI	British India Steam Navigation Company
EIC	East India Company
GD & Co.	Gray Dawes & Co.
GM & Co.	Gray Mackenzie & Co.
GP & Co.	Gray Paul & Co.
HA	*History of Acquisitions, internal memo*
IA	*Inchcape Archives*
MEA	*Mann Egerton Archives*
MM & Co.	Mackinnon Mackenzie & Co.
MPC	Mesopotamia Persia Corporation Ltd
NMM	*National Maritime Museum*
P & O	Peninsular & Oriental Steam Navigation Co.
PP	*Parliamentary Papers*
RC	*Royal Commission*
RSN	Rivers Steam Navigation Co.
SM & Co.	Smith Mackenzie & Co.
SSI	Specialist Services International
VYB	Vivian, Younger and Bond
ZNA	*Zanzibar National Archives*

Foreword

The evolution of the Inchcape Group is a fascinating and complex story. I am therefore delighted to recommend this history to you as a remarkable study of commercial growth since the early nineteenth century. As traders and merchants, Inchcape has played a unique role in developing Britain's commercial links overseas, initially with the Indian Ocean and latterly with the Far East.

It is remarkable that comprehensive records of the histories of the various companies in the Inchcape Group have been retained. Dr Stephanie Jones has used this material in a thorough and imaginative way to reconstruct this picture of the Group which will, I am sure, earn a distinguished place in this series of *Studies in Business History*.

David Orr

Preface

This series of *Studies in Business History* sets out to concentrate on 'general issues in the history of business rather than on the biographies of individual companies or businessmen'. Why then does it include a history of the Inchcape Group? Basically, because it seeks to examine a vital, but neglected, subject: the marketing overseas of consumer goods mainly exported from Britain.

The Inchcape Group of Companies was formed as recently as 1958, from a large number of merchant partnerships established at home and overseas in the late eighteenth and the nineteenth centuries. Marketing was the common feature of most of these firms. They were set up at trading posts overseas by British (mainly Scottish) entrepreneurs, as new enterprises or branches of existing businesses at home or in other countries. They represented the owners of British transport, mainly shipping companies (especially the British India Steam Navigation Company) and later airlines, acting as early travel agents for passengers and goods. They imported Western products and distributed them to satisfy local demand, whether they were made in Britain or elsewhere. They exported locally-produced goods, seeking to develop export crops and, later, manufacturing industry. They represented British and foreign services, such as insurance companies, banks and information agencies. They invested directly in land, property, industry, housing, shipping and port developments overseas. They provided specific services in foreign ports, such as lighterage, towing and other marine facilities, including cargo inspection. They offered many aspects of management expertise, of tea estates and river steamers.

Many of these common features are still evident in the Group today. Its primary aim, distributing other people's products and technologies and providing skilled specialist services, is in many ways based on the traditional activities of its most old-established subsidiaries. The principal changes which have taken place since Inchcape was launched in 1958 have been in scale rather than purpose. The number of subsidiaries and associated companies has increased from 17 to over

800. The range of products marketed has expanded from a few hundred to 2300. The number of countries in which the Group operates has risen from six to over sixty. This great multitude of companies has been, and continues to be, essentially middlemen, those who oil the wheels of commerce, concentrating on the handling of goods and the provision of services.

The problem of marketing overseas, which this study seeks to illustrate, has but rarely featured in the dramatic recent growth of business history. A recently compiled bibliography shows a pronounced concentration of manufacturing concerns and the ownership of transport and other services.[1] The rich, original records of companies which have come into the Inchcape Group are especially appropriate in filling this gap. Other British international trading companies have reached prominence, such as Gill and Duffus, Harrison Crosfield, Lonrho, Sime Darby, Tozer Kemsley, Yule Catto and James Finley,[2] but none has Inchcape's geographical spread and diversity of interests.

Present-day management in the Group recognises the significance of the historical development and old-established traditions of many of the most important of its member companies: 'the long-standing relationships with business associates are of major importance to the Group, which offers established distribution facilities and experience of business conditions in areas with which its principals are not necessarily so familiar'[3]. In this sense, the entire history of each particular company is important, and not just its experience (often brief) as a member of the Group. An 'Inchcape company' is defined here as a business which has been, or still is, a member of the Group, and thus its development, from its origins to the present, is included here, irrespective of its date of joining the organisation.

It is thus as a study of a large range of middlemen, diverse in activity and geographical location, that this work seeks to make its contribution to economic and business history. In the process we shall encounter some personalities as dynamic as any who feature in British industrial life.

NOTES

1. T. C. Barker, R. H. Campbell and P. Mathias, *Business History*, revised edition published by Debrett's Business History Research Limited (London, 1984).
2. *The Financial Times*, Daily Stock Exchange Prices, list of 'international traders'.
3. *Report and Accounts, Inchcape PLC*, 31 December 1984, p.4.

Acknowledgements

First, I would like to thank all those at Inchcape's Head Office who helped in providing access to all the historical records at their disposal, and freely gave of their time and advice in interpreting them. I am particularly indebted to Lord Inchcape himself, Sir David Orr, Sir Edward Studd, Commander Michael Wall and Mr Len Bishop. Difficulties with company corporate and financial matters were resolved with the help of Mr Ian Reid, Mrs Margaret Guy and Miss Bonny Oxenham, and Mr Ian Bebbington assisted greatly in the computer-drawn graphs. Secretarial help from Mrs Brenda Mobey and Mrs Lesley Leporati has been much appreciated. Retired employees of the Group gave particularly enthusiastic help on this project, especially Mr Hugh Waters, Mr Donald Caswell, Mr Peter Heath, Mr Alan Ledger and Mr John Hall. At Mann Egerton's base in Norwich, Mrs Marie Lee and Mr Jim Campbell gave every assistance.

Staff in many libraries, museums and archives (which are listed in the notes and in the bibliography) were always helpful. It was a great privilege to be admitted to the Zanzibar National Archives, and I would particularly like to acknowledge the interest shown and help given there.

Finally, friends and colleagues from my student days helped tremendously in advising me on my manuscript and the presentation of my findings. Dr J. Forbes Munro, Dr Bill Reader and Mr John Armstrong, a few among many, were especially sympathetic and helpful. Professor Theo Barker read the entire volume in various stages of its progress; to him I owe an exceptional debt of gratitude.

Inchcape PLC STEPHANIE JONES
40 St. Mary Axe *June 1985*
London EC3A 8EN

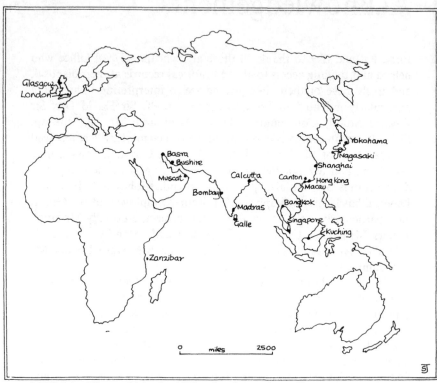

MAP 1.1   The world in the 1870s, showing early trading posts

1 Introduction: The Early Pioneers, from the Eighteenth Century to *c*.1870

The first pioneering merchant partnerships – the foundations on which the modern Group has been built – originated two centuries ago when world trade was marked by the growth of early industrial capitalism, especially in Britain. Much earlier, overseas trading had been confined to the limited movement of a small quantity of luxurious and exotic products, such as spices, silks, jewellery, ceramics and precious stones and metals, between the oldest cultural areas of the known world. After the sixteenth century, the modern features of world commerce were slowly emerging. An increased volume of shipments of basic consumer goods such as tea, sugar and tobacco was the result of the specialisation of particular regions in certain products to meet this wider popular demand. World trading developed its own infrastructure: cosmopolitan communities of merchants grew in number; credit and banking systems became established, with the international use of bills of exchange;

1

shipping tonnage increased, and the first commercial newspapers listed the movements of vessels and their cargoes.

This encouraged and sustained the increased production of industrial goods in the towns and the concomitant need for greater supplies of raw materials and foodstuffs.[1] The export of these goods overseas in addition to fulfilling the home demand was vital to ensure a constant supply of bullion into Britain, necessary to pay for the costly foreign wars of the eighteenth century. Many British industries were thus geared for the export market from this early period. For example, the East Anglian wool industry concentrated on producing goods for overseas, enjoying protection by restrictions. not only on the imports of competing textiles from abroad, to encourage home demand, but the export of raw wool, sheep and textile machinery was prohibited until 1843.

The establishment of the earliest companies which were ultimately to form part of the Inchcape Group took place against the background of the dramatic growth of British overseas trade. The value of exports rose from £6.5m in 1700 to over £40m a century later, whilst imports grew from £6m to £28m. Woollen goods accounted for over half of Britain's export trade at the beginning of the eighteenth century, but by its end, cotton had become a close rival. The enormous level of production of cotton piece goods from British mills, especially in Manchester, is one of the most significant features in the expansion of British overseas trading in the eighteenth and nineteenth centuries. By 1829 cotton exports were valued at nearly £30m per year, and by 1870, £70m.[2]

In seeking a market to sustain this output, and to ensure a constant source of supply of raw materials, Britain looked increasingly overseas, especially to her newly-acquired territories and spheres of influence in the East. British trading posts had been established at Madras in 1639, Galle in 1640, Bombay in 1661 and Calcutta in 1690, and India was further opened to trade with Britain with the steady erosion of the monopoly enjoyed by the East India Company [EIC] which had originally been established in 1600. Commerce between India and the UK was thrown open to free merchants after 1813. and the EIC was finally dissolved after the Mutiny of 1857.[3]

India's existing cotton piece goods and dyestuffs industry was largely held in check and restricted in its growth by Britain's export policies. India's cheap cotton goods were in great demand in Britain despite the heavy import duties imposed, but soon declined when faced with increased competition from the factory-produced versions from Britain. Disrupted by war and internal instability, and affected by the discriminatory tariffs, India's export trade fell as her imports of British goods rose. Table 1.1 shows how, by 1850, imports of British goods to India overtook Indian exports to Britain in value. Britain's preference for West Indian sugar also had the effect of stifling India's early sugar refining business, based around Madras, for only unrefined sugar would be imported into Britain. India's indigo trade collapsed by the later nineteenth century, her copper-mining industry was short-lived and coffee planting was one of the few successful economic developments, to be followed by the growth of the tea industry in the later nineteenth century. Only when the export of British textile machinery was permitted in 1843 did India's own cotton industry re-emerge. The first steam cotton press in Bombay was established in 1853.[4]

Because of its colonial status and the absence of competition from other Western economies in her trade, India was especially valuable to early British overseas traders. From Table 1.1 it is clear that Britain (with the exception of Hong Kong, a British colony from 1842) dominated India's foreign trade. But more distant and unknown markets also attracted these merchants. The demand in the West for tea and silk was such that the commercial possibilities of the Far East were also explored by traders, not only from Britain but also from Germany and other European countries, and from New England. Trade between the West and China before the Treaty of Nanking in 1842, however, was restricted to the ports of Macao and Canton, and only members of the exclusive *Cohong* were permitted to make transactions with foreign merchants. Western goods were still unknown in China in the early nineteenth century, because the large local market for opium provided a 'currency' with which foreign traders could purchase tea and silk. The attempts of the Chinese authorities to restrict opium imports into the main settlements, the 'Opium Wars' and the resultant treaty of Nanking, reduced the importance of this drug and therefore assisted in encouraging the imports of Western products, such as the ubiquitous cotton piece goods. The cession of the colony of Hong Kong to Britain and the inauguration of the Treaty Port System in China further opened the area to trade. The port of Shanghai, centre for the commercial development of the Yangtse, became one of the most important and prosperous of the foreign settlements, whilst Hong Kong became the centre of the entrepôt trade of south China generally.

The rigid social structure of mid-nineteenth century Japan strongly discouraged all contact with foreign merchants, who were concentrated particularly at the Western port of Nagaski. The building of large sailing vessels capable of distant voyages, which would have enabled Japanese entrepreneurs to make contact with the West, was expressly banned.

TABLE 1.1 Imports from Britain, and exports to Britain, of India, Ceylon, China, Japan and Singapore, 1849–1875, sample years, showing UK as percentages of total trade.

Year	India Imports (millions rupees)	Exports	Ceylon Imports (thousand pounds)	Exports	China Imports (millions taels)	Exports	Japan Imports (millions yen)	Exports	Singapore Imports (millions/Straits dollars)	Exports
1840	61 (77%)	71 (74%)	127 (19%)	298 (74%)	—	—	—	—	—	—
1845	65 (72%)	66 (49%)	306 (22%)	439 (78%)	—	—	—	—	—	—
1850	88 (74%)	81 (54%)	267 (20%)	730 (78%)	—	—	—	—	—	—
1855	147 (83%)	103 (56%)	448 (20%)	1015 (64%)	—	—	—	—	—	—
1860	217 (85%)	142 (49%)	1043 (38%)	1639 (70%)	—	—	—	—	—	—
1865	249 (67%)	434 (77%)	904 (21%)	2420 (71%)	22 (56%)	38* (72%)	—	—	8.8 (45%)	4.7 (29%)
1870	259 (84%)	313 (67%)	1531 (37%)	2907 (80%)	24 (55%)	29 (59%)	12 (44%)	5.2 (29%)	12.0 (49%)	8.3 (37%)
1875	345 (91%)	284 (66%)	1417 (30%)	3709 (81%)	21 (40%)	29 (59%)	15 (50%)	2.5 (15%)	10.0 (33%)	10.0 (32%)

*1868 figures.

SOURCE Adapted from B. R. Mitchell, *International Historical Statistics: Africa and Asia* (London, 1982) pp.432–8.

Only with the gradual demise of the *Daimyo* (the territorial lords) and the rising prosperity of the *Chomin* (the merchant class), which contributed to the collapse of the Tokugawa Shogunate and the Meiji Restoration in 1868, did Japan accept the growing influence of foreign trade on her society and economy. The Far East, another region of great trading possibilities for the British merchant, was not a captive market like India – as seen in Table 1.1 – but with the potential demand from its huge, largely untapped population and rich resources, was to contribute significantly to British overseas trading enterprise.[5]

The area broadly known as the South China Sea also came under the purview of the British merchant. Three developments encouraged this; the founding of Singapore in 1819 by Sir Stamford Raffles; the ceding of Sarawak to its first Rajah, Sir James Brooke in 1841; and Sir John Bowring's negotiation of a favourable commercial treaty between Britain and Siam in 1855. Singapore, originally just wasteland when the EIC granted it to Raffles, became an established trading post for the import of British goods, exporting in return such commodities as coffee, gambier, hides, sago and pepper. Sarawak, in the early nineteenth century, was known only for its Dyak head-hunters, pirates and slavery. British merchants settled in Singapore became acquainted with the Rajah's efforts to develop this part of Borneo: he had declared Kuching, which lay at the mouth of a large, navigable river, to be a free port, and he provided the country with a relatively stable government. Such valuable resources as antimony, gold, rice, coffee, nutmegs and coal were available. A British protectorate was not formally established there until 1888, but long before then, through Brooke's rule, the area was practically a British colony. Its trade with Britain rapidly grew. Migrants from Dutch Borneo, China, Java and Singapore were attracted there, and the population of Kuching swelled from a mere village in the early nineteenth century to a small but thriving town of 20 000 by the 1860s.

A royal trading monopoly imposed by the King of Siam, and his refusal to permit the settlement of foreign merchants, thwarted British trading ventures to this country in the early nineteenth century. Sir James Brooke of Sarawak had been sent by the British Government in 1850 in an attempt to open commercial relations, but this had come to nothing. Only with the accession of King Mongkut in 1856 was this objective realised. Through Bowring's treaty, the British played an important part in the development of Siam. For example, British merchants won the contract to build a telegraph link between Bangkok, Burma and Penang, and they reorganised the local currency, even to the extent of providing new coin-minting machines. A British sugar factory at Nakorn Chaisri was protected against disgruntled Chinese sugar workers (facing what they considered unfair competition) by the Siamese authorities. British imports made considerable headway but, as in China and Japan but unlike India and Singapore, Siam was also open to commercial competition from other nations. British goods thus completed against those of France, Prussia, the USA, Sweden and Norway in the 1860s and 1870s.[6]

The Persian Gulf became of interest to British merchants through its location on the route between Britain and India. Captain Chesney's expedition up the Tigris was ultimately to lead to the establishment of a number of British trading posts. The area became important as a supplier of raw cotton, when American supplies were interrupted by their civil war. Bushire and Basra became significant markets for British goods. From the hinterland of these ports came pearls, silk, nuts, spices, dates and other dried fruit, wool and carpets.[7]

The port of Muscat had acted as an entrepôt centre for much of the wool trade of this region, and the establishment by its ruler of an African Sultanate at Zanzibar helped considerably in drawing the attention of British and other Western merchants to East Africa. EIC ships had plied their trades off the Arab/Persian Gulf and African coasts of the Indian Ocean since the seventeenth century, and a British consular office had been opened at Zanzibar in 1841. British naval vessels were a common sight in these waters, combating the slave trade and the pillaging of Zanzibar by pirates from the Gulf. To a greater degree than at Gulf ports, Britain shared the trade of Zanzibar with the merchants of France, Germany, Italy and the USA, who were also attracted to this island entrepôt centre. With its large re-export trade Zanzibar acted as a market for Western goods. A major world source of cloves, it also exported ivory, coconuts, gum, molasses, shells, cassava root, ghee and cereals.[8]

I

The modern Inchcape Group has been built upon the enterprise of a group of British merchants who ventured overseas to these early trading posts, the location of which is shown in Map 1.1. This enterprise, and the capital that went with it, was Scottish rather than English, though most of these Scots had come south to London to establish their partnerships. Most had to leave their native land to make their fortunes (and those of their firms). Besides the entrepreneurs who set out for the East were those who stayed at home to run the equally important London end of the business. Who were these enterprising merchants? Why did they seek to set up businesses in remote parts of the world? How successful were they?

Studies of British traders operating overseas in this period are comparatively rare: most works on the growth of the British economy concentrate on home-based enterpreneurs, ignoring the contribution of those who went abroad to market her exports and buy her imports. Before the arrival of the telegraph in the second half of the nineteenth century, success depended more than it was later to do upon the decisions taken by men on the spot. Yet, in an analysis of the early British entrepreneur, a leading economic history textbook gives only examples of those who made their fortunes at home, not overseas, although credit is given to the importance of Scots in British trading colonies abroad.[9] Only in studies dealing with particular foreign trades does the merchant receive due credit. In a discussion of the English merchant community of Lisbon in the eighteenth century, for instance, it is emphasised that 'in assessing the record of English mercantile and shipping enterprise in this [the eighteenth] century there is surely a need to look more at the local activities of Englishmen domiciled abroad', for this aspect of Britain's success is of 'a little studied kind'.[10] Precise details of such individual merchants are seen only rarely in specialised works which, tending to view their subjects in isolation, can only give a limited contribution to the broad issue of the nature of British overseas trading partnerships.[11]

By studying the origins of a large number of overseas merchant houses together, this chapter aims to help to fill this gap, by identifying the most prominent merchants and the founders of each firm which eventually came to form the Inchcape Group. Together they present a wide spectrum of individual activities and areas of business. Appendix 1.1 lists over fifty entrepreneurs, again drawing attention to the high incidence of Scots. Checkland, in describing Gillanders, a typical early entrepreneur, and one of the partners in a business destined to become eventually the Anglo-Thai Corporation, wrote 'A tall, well-built young Highlander, an obvious Scotsman in manner and speech, Gillanders did well in a trade in which Scots connections were strong'.[12] Of the eleven trading houses which founded the Bombay Chamber of Commerce in 1836, at least nine were Scots-owned.[13] No quantification of this tendency has previously been attempted. This present study shows that in a sample of fifty-six merchants based overseas in this period, at least thirty-four were originally from Scotland.

The importance of kinship in the establishment of these communities of traders is also shown in Appendix 1.1. Nine cases of direct family links in a business may be discerned, not including more distant ties concealed by the absence of a common surname. This factor was typical of many overseas enterprises. Maggie Keswick, in describing Jardine and Matheson, wrote that they 'were unmarried . . . but they had their family interests at heart. Family solidarity runs strong in Scotland, and both Jardine and Matheson wanted to ensure continuity of control and the continuing influence of their families in the business. This principle carried the firm through a vital period of growth. Before long James Matheson produced his nephew Alexander as an assistant in the office'.[14]

Appendix 1.1 also summarises the timing of these first overseas ventures. This seems to have been largely determined by region, following the establishment of trading bases. In India, they were founded in the late eighteenth and early nineteenth centuries; in the Far East, in the middle decades of the nineteenth; and firms based in what is now Malaysia followed in the subsequent half century. The Gulf and East Africa were the most recently settled: firms were set up there in the last quarter of the nineteenth century.

The earliest activities of these partnerships may be considered in relation to their date of formation. The oldest companies were usually involved in the most varied work. Before the establishment of a sophisticated commercial infrastructure, each company had to concern itself with all aspects of its business: not just importing and exporting with general agency work, but providing its own banking, exchange and insurance facilities. By the late nineteenth century, it became possible for firms to specialise in particular commodities and services. Before the present century, however, these firms acted primarily as general traders, handling any commodity or providing any service for which there was a demand. In all the regions, the import of British goods, the export of local products and the organisation of the necessary transport arrangements acted as a common link between the firms.

Twenty-five of the sample of fifty-six merchants listed in Appendix 1.1 were the original founders of their companies: the remainder were partners and assistants. Of these entrepreneurs, three distinct types may be defined: first, those who ventured out with their own capital, alone, to seek their fortunes abroad; second, those sent out by the British office (usually London-based) of an overseas firm to its branches, to help set up new offices or join an established branch; and third, those who were already based in these places, either with the EIC or the army or navy.

Those falling into the first category were rare, comprising less than a quarter of this sample. It took great courage and confidence to set out for an unknown land without assured employment on arrival, to say nothing of the capital required for the voyage and initial expenses. These most daring of pioneers usually enjoyed the presence of some family contacts at least. The majority of the sample joined existing businesses or were sent out to make surveys with a view to establishing firms. The remainder, less than a quarter, became aware of the commercial opportunities of these countries through their experience of working for the authorities: it is likely that they dabbled in trade using the privileges of their positions before formally starting businesses. The region involved had a bearing on the type of merchant it attracted. In India, examples of the three categories may be found, but in the case of the Far East, it was rare for a potential merchant to venture out without the benefit of previous surveys, knowledge of the area from government service or contacts on the spot.

II

Appendix 1.1 serves as an introduction to, and summary of, a more detailed appraisal of the formation of the firms under review. In India, the oldest enterprises were those which were ultimately to form the Binny group of companies, and the Anglo-Thai Corporation. John Binny, who originally hailed from Forfar, near Dundee, may be seen as one of the first category of entrepreneurs. He sailed from London in 1796, aged 27, aboard an East Indiaman, for a six-month voyage which took him to Madeira, the Cape and Ceylon. His ordinary cabin, with simple canvas screen, cost the sizeable sum of £350, which suggests that not only had he already made a significant profit from a previous venture, or inherited a large sum, but that he was dissatisfied with life in Scotland. Although he did not join an existing family firm, ties of kinship helped to attract him to the early English trading post of Madras: an ancestor, Thomas Binny, had married in Madras in 1682; a member of another branch of the Binny family had acted as the English secretary to the Nawab Walajah since 1769, and two of Binny's brothers served on board the Nawab's ships, one as a purser and the other as a captain. Thus, with relations already in senior posts in the Nawab's service, John Binny was enabled to obtain initial security and an income by becoming the Nawab's surgeon. However, by 1799, influenced by the Nawab's steady decline of power, the lack of work and interest in his job of Palace Surgeon, together with the growing peace and prosperity now enjoyed in the area after the constant wars and political unrest of the mid-eighteenth century, he had established his House of Agency in Madras. From the firm's early days private banking became an important part of Binny's business, prompted by the limit on remittances sent home by EIC employees. The latter were not allowed to trade on their own account after 1800 – another inducement to leave and set themselves up in business – so the private banks provided a much-needed service in investing this surplus capital. The monopoly maintained by the Company, although coming under increasing attack, was such that when Binny founded his firm, he could act only as an agent rather than a free merchant, selling merchandise on consignment only.[15]

In the period up to 1870, Binny's enterprise grew dramatically. From an initial capital outlay of Rs 50 000 and an original staff of six in 1799, Binny & Co. was described by the late nineteenth century as 'perhaps the largest general merchants in the City of Madras, and they have a substantial banking establishment for the furtherance of business transactions with their many clients'.[16] The number of Houses of Agency had increased from ten in 1802 to twenty by 1858, and Binny's is the only name common to both lists.[17] As early as 1804, Binny and his partner Dennison had purchased a house and grounds in the prestigious Armenian Street for Rs 35 000, and in 1811, a surviving ledger records an overall profit for that year of Rs 140 000. When the senior Binny, the founder, voyaged back to Britain to retire in 1816, his prosperity was such that he was able to afford £1000 for the best cabin available. In the mid-nineteenth century, Binnys ventured into sugar refining, indigo cultivation and textile production. They assisted in the flotation of the Manjunhalla Coffee Co. Ltd, contributing substantially towards its capital of Rs 240 000.[18] Thus Binnys played an increasingly important part in the mercantile community of Madras.

Meanwhile, a large and recent addition to the Inchcape Group, now known as the Anglo-Thai Corporation, had begun as six separate merchant houses trading in Bombay, Calcutta and Karachi. John Gladstone, prominent Liverpool merchant, father of the future Prime Minister and pioneer of free trade to India and China against the London-based EIC monopoly, provided the impetus to this enterprise: deciding to investigate the trading possibilities of Bengal, as an adjunct to his existing West Indian business, he employed his wife's cousin, F. M. Gillanders as a supercargo, on a voyage to Bombay in 1818.[19] Gillanders may be seen as typical of many of the entrepreneurs considered in

Appendix 1.1 in so far that he ventured overseas on behalf of an existing business venture, he was a Scotsman, and ties of kinship played an important part in determining his future employment.

Originally, Gillanders acted as a seaborne merchant and agent aboard the ships of Gladstone's fleet, which comprised six vessels in the India trade owned by John Gladstone and his brother Robert. Gillanders soon became dissatisfied with his 1 per cent commission on purchases and sales and one-eighth share in the net profits of the voyages and, with his early sponsor losing interest in the India trade, Gillanders set up there on his own account. Already experienced in investigating trading possibilities through new commodities and services, he soon made his mark, sharing the offices of McIntyre & Co. in Bombay. Aided by the news of free trade which followed the Napoleonic Wars, and by a loan of £5000 from Gladstone to himself and his partner Thomas Ogilvy, their business grew. It comprised the consigning of vessels, receipt and disposal of goods despatched by others for sale on commission, and agency business generally. They also took an interest in 'when expedient, such moderate adventures in merchandise for account of the co-partnership as may be desirable for making more favourable remittances than the current rate of exchange in returning the co-partners' capital to England from time to time'.[20] An early partner was Robert Byrne who, from 1851, expanded the firm's activities by dealing in the wool of North West India, 'adventures' in rice, sugar and cotton, and by importing British goods wholesale on behalf of the bazaar traders. A contemporary in the firm, G. C. Arbuthnot, left detailed notes about the business, concluding that 'India could supply Britain in much greater abundance with sugar and cotton, and now that the tea plant had been found to be indigenous in large parts of the district of Assam, with tea also'. The partnership soon appreciated the potential of Bengal labour, recruiting 250 men to send to Arbuthnot's brother, to work as indentured labour on plantations in Mauritius: 'their cost,' he wrote, is not one-half that of a slave'.[21]

Details of these partnerships' profits and turnover have not survived, but their prominence is seen in the fact that a further partner, Edward Lyon, was a member of the Bombay Chamber of Commerce Committee and that Gillanders, Ewart and Co. was one of the twenty-eight most prominent European firms in Bombay by 1841. In Bombay and in Calcutta by 1852, these partnerships represented the Oriental Insurance Society, the London Assurance Corporation, the Victoria Insurance Society and the Albion Life Insurance Company.[22]

The most significant early entrepreneur in our sample, in terms of his role in the formation of partnerships which were subsequently to join the Inchcape Group, was William Mackinnon. Originally employed by a Portuguese East India merchant in Glasgow, in 1847 he ventured out to Calcutta, at first working at a sugar refinery in nearby Cossipore. It is not known whether or not he paid his own passage out. Shortly afterwards, he joined a fellow Campbeltown man who already managed a general mercantile business, dealing in importing British piece goods and exporting local tea, sugar, hides, saltpetre, indigo, shellac and rice.[23] A private ledger, with first entries dating from March 1850, records that the senior partner, Robert Mackenzie, had invested Rs 32 505 (nearly £2500), William Mackinnon Rs 20 530 (nearly £1500) and James Hall, who also joined the company in its early days, Rs 19 082 (or just over £1000). The net profit for 1850 was calculated as Rs 16 171 and for 1851, Rs 68 604, equivalent to nearly £5000, which was distributed among the partners according to their initial investment. Thus, after approximately four years of trading (dating from 1847) the partners had received dividends in excess of the value of their original investment.

1.1 William Mackinnon, Robert Mackenzie and James McAlister Hall, the original founders of Mackinnon Mackenzie & Co.: an early photograph, possibly of the late 1860s or 1870s

1.2 The First Earl of Inchcape who, as James Lyle Mackay, joined Mackinnon Mackenzie & Co. in 1874. A photograph by Van Dyke

The business was further expanded after Mackenzie's visit to Australia in 1852, by which time it had been reorganised into two complementary firms: Mackinnon Mackenzie & Co. [MM & Co.] at Calcutta, and Wm. Mackinnon & Co. at Glasgow. The Company's assets, valued at Rs 158 302 (over £11 300) in 1850, had shot up dramatically to Rs 670 105 (or nearly £50 000) by 1852. It then specialised in three principal activities: the shipping of cotton goods from Glasgow and Manchester for sale in Calcutta; a trade in general goods between Calcutta and Australia; and the running of a few sailing ships on the Glasgow–Sydney–Melbourne routes. Details of each 'adventure' have survived for these early years, giving the name of each ship consigned and the appropriate earnings, together with port charges, payments to other merchants, and purchases of commodities. A total of sixty-three shiploads, mainly destined for Britain, were handled by the firm in 1852 alone.

The principal activity which transformed these partnerships from two among several trading houses located in Glasgow and Calcutta into the base of a world-wide network of companies, was their direct investment in steam shipping, at a time when the steamship was just achieving economic viability. They successfully won the contract to carry mails from Calcutta to the Burmese ports, put out to tender by the Government of Bengal. Mackinnon's Calcutta and Burmah Steam Navigation Company was then established in 1856, and its early success enabled its founder to obtain further funds in Britain to increase its paid-up capital from £39 800 in 1857 to £342 685 by 1865. Then bearing the much more familiar name of the British India Steam Navigation Company [BI], the firm gained further contracts enabling it to operate lines from Calcutta eastwards to Burma and Singapore, from Calcutta round the coasts of India to Bombay, and from Bombay to the Persian Gulf. A sister enterprise, the Netherlands India Steam Navigation Company, covered the coasts of Java for the Government of the Netherlands East Indies. These enterprises were largely financed from profits earned by MM & Co., who acted as the BI's Calcutta agents. They enjoyed particularly high earnings from large shipments of raw cotton from India during the American Civil War.[24] A letter of 1850 records that this firm was allowed 'a continual supply of credit, to the extent in all of £10 000' from the City of Glasgow Bank.[25]

Other relevant companies formed in India in the middle decades of the nineteenth century were founded as a result of the discovery and early cultivation of the tea plant in India, credited to C. A. Bruce. The Assam Company, established in London in 1839, had been promoted by a

London merchant and businessman, George de Hochpied Larpent, together with a group of merchants and traders who included Richard Twining. Bruce had previously been employed by the EIC and then commanded gunboats as a naval lieutenant. His brother, also a naval officer, had first noted the existence of the tea plant in India in 1823. Employed as the Northern Division Gardens Superintendent of the Assam Company in 1840–5, C. A. Bruce may be seen as a combination of two of the types of entrepreneur classified in Appendix 1.1 in the fact that he was in India working for the EIC, and that he was to join an established enterprise. J. W. Masters, sent out from England in 1839, joined him to clear jungle, build huts and organise coolie labour.[26]

Albert de Hochpied Larpent, a Calcutta merchant and relation of George, became a director of the India General Steam Navigation Company, established in 1844, supported by Larpent and nine other Calcutta merchants. This was followed in 1862 by the founding of a rival firm, the Rivers Steam Navigation Company [RSN], by an ex-captain of the India General, J. W. Williamson.[27]

These enterprises were encouraged not only by the technological improvements in steamers, but also by the dramatic expansion of river-borne trade, mainly brought about by the increase in India's tea output from $2\frac{1}{4}$ million lb. in 1862 to $6\frac{1}{4}$ million lb. by 1867. The Assam Company, recovering from a period of losses due to the falling price of tea on the London market from $1s\,7d$ to $1s\,0\frac{3}{4}d$, recovered by 1870, declaring a profit of £23 342 and a 6 per cent dividend.[28] The trading accounts of the India General, which was heavily involved in the shipment of tea have survived in sufficient detail to see that the company enjoyed increasing prosperity: from a loss of Rs 16 803 (or over £1200) in the first half year of 1850, its net earnings increased to nearly Rs 100 000 (over £7000) by the end of 1854, when a 12 per cent dividend was paid. The company suffered from heavy competition from the Irrawadi Flotilla Company when it entered Burmese waters, but otherwise its level of profits and dividends was maintained, with net earnings of Rs 1 052 728 in the second half of 1858 and Rs 218 260 in the second half of 1862. Dividends of up to 44 per cent per annum were paid out. Meanwhile, the RSN concentrated on the Allahabad route rather than venturing into Assam and made relatively slow progress, offering no serious rivalry to the India General until the late 1870s.

A number of managing agencies, which acted for the river steamer companies and invested in many local tea estates, also emerged in the middle decades of the nineteenth century. Shoene, Kilburn & Co. originated when C. E. Shoene's import and export business, which began in Calcutta in 1842, was joined by E. D. Kilburn in 1849. Kilburn, yet another Scot, made a thorough survey of the climate and conditions for business in Calcutta before agreeing to join the partnership. The importance of kinship in these early firms is seen in the appointment of the co-founder's nephew in 1876. The import of cotton goods and yarn, and the export of local silk, hides, jute, indigo and shellac dominated the partnership's early activities. It acquired the agencies of two important insurance companies in the 1860s, together with the Assam Company agency in 1865, and that of the India General in 1875.

Meanwhile, J. B. Barry, an Irish surgeon with an official appointment in Assam, formed a partnership in the early 1860s, purchasing a tract of land in Chittagong for tea cultivation. His son then opened a London office to handle the estate's exports. A third partnership involved in India's tea trade was sponsored by William Mackinnon. Two of his nephews, employed by Mackinnon's Glasgow firm, had originally ventured out to India to join the shipping agency firm of Begg, Dunlop and Company in Calcutta, and then founded their own partnership, Macneill & Co. in 1872. By 1855, Barry's had entered the jute milling business, after an earlier successful diversification into distilling gin in 1852. Barry's son had played an important part in producing the first automatic tea dryer in India, and by the 1870s the firm had increased its tea estate holdings. Macneills meanwhile was also expanding its interests in tea shipment. From their ex-employers, Begg Dunlop, the partners took over the agency for the RSN, followed by that of the Kalline Tea Co., and formed an associated partnership, Duncan Macneill & Co., to manage the London end of their affairs.[29]

Ceylon, as shown in Table 1.1, was of considerable importance as a source of imports (principally raw cotton) to the UK by the late nineteenth century. Combined with the products of its sugar, coffee and cinnamon estates, its trade was such that nearly 400 000 tons of shipping, mainly from Britain and the colonies, cleared outwards with cargoes in 1859. The merchant house of Reid & Co. was founded at the port of Galle in 1850. Its original partner was another Scott, Alexander Reid, who was joined by an American, E. T. Delmege, who settled at Galle in 1865 after acquiring capital as a Mississippi pilot engaged in blockade running during the American Civil War. The importance of kinship in this shipping and coaling enterprise is shown by the fact that both were soon joined by their brothers, James Reid and A. A. Delmege respectively. In 1861, Reid was one of thirteen European merchants based at Galle, with four employees, the brothers A. and B. Scott, E. McKellar and J. K. Molison. He was one of three British traders who each owned a bonded warehouse at the port, storing rice, wheat, and produce of the East Indies generally. A fortnightly service by the Peninsular and Oriental Steam Navigation Company Limited [P & O], linking Galle to Calcutta, Bombay, China and London, stimulated the company's business. It became officially known as Delmege, Forsyth & Co. when, after the Reids' retirement, the Delmege brothers separated. The older Delmege successfully secured the firm's agencies, specialising in the import of flour and sugar.[30]

III

Table 1.1 shows that China was developing a significant trade with Britain by the mid-nineteenth century: exports to the UK were valued at 38m taels in 1868, equivalent to £11m, over four times the value of goods sent to Britain from Ceylon, and more than half the value of all India exports to this country. The value of imports from Britain into China has been estimated as 22m taels, or nearly £7m. By the second half of the nineteenth century, China's imports from the UK approached the value of its exports. Exports to the UK from Japan were less significant in this period for reasons already discussed at the beginning of this chapter, but Britain supplied half of Japan's imports by 1875, and its trade generally increased by leaps and bounds in the later nineteenth century.

Four companies which were subsequently to form a vital part of the Inchcape Group were established in China in the middle decades of the nineteenth century. First, two ex-E1C merchants, Thomas Augustus Gibb and William Potter Livingston, founded a 'factory' in Canton in 1836. In a base which combined in one building the functions of office, warehouse and residence, they imported English cottons and woollens and exported tea, with silk and silver bullion used in payment for exports. An account book dating from 1844 shows that the partners also dealt in grey shirtings, velveteens, nankeens, chintz, leather, tin plate and saltpetre, acting as agents for a large number of sailing ships, organising the payment of their port charges, consular fees, import and export duties, landing charges, and the cost of boat hire and storage of cargoes on shore. The firm, known as Gibb, Livingston and Co., imported goods on behalf of Chinese and other British merchants which were handled by their compradores – Chinese middlemen – who collected their commissions and earnings and advised on the state of the market. In one month alone, March 1845, the turnover of the partners' business exceeded 13 000 taels or nearly £4000, and their net profit equalled nearly £150.

This figure could be increased at least tenfold to equal present values. Despite the restrictions on the opium trade after 1842, the account book mentions several transactions involving opium, such as in May 1845: 'received from Capt. Hy. Forman of the *Thomas Crisp*, schooner, demurrage and sale charges on 40 chests of Malwa opium per agreement at Ts.16 per chest, Ts.640'. By this date, the partners were trading in Shanghai and Woosung in addition to Canton.[31] A China Directory of 1863 lists Gibb, Livingston & Co.'s branches at Kuikiang (W. F. B. Sams and R. R. Rothwell), Hankow (J. T. Hudson and E. H. Hancock). They employed a total of twenty-seven Europeans in China as a whole, including four members of the Gibb family. An advertisement of the Imperial Fire Insurance Company of London (which mentions T. A. Gibb as a director) was undersigned by Gibb, Livingstone & Co., as agents for the company at Canton, Hongkong, Amoy and Shanghai, 'prepared to grant . . . against FIRE to the extent of Ts.40 000 on any one First Class Risk'.[32]

A tea-taster, Richard James Gilman, from the old-established firm of Dents, was responsible for the formation of a second partnership which was later to join the Group. It was known as Gilman & Bowman from 1840, when, joined by Abram Bowman, Gilman also occupied a Canton 'factory'. By 1863 the firm was also represented at Kiukiang, Hankow and Tientsin, employing twenty-one staff in all, including three members of the Brand family and two Lemanns, again showing the part played by ties of kinship in these enterprises. Gibb Livingston's and Gilman's were both formed by British traders already involved in the commercial life of China. W. R. Adamson & Co., however, was founded as a result of the efforts of a group of Cheshire silk-weavers to increase supplies of raw silk for their mills. Adamson, who arrived in Shanghai on their behalf in 1852, soon branched out into the export of tea and the import of general merchandise. He established his own company, W. R. Adamson & Co. in 1858, based at Shanghai, with branches in Foochow, Hangkow and Hong Kong, with ten European employees. Caldbeck, Macgregor and Co., a firm which differed from those described above, because it specialised exclusively in wines and spirits, rather than general merchanting,[33] was formed after the purchase by John Macgregor and Jack Caldbeck, of the business of George Smith & Co. of Shanghai. Macgregor had originally gone East to seek his fortune after serving in the Navy during the Crimean War. Caldbeck had been the P & O Agent in Singapore. In 1863 he was recorded as a director, with H. B. Gibb, of the Sailors' Home in Hong Kong, showing evidence of his wide influence. They subsequently built up a thriving wines and spirits business throughout the East, representing many prominent European and British principals. W. R. Adamson & Co., which became Adamson, Bell & Co. in 1867, was the first of these firms to venture into Japan, opening a branch in Yokohoma in the early 1860s. All these partnerships retained close ties with London. Gilmans was represented by Ashton & Co., of which Richard Gilman's brother, Ellis, was a partner. Caldbeck MacGregor opened a London office in 1882. With the exception of Caldbeck's, all these firms acted as agents for British shipping and insurance companies, and played an important part in the China tea trade.

IV

The opening-up of British trade in the South China Seas led to the remarkable expansion in the foreign commerce of Singapore, Sarawak and Siam. The overseas trade of the Straits Settlements nearly doubled in value between about 1860 and 1880; imports rose from 40m to 74m Straits dollars, and exports from 37m to 64m. The value of Siam's exports more than tripled in roughly the same period, from 4.2m to 15m ticuls. Sarawak and Sabah were then only just emerging as commercial centres, but by 1885 exports from the former exceeded 1m Straits dollars in value. The Borneo Company originated from the establishment of a branch of a Glasgow firm in Singapore. In 1846, W. R. Paterson & Co. sent Robert MacEwan from the west coast of Scotland, to expand their business interests overseas. A clerk, John Harvey, who hailed from Renfrewshire, accompanied MacEwan and was to take his place when the latter returned to Glasgow on the retirement of the original senior partner. Branches were shortly opened at Manila and Batavia. It was, however, the opportunity to contribute to the economic expansion of Sarawak which was most instrumental in leading to the decision to float the Borneo Company Limited in 1856.

Registered in London to take advantage of the limited liability status which had been introduced earlier in that year, this firm was unique among the businesses so far considered, in that most preferred the less formal, more flexible style of a partnership. Merchant trading companies, in contrast with manufacturing concerns, were able to continue until even the mid-twentieth century as partnerships, for they required much less capital, working as well as fixed. In the commission business, shipping agency work, and the representation of principals such as British manufacturers and insurance firms, those for whom they acted provided the capital: they lived by taking their percentages , usually operating from modest premises, often shared with other firms. The Borneo Company's capital of £60 000 however, was not financed by a Stock Exchange issue but subscribed by the partners and employees of the original W. R. Paterson & Co. together with by Robert Henderson of R. & J. Henderson, merchants of Glasgow and London, and John Charles Templer, a lifelong friend of Rajah Brooke of Sarawak.[34] Brooke's offer of far-reaching development rights to the Borneo Company acted as an irresistible magnet. Under a royalty arrangement with the Sarawak treasury, the new firm took over the 'mines, ores, veins or seams of all descriptions of minerals in the Island of Borneo, and to barter or sell the produce of such workings'.[35]

Meanwhile, in the year of its formation, 1856, the company opened a branch in Bangkok. Ludvig Verner Helms, a Danish explorer who had visited Sarawak before Brooke and subsequently worked for the Borneo Company there, had been sent to Bangkok on the death of the old king, to investigate the truth in the rumours that his successor was keen to open the country to foreign trade. Samuel Gilfillan, previously of a rival firm, Gilfillan, Wood & Co., merchants of Singapore, was sent to manage the Siam branch.[36] As early as March 1858 the King of Siam himself expressed his satisfaction at the opening of the branch, and a deputation of the Board duly returned their thanks and assured the King of their willingness to help in the further commercial development of his dominions.[37]

The Singapore branch, as the Company's original base and jumping-off point, continued to thrive, especially with the prominence of British shipping at the port, which represented nearly 70 per cent of the total in 1871. As Lloyd's Singapore Agents, the firm dealt closely with these ships, primarily those of the P & O, who competed against French and Dutch steamers and German and American sailing ships. The Borneo Company was one of thirty-eight merchant houses established by 1872, twelve of them British. Other British firms were Boustead & Co. of London, operating here since 1830; Brown & Co., and Cameron, John & Co. since 1861; Gilfillan, Wood & Co. of London; Greenshields, Ledward & Co. of Liverpool; Hamilton, Gray & Co. since 1832, of Glasgow; A. L. Johnston & Co., the oldest firm in Singapore, dating from 1820; Scott, Witham & Co. of London since 1832; W. Mansfield & Co; Martin, Dyce & Co. of Glasgow, since 1843; Paterson, Simons & Co. of London, since 1858, who were possibly linked to the original W. R. Paterson of Glasgow; Shaw, Schofield & Co. of London and Liverpool, since 1860 and Syme & Co. Since 1823, of Glasgow and

Liverpool. The Borneo Company's Singapore office represented the Indo-Chinese Sugar Co. Ltd, the Norwich Fire Insurance Company, the North China Insurance Company, the Chinese Insurance Co. Ltd, the Standard Life Assurance Co., not to mention HM Government of Labuan. They were founder-members of the Singapore Chamber of Commerce, and Robert Harvey was appointed as the Inspector of Police at Malacca in 1869, with a remuneration of 840 Mexican dollars. Despite all these activities, only nine Europeans were employed by the Borneo Company in Singapore by 1872.[38]

Sarawak was seen as among the most promising of the company's outposts, where they enjoyed a particularly prominent position in the commercial community. By 1872, Helms acted as the general manager, with an acting manager, assistant, clerk, cashier and storekeeper and an agent at Muka. Three local employees operated the antimony mines at Jambusan and Busan and a further fifteen worked at the cinnabar mines at Tegora. The company also played an important part in the coffee, pepper, gambier, sugar, indigo and coconut estates, and in brick kilns and factories at Kuching and Muka. They employed diamond and gold workers and managed two wharves. They purchased a steamer, the *Victor Emanuel*, and renamed it the *Sir James Brooke*. The Company's minute books record that a sample of a wooden sleeper from the railway track used by the London and North Eastern Railway was being brought to Borneo to see if 'they can produce similar'. Shipwrights and millwrights were engaged, encouraged by the Rajah who attended many of the Company's meetings.[39] Although they suffered heavy losses at the outset because of the Chinese insurrection of 1857 (the 1857 accounts record an overall loss of $7927) the Company soon enjoyed considerable prosperity. The 1860 accounts show a profit of £21 257, listing a total of ninety-three shiploads of 'homeward adventures' carrying Japan wood, sago, hides, dragon's blood, gambier, pepper, rattans, coffee, tortoise-shell and gutta-percha, and nine inward shipments of cottons, together with coal imports. As has been seen, the Company's original paid-up capital was £60 000; within four years, this had risen to £200 000. Its property and assets were then valued at £672 309.[40]

V

Gray Paul & Co. and Gray Mackenzie & Co., later to become founder members of the Inchcape Group, were the most important European merchant houses of the Persian Gulf, when the region was opened to wider trade with the award of the mail contract of 1862 and the arrival of BI steamers, for which they acted as agents. The eight voyages per year provided by the BI in this year was increased to fortnightly by 1866, when the subsidy was raised from Rs 80 000 (nearly £6000) to Rs 160 000 (nearly £11 500). Imports of cotton piece goods into the Gulf were to rise dramatically as a result.

An insight into the export commodities from this region shipped to Britain is seen in a return of 1866 to 1869 kept by Gray Paul & Co. at Bushire. It records cargoes of specie, pearls, cotton, silk, almonds, grain, gallnuts, cumin seeds, opium, safflower, ghee, rosewater, horses, carpets, dried fruit and wool.[41] The value of imports into the area from Britain nearly always exceeded the value of homeward shipments. In order to correct this imbalance and fill vacant cargo space in returning vessels, Gray Paul & Co. and Gray Mackenzie & Co. were encouraged to develop local trades, such as opium. Gray Paul & Co.'s office at Bushire was effectively the headquarters of the BI Gulf Service, and was operated by only one manager, Robert Paul, with two Persian clerks, six Persian servants and seven Indian assistants. British Indians enjoyed an important position among merchants and traders in the Gulf, acting as shopkeepers, clerks and 'Dubashs', who were foremen of local labour. Their prominence in the early Gulf economy explains the use of rupees as the official currency of the area used in statistical returns.

The British community at Bushire in the 1860s comprised the political resident, his two assistants, four clerks, an apothecary and the postmaster. Ten other Britons worked in the telegraph department and four military personnel were stationed there.[42] In 1865, when he founded the branch, Robert Paul, who had originally worked in MM & Co.'s piece goods department in Calcutta, was the only European merchant established there. He had been sent by Mackinnon and the London partners who had originally invested in this agency, Archibald Gray and Edwin Sandys Dawes. At the Lingah office, opened in 1875, Gray Paul & Co.'s branch manager was again the only British resident at the port. This was also the case at Bandar Abbas and Bahrain. The latter port was to become the centre of the pearl fishery.

The Basra branch was opened in 1869 by George Mackenzie, who had originally helped Robert Paul set up the Bushire office. Their two partnerships in effect acted as one company, keeping one set of accounts and maintaining a close correspondence. In decline in the first half of the nineteenth century, Basra was revived when the river steamer service on the Tigris and Euphrates was started. This connected the Gulf more effectively with the hinterland. These steamers, operated by the firm of

Lynch Brothers, brought down wood, cereals, dates, liquorice and horses for export, and took back British goods for central Iraq. The expansion of British commerce into the Gulf, in which Gray Paul & Co. and Gray Mackenzie & Co. played such a significant part, was seen as of great benefit to the export trade of both Britain and British India.

VI

Another founder company of the Group which acted as agents for the BI was Smith Mackenzie & Co. They established a merchant house in Zanzibar after the award of the East Africa Mail Contract in 1872. With a monthly service, and with a £10 000 subsidy, BI steamers dominated the traffic at the port in this early period. The opening of the Suez canal in 1869, the success of the Persia Gulf contract, the need to establish a British presence in the area and the popular clamour to fight against slavery, all contributed to British interest in Zanzibar. Smith Mackenzie & Co. were involved in actively developing an existing trade: by 1867–8, imports from Britain were already valued at £153 305, and exports of local produce at £321 642. The value of the annual clove trade, for which Zanzibar became justly famous, was already approaching £100 000 per year.[43]

Expatriate firms based in East Africa before 1870 were rare, so Sir William Mackinnon appointed Captain H. A. Fraser, a retired naval officer, living in Zanzibar as the first local representative of the BI service. Fraser proved to be a disreputable character, heavily indebted to prominent British residents at the port. He owed a Dr Christie $13 000 (equivalent to £2600); Christie's solicitor wrote to the British consul in protest when Fraser tried to sell properties already mortgaged to his client. The BI eventually purchased two houses and two yards from Fraser to enable him to pay off his creditors.[44] Meanwhile, Mackinnon had sent Archibald Smith to Zanzibar from his Glasgow firm to act as Fraser's assistant.

On Fraser's failure to return from an extended visit to Natal in 1874, Smith conveniently presumed him dead and took over the running of the business. Edmund N. Mackenzie, who had worked for Gray Dawes & Co. in London, was then sent to join Smith in Zanzibar, and with capital from Archibald Gray and Edwin Sandys Dawes, they operated jointly as Smith Mackenzie & Co. from 1875.[45] In addition to acting as BI agents, Smith Mackenzie represented the Union Steam Navigation Company, British insurance companies and various British exporters. They also supplied coal to naval vessels. The firm played an important role in representing British commerce at the port, where other merchant concerns, such as the German firms of Widmer, Hansing and O'swald, the Americans Arnold Cheney and James Whyte, the Norway and East Africa Trading Co. and Kilinado of Italy were also established. This was especially important when commercial feelers were being put out from Zanzibar to the mainland of East Africa.

VII

These overseas merchants required representation in London and other cities of Britain if they were to manage their import/export businesses and agency work most effectively. Binny's maintained trading links in Scotland; the Calcutta and Bombay houses set up by Gillanders, Ogilvy and their associates kept strong ties with their Liverpool office; MM & Co. of Calcutta worked closely with William Mackinnon & Co. of Glasgow; the Assam Company was registered in London, as was the India General and the RSN. Kilburn's and Barry's were to establish London offices soon after their formation in India while Macneills were represented there by Duncan Macneill & Co. The companies in China maintained their economic links with Britain through the insurance companies and principals they represented, and the Borneo Company was originally registered in London where its affairs came under close scrutiny. Gray Dawes & Co. (founded by Archibald Gray and Edwin Sandys Dawes in 1865), the London agents of the BI, who, as we have seen, had invested in agencies in the Gulf and at Zanzibar, worked closely with them. Surviving notebooks show their dependence on each other in their day-to-day work.

In addition to the overseas firms, a relatively small number of companies which were to play a part in the history of the Group operated mainly from Britain in this period. They are summarised in Appendix 1.2. These include Rucker and Slann, who were first registered as merchants in Cannon Street, London, in 1767, and were to deal in spices, bristles, pepper, coffee and rubber. Surviving bills of exchange show that the company, first known as Rucker Brothers and then as Rucker and Bencraft, consigned vessels to trade at such ports as St Petersburg. At the end of the eighteenth century, their prosperity was such that the splendid Melrose Hall, on the West Hill, Wandsworth, was 'purchased by John Arthur Rucker, a wealthy merchant in the Baltic trade'.[46]

Gellatly, Hankey & Sewell, established in May 1862, developed from Duncan Dunbar's wine- and beer-shipping business which operated from Limehouse in the late eighteenth century. Selling his brewery which specialised in India Pale Ale for export, Dunbar's son ventured into shipbroking and coaling, owning a large number of sailing vessels, and establishing shipyards at Moulmein in Burma and at Calcutta. He died, leaving a fortune of £1.15m, in 1862. The business was taken over by his shipping manager and an associate.[47]

* * *

In the years 1958–84, all these companies became associated with the Inchcape Group, either as original subsidiaries or as later acquisitions.[48] In considering the history of this Group as a whole, it has been possible to attempt a wide-ranging look at the origins of a large number of merchant partnerships scattered throughout the world. During the last quarter of a century, these firms have been formally linked together; but it is possible to argue that they already had many similarities, activities and contacts in common. From their earliest ventures, many of these companies worked together and shared common directors and investors. For example, in India, we have seen how Albert de Hochpied Larpent of the India General was related to George de Hochpied Larpent of the Assam Company, and John Storm, the first chairman of the India General in 1844, was also a director of the Assam Company. John Jackson, who worked with Ogilvy and Gillanders, ultimately joined the Assam Company and was buried in its cemetery on his death. In Ceylon, A. and B. Scott, employees of Delmege, Reid & Co., formed a branch at Colombo in association with Binny & Co. The partnerships which were ultimately to form the Anglo-Thai Corporation opened a sub-branch in Zanzibar, and Robert Ryrie was to become one of the original investors in the Imperial British East Africa Company. The Borneo Company maintained branches in Hong Kong, Shanghai and Calcultta and Caldbeck originally worked in Singapore. Thus, many of these merchants would have been closely acquainted with each other, in the small British trading communities of Calcutta, Bombay, Singapore, Shanghai, Hong Kong and Zanzibar. The organisation of the carriage of British goods overseas, and the export of local products together with representation of British shipping lines, insurance companies and exporters preoccupied the vast majority of these firms. Many also invested and took an interest in a variety of local commercial opportunities.

By 1870, most of these businesses already enjoyed considerable prominence at their chosen trading posts. Binny's was regarded as one of the most important merchant houses of Madras, involved in sugar, textiles and coffee production. Gillanders and his successors were well established in Bombay and Calcutta; MM & Co. were at the hub of the growing network of BI steamship services on the Indian coast, the Persian Gulf, and in the East African trade. The Assam Company, the oldest tea-producing enterprise in India, was earning substantial profits, as was the India General, and the RSN was soon to prove itself. The firms which managed these tea estates and steamers, Kilburn's, Barry's and Macneill's, were by then well established. The businesses in China – Dodwell's, Gilman's and Gibb Livingston's – were prominent in the tea trade and in shipping, and Caldbeck Macgregor were already famous for their wines and spirits. The Borneo Company had already achieved fame through its near-monopolistic position in Sarawak, and was well respected in Singapore and Siam. In the Gulf and in Zanzibar, the BI agencies enjoyed great prestige through representing this powerful shipping line. These enterprises had all shown that they could cope with the problems of setting up in business in a strange and unknown place, and survive the financial instability, harvest fluctuations and political uncertainties of the countries where they traded. For every successful firm, many more failed and have long since disappeared; the survivors were exceptional. One of the most remarkable of them, MM & Co., welcomed a new employee in 1874 who was to continue this process of gradually drawing these companies and partnerships together into a group: James Lyle Mackay.

NOTES

1. J. Forbes Munro, *Africa and the International Economy, 1800–1960* (London, 1976) pp.9–12.
2. Peter Mathias, *The First Industrial Nation: An Economic History of Britain, 1700–1914* (London, 1969) pp.83–97. See also W. Schlone, *British Overseas Trade from 1700 to the 1930s* (Oxford, 1952); E. B. Schumpeter, *English Overseas Trade Statistics, 1697–1800* (Oxford, 1960); P. J. Cain, *Economic Foundations of British Overseas Trade, 1815–1914* (London, 1980) and D. A. Farnie, *The English Cotton Industry and the World Market 1815–1896* (Oxford, 1979).
3. *Penguin Atlas of Modern History, Part 2* (Harmondsworth, 1974).
4. Binny & Co. Ltd, *The House of Binny* (London, 1969) chap. 2, pp.40–77, and P. J. Griffiths, *The British Impact on India* (London, 1952) chap. 42, pp.391–404.
5. See C. D. Cowan, *The Economic Development of China and Japan* (London,

1964); G. C. Allen and Audrey Donnithorne, *Western Enterprise in Far Eastern Economic Development* (London, 1954) and W. W. Lockwood, *The Economic Development of Japan – Growth and Structual Change, 1868 – 1938* (Princeton, 1954).

6. H. H. The Ranee of Sarawak, *The Three White Rajahs* (London, 1939); Vernon Mullen, *The Story of Sarawak* (Oxford, 1960); Henry Longhurst, *The Borneo Story: The First Hundred Years of the The Borneo Company Limited* (London, 1956) and M. L. Manich-Jumsai, *A Popular History of Thailand* (Chalermnit, 1976).

7. See references in Chapter 3.

8. See references in Chapter 4.

9. Peter Mathias, *The First Industrial Nation*, pp.156–65. However, see R. A. Cage (ed.) *The Scots Abroad* (London, 1985).

10. H. E. S. Fisher, 'The Portuguese Trade' in Philip L. Cottrell and Derek H. Aldcroft (eds) *Shipping, Trade and Commerce: Essays in Memory of Ralph Davis* (Leicester, 1981).

11. See, for example, S. G. Checkland, *The Gladstones: a Family Biography, 1764 – 1851* (Cambridge, 1971); P. N. Davies, *The Trade Makers: Elder Dempster in West Africa, 1852 – 1972* (London, 1973) and Henry Tyrer, *A Liverpool Shipping Agent and His Enterprise, 1879 – 1979* (London, 1979); Sheila Marriner and Francis E. Hyde, *The Senior: John Samuel Swire, 1825 – 1898* (Liverpool, 1967); Maggie Keswick (ed.) *The Thistle and the Jade: A Celebration of Jardine, Matheson & Co.* (London, 1982); R. Pares, *A West India Fortune* (London, 1950) and L. S. Sutherland, *A London Merchant 1695 – 1774* (Oxford, 1962). Two useful general studies of entrepreneurs are D. Aldcroft, 'The Entrepreneur and the British Economy, 1870 – 1914', *Economic History Review* 2nd Series, XII (1964) and Peter Payne, *British Entrepreneurship in the Nineteenth Century* (London, 1974). A rare article on the marketing overseas of British goods by British merchants, which argues that this was more successful and efficient than previously suggested, is Stephen J. Nicholas, 'The Overseas Marketing Performance of British Industry, 1870 – 1914', *Economic History Review*, 2nd Series, XXXVII (1984).

12. Checkland, *The Gladstones*, pp.121 – 3, 181, 318, 341.

13. *The Bombay Almanac, Directory and Register for the Year 1842* (Bombay, 1841) p.9, Bombay Chamber of Commerce list.

14. Keswick, *The Thistle and the Jade*, pp.18 – 19.

15. Binny & Co. Ltd, *The House of Binny*, p.15.

16. Arnold Wright (ed.) Somerset Payne (Compiler) *Southern India: Its History, People, Commerce and Industrial Resources* (London, 1914 – 15) pp.138 – 141, 212.

17. *The Madras Almanac* (Madras, 1802) pp.120, 139 – 48 and *The East India Register and Army list for 1858* (Bombay, 1858) p.136.

18. Binny & Co. Ltd, *The House of Binny*, pp.40 – 77. Rs 100 = approx. £7.

19. Checkland, *The Gladstones*, see note 13, and Anthony Goodinge, 'History of the Anglo-Thai Corporation Limited, 1834 – 1971', unpublished typed Ms., 1973, p.1.

20. *Inchcape Archives [IA]*, Anglo-Thai, Gillanders, Ewart and Company. Deed of Partnership, 19 August 1836.

21. Checkland, *The Gladstones*, pp.121–3, 181, 318, 341.
22. *The Bombay Almanac 1842*, pp.11–13 and *The Bombay Calendar and Almanac for 1853* (Bombay 1852) pp.242–4.
23. *IA*, Mackinnon Mackenzie & Co., private ledger, 1850–3.
24. J. Forbes Munro, entry on Sir William Mackinnon in *Dictionary of Scottish Business Biography* (Aberdeen, forthcoming).
25. *IA*, MM & Co., private ledger, 1850–3, loose letter attached to front page.
26. H. A. Antrobus, *A History of the Assam Company, 1839–1953* (Edinburgh, 1957) pp.17, 35–7 and see P. J. Griffiths, *A History of the Indian Tea Industry* (London, 1967).
27. Alfred Brame, *The India General Steam Navigation Company Limited* (London, 1900) pp.9–12, and P. J. Griffiths, *A History of the Joint Steamer Companies* (London, 1979) chap. 4.
28. Antrobus, *History of the Assam Company*, chap. 12, pp.144–63.
29. P. J. Griffiths, *A History of the Inchcape Group* (London, 1977) chap. 2.
30. *Ceylon Almanac and Annual Register* (Colombo, 1861), pp.204–7, 299, 320.
31. *IA*, Gibb Livingston & Co., Account Book 1844–5.
32. *The China Directory for 1863* (Hong Kong, 1863).
33. 'Caldbecks Celebrate Ten Cycles', *Inchcape Magazine 17*, Spring 1984, pp.10–11.
34. Henry Longhurst, *The Borneo Story*.
35. *IA*, The Borneo Company Limited [BCL], agreements with Rajah Brooke, 1857–9.
36. *The Colonial Directory of the Straits Settlements including Sarawak, Labuan, Bangkok and Saigon* (Singapore, 1873).
37. *IA*, BCL, Minute Book Summary, 1856–71.
38. *Annual Report on the Administration of the Straits Settlement, 1865–6* (Singapore, 1866) and *Straits Settlement Blue Book 1871* (Singapore, 1872).
39. *IA*, BCL, Minute Book Summary, 1856–71.
40. *IA*, BCL, Reports and Accounts, 1860.
41. J. A. Saldanha, *Precis of Commerce and Communication in the Persian Gulf, 1801–1905* (Calcutta, 1906) app. D.
42. Ibid, app. E, Returns of British Subjects Resident in Bushire, 1869.
43. *Reports from HM Consuls on the manufacturers and Commerce of their Consular Dsitricts, Parliamentary Papers*, 1876, LXXIV (*c*.1421), report on the trade of Zanzibar by Captain Prideaux.
44. *Zanzibar National Archives*, in letters to British Consul, vol. E66, 1874, and in letters vol. E70, 1875.
45. Smith, Mackenzie & Co. Ltd, *The History of Smith, Mackenzie and Company Limited* (London, 1937).
46. 'More than Two Hundred Years of A History of Trading', *Inchcape Magazine 12*, p.11, and information kindly supplied by Mr Button of Rucker & Slann, including the reference to Melrose Hall, in *The Wandsworth Historian*, February 1979, no. 21, p.1.
47. George Blake, *Gellatly's 1862–1962* (London, 1962) pp.1–19 and *Inchcape Magazine 17* pp.4–5.
48. See Appendix of Principal Subsidiaries and Associated Companies of the Group in 1984, at the end of this book, which also shows the year in which these businesses were acquired.

APPENDIX 1.1 THE ORIGINAL FOUNDERS OF THE INCHCAPE GROUP: 56 OF THE EARLIEST ENTREPRENEURS, 1796–1874, BASED OVERSEAS

	Place of Birth	Place first worked at overseas	Date of arrival	Activities when first arrived	Ultimate position in Co.
1. John Binny	Forfar	Madras	1796	Surgeon	Founder, Binny & Co.
2. Robert Dennison	Scotland	Madras	pre-1796	Coffee trader and sold army clothing	Partner, Binny & Co.
3. John Binny, Jnr	Forfar	Madras	1810	Merchant	Partner, half share in Binny's, 1836
4. F. M. Gillanders	Highlands, Scotland	Bombay	1818	Representative of Gladstone family	Founder, Ewart & Co.
5. Thomas Ogilvy	Scotland	?	?	?	Director, Ewart & Co. till 1842
6. William K. Ewart	Scotland	Bombay	1834	Local Manager	First Bombay Manager
7. Peter Ewart	Scotland	Bombay	1836	Local Manager	Second Bombay Manager
8. Edward Lyon	Scotland	Bombay	1836	Assistant to P. Ewart	With Ewart, till 1847, then Partner in Lyon & Co.
9. John Jackson	Liverpool	?	?	Merchant	Worked for Assam. Co.
10. Robert Brown	Liverpool	Bombay	1848	Merchant/Partner at Bombay	Third Bombay Partner
11. George Clark Arbuthnot	Scotland	?	?	Captain in EIC	Senior Partner to 1857
12. Arthur George Latham	Scotland	Bombay	1847	Merchant	Senior Partner
13. Robert Ryrie	Caithness	Bombay	1851	Merchant	Senior Partner until 1888
14. William Mackinnon	Campbeltown	Calcutta	1847	Sugar factory worker	Founder, MM & Co., 1847

Continued overleaf

APPENDIX 1.1—*continued*

	Place of Birth	Place first worked at overseas	Date of arrival	Activities when first arrived	Ultimate position in Co.
15. Robert Mackenzie	Campbeltown	Calcutta	c.1830s	Merchant	Founder, MM & Co., 1847
16. James McAlister Hall	Scotland	Calcutta	c.1840s	Merchant	Partner, MM & Co.
17. James Lyle Mackay	Arbroath	Calcutta	1874	Merchant	Partner, MM & Co.
18. Charles Alexander Bruce	Scotland	Assam	c.1836	EIC Naval Officer	Manager, Assam & Co.
19. J. W. Masters	?	Assam	1839	Local Manager Assam Co.	Manager, Assam & Co.
20. Albert de Hochepied Larpent		?	?	Merchant	Director, India General
21. Captain A. G. Mackenzie	Scotland	India	1820s	EIC 2nd officer	Founder, India General and Partner
22. Captain J. H. Williamson		India	?	IGNR Commander	Founder and Partner, India General
23. C. E. Shoene		Calcutta	pre-1842	Merchant	Founder, Schoene, Kilburn & Co.
24. Edward Dunbar Kilburn	London	Calcutta	1847	Merchant	Founder, Schoene, Kilburn & Co.
25. Dr J. B. Barry		Calcutta	1860s	Surgeon in Assam	Founder, J. B. Barry & Co.
26. Duncan Macneill	Scotland	Calcutta	1858	Assistant, Begg, Dunlop & Company	Founder, Duncan Macneill & Co.

	Origin	Location	Date	Occupation	Firm
27. John Mackinnon	Scotland	Calcutta	1858	Assistant, Begg, Dunlop & Company	Founder, Duncan Macneill & Co.
28. Alexander Reid	Scotland	Galle/Ceylon	1850	Merchant, trader	Founder, Reid & Co.
29. James Reid	Scotland	Galle/Ceylon	1850s	Merchant, trader	Assistant to brother
30. E. T. Delmege	USA	Galle/Ceylon	1865	Merchant, trader	Founder, Delmege, Forsyth & Co.
31. A. A. Delmege	USA	Galle/Ceylon	post-1865	Merchant, trader	Assistant to brother
32. Thomas Augustus Gibb	Scotland	Canton	1835	EIC merchant	Founder, Gibb Livingston & Co.
33. William Potter Livingston	Scotland	Canton	1835	EIC merchant	Founder, Gibb Livingston & Co.
34. Abram Bowman	?	Canton	c.1830s, 1840s	Merchant	Founder, Gilman Bowman & Co.
35. Richard James Gilman	?	Canton	1840	Tea taster	Founder, Gilman Bowman & Co.
36. Jack Caldbeck	Scotland	Hong Kong	1850s	Army-Crimean War	Founder, Caldbeck Macgregor & Co.
37. John Macgregor	Scotland	Hong Kong	1850s	Army-Crimean War	Founder, Caldbeck Macgregor & Co.
38. W. R. Adamson	Macclesfield?	Shanghai	early 1850s	representative of silk manufacturer in Cheshire	Founder, W. R. Adamson & Co.

Continued overleaf

	Place of Birth	Place first worked at overseas	Date of arrival	Activities when first arrived	Ultimate position in Co.
39. George Benjamin Dodwell	Derby	Shanghai	1872	Shipping agent, trader	Founder, Dodwell & Co., Ltd.
40. A. J. H. Carlill	?	Foochow	1870s	Tea taster	Partner, Dodwell, Carlill & Co.
41. Ludvig Verner Helms	Denmark	Bali	1846	Explorer, pioneer	Local manager, Borneo Company
42. Robert MacEwan	W. Coast of Scotland	Singapore	1840s	Trader, merchant	Manager, Singapore branch, Paterson & Co.
43. John Harvey	Renfrewshire	Singapore	1840s, 1850s	Merchant	Succeeded MacEwan
44. Robert Harvey	Renfrewshire	Singapore	1840s, 1850s	Clerk, Assistant	Assistant to J. Harvey
45. John Charles Templer	?	?	?	Merchant	Friend of Rajah Brooke, Vice Chairman BCL
46. Francis Richardson	?	Manila	?	Local manager Manilla-merchant	Partner, MacEwan & Co.
47. Samuel Gilfillan	?	Bangkok	?	Merchant, trader	Borneo Company Manager, Siam
48. William Adamson	?	Singapore	1862	Merchant, trader	Borneo Company Manager, Singapore
49. Louis T. Leonowens	?	?	?	Merchant, originally with Borneo Company	Founder, Leonowens & Co., traders
50. John and Henry Lynch	?	Basra	1840s	Traders, shippers	Formed Euphrates & Tigris SN & Co.
51. Robert Paul	Scotland	Bushire	1865	Merchant, trader	Partner, Gray Paul & Co. Manager, Bushire

52. George S. Mackenzie	India-of Scottish percentage	Bushire	1865	Merchant, trader	Partner, Gray Mackenzie & Co. Manager, Basra
53. Capt. H. A. Fraser	?	Zanzibar	1860s	Merchant, shipping agent	First BI Agent, Zanzibar
54. Edmund N. Mackenzie	Scotland?	Zanzibar	1872–3	Merchant, shipping agent	Partner, Smith Mackenzie & Co., Manager Zanzibar
55. Archibald Smith	Scotland	Zanzibar	1873–4	Merchant, shipping agent	Partner, Smith Mackenzie & Co. Assistant, Zanzibar
56. Stephen Williamson	Scotland	Valparaiso	1853	Merchant, shipping agent	Founder, Balfour Williamson & Co.*

*See Appendix 6.1

SOURCES Various company histories and archives listed in notes.

APPENDIX 1.2 THE ORIGINAL FOUNDERS OF THE INCHCAPE GROUP: THOSE REMAINING IN BRITAIN

	Place of Birth	Original Position	Involvement in Inchcape Co.
1. Archibald Gray	Scotland	Merchant, India	Director, GD & Co., GP & Co., GM & Co., SM & Co.
2. Edwin Sandys Dawes	Staffordshire, England	Merchant, India	Director, GD & Co., GP & Co., GM & Co., SM & Co.
3. George de Hochepied Larpent		Merchant, tea trade London	Director, Assam Company
4. W. R. Paterson	Glasgow	Merchant trader	Founder, W. R. Paterson & Co.
5. William Morgan	Glasgow	Merchant, trader	Director, Borneo Company
6. Robert Henderson	Scotland	Merchant, trader	Director, Borneo Company
7. Edward Younger	London	Worked in London non-smelting firm	Founded metal-broking firm in London 1865 – Vivian, Younger & Bond
8. James Edward Vivian	London	Joined family smelting business	Founded metal-broking firm in London 1865 – Vivian, Younger & Bond
9. Frank Walters Bond	London	Metal broker, tin-maker	Founded metal-broking firm in London 1865 – Vivian, Younger & Bond
10. Duncan Dunbar	Moray, Scotland	Brewer, skipper	Founder, Duncan Dunbar & Co.
11. Duncan Dunbar, Jnr.	Limehouse, London	Shipowner	Succeeded as Chairman
12. Edward Gellatly	London	Originally for Dunbars Shipbroker & Manager	Founder, Gellatly, Hankey & Sewell
13. Jameson Alers Hankey	London	Merchant banker	Founder, Gellatly, Hankey & Sewell
14. Frederic Sewell	London	Brewer, Taylor Walker's	Founder, Gellatly, Hankey & Sewell
15. John Arthur Rucker	London	Merchant	Founder, Rucker Brothers
16. Jonathan Rucker	London	Merchant	Founder, Rucker Brothers

17. William Bencraft	London	Merchant-brother of Jonathan	Partner, Rucker & Bencraft
18. G. N. C. Mann	Cornwall	Electrical engineer, Norwich	Founder, Mann Egerton & Co.*
19. Hubert Egerton	?	Early motoring pioneer	Founder, Mann Egerton & Co.*
20. Alexander Balfour	Scotland	Merchant	Founder, Balfour Williamson & Co.**

*See Appendix 2.2
**See Appendix 6.1
SOURCES Various company histories and archives listed in footnotes.

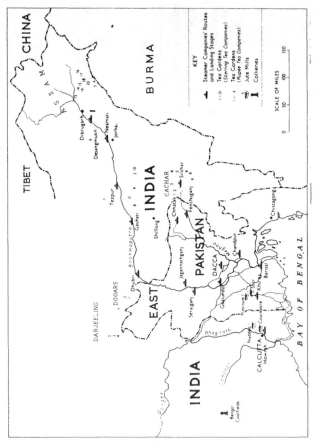

MAP 2.1 North East India and East Pakistan, showing joint steamer companies' routes and ports of call, location of sterling and rupee tea estates, jute mills, etc., at the time of the formation of the Group.

NOTE At the end of 1984, the Group's only interest is in the Assam Company (India) Ltd.

2 An Entrepreneur *par excellence*: The First Lord Inchcape and the Growth of the Companies in India and at Home, c.1870–1939

By 1870, the core companies of the Inchcape Group today were slowly expanding their commercial activities on the trading routes of the Indian Ocean and the Far East. In the decades before the First World War, these enterprises grew dramatically through improvements in communications accelerated by the opening of the Suez Canal in 1869 and the development of the compound steamship engine. Their growth was sustained by the resultant increase in the world carrying-trade, enabling them to survive and prosper despite the First World War, which completely ruptured existing trading arrangements and led to a world depression of unprecedented magnitude. The links which these independent companies had already built up during the earlier nineteenth century through their dealings in the same ports, and handling the same commodities, were to be further strengthened in one of two ways. Either they became part of the future Lord Inchcape's portfolio during his lifetime or, much more recently, became members of the Inchcape Group after it was formed in 1958. The following chapters will consider these growing Inchcape interests in various parts of the world. We shall first focus on the two places with which the Group has been most strongly associated – India and London – and on the activities of its most prominent enterpreneur.

I

In many ways, James Lyle Mackay (who became the first Lord Inchcape in 1911) was typical of the earliest Group enterpreneurs discussed in Chapter 1. Like many other able Scots, he had become disenchanted with the lack of commercial opportunities that he had experienced in his homeland, working as a scrivener in Arbroath, then for a local firm of rope and canvas makers. He earned £5 in his first year of office life, £10 in the second, and £15 in the third, working each day from nine in the morning to eight at night, and often ten and eleven o'clock, with occasional unremunerative extra labour, consisting of flax-weighing from a ship in harbour beginning at six in the morning. His employer, named Webster, had described him thus: 'Jeemie is no a bad laddie, but he's a damned sicht ower-ambitious'.[1] His negative reasons for leaving his homeland were to be emphasised in much later life in a speech at his old school:

> let me recommend you not to be afraid to go out into the world. There is no scope in Scotland for the energy, the brains, the initiative and the ambition of all the youth in the country . . . if there is no prospect for you here, the sooner you get away the better.[2]

Meanwhile, Mackay, in common with many of the other early entrepreneurs mentioned in Chapter 1, had positive reasons to seek more remunerative employment. He had already gained some experience of shipping and trading: his father, a well-to-do Arbroath shipmaster, had taken his second son and fourth child on a voyage from Montrose to Archangel in the flax trade in celebration of his eighth birthday. Subsequently the young man never missed an opportunity to converse with captains in port whilst working for the Arbroath rope and canvas makers. Moreover, the death of his parents when he was only twelve not only made him independent of the usual home ties but one of the beneficiaries of his father's substantial will. A patrimony of £2000 was prudently invested by his guardian in three East Indian barques (which his elder brother managed and often commanded), bringing in a reassuring income of £100 a year. So, in 1871, at the age of 19, the young Mackay searched through the columns of the London shipping press for an opening in the metropolis. He found a post with the well-known and old-established ship-brokers and agents, Gellatly, Hankey and Sewell, who enjoyed growing links with the newly-formed BI. Thus, like many of these entrepreneurs, he was to gain further valuable experience in the London office of his future employers overseas. This involved working as a bill-of-lading clerk, then in dealing with the customs authorities, supervising the entrance and clearance of all vessels consigned to the firm and organising the handling of their cargoes, together with paying all port and Trinity Light dues.[3]

2.1 A steamer going through the Suez Canal in the late nineteenth century

Meanwhile, the attractions of the East had become even stronger and more popular through the impact of the recent opening and greater use of the Suez Canal. Previously, to carry the cargo of a single steamer overland to Suez, a caravan of at least 3000 camels and as many men were required.[4] The BI's Calcutta agents, Mackinnon Mackenzie & Co. [MM & Co.], who acted as the hub of their overseas operations, asked the London agents, Gray Dawes & Co. [GD & Co.] for a new assistant to handle their increasing business. Mackay was in fact their third choice. He was helped by his dedication and independent status: the first young man wanted to have his summer holidays first, and the second had to ask parental permission.[5]

A voyage to Calcutta lasting nearly three months (lengthened by the refusal of the Post Office to allow mail steamers to use the Canal until 1888 and by calling and landing at thirty-two ports between Bombay and Calcutta)[6] further severed his ties with his already distant homeland. MM & Co. at Calcutta were already a prosperous and influential firm.

2.2 Calcutta street scene, c.1900: note the electric tramway

The senior partners had amassed large personal fortunes and had returned to Scotland by the time that Mackay was finding his feet in Calcutta. William Mackinnon had purchased extensive lands at Balnakill and Loup and at Strathaird in Skye, the hereditary home of the clan Mackinnon. Peter Hall, who had joined MM & Co. in 1851, had bought Torrisdale Castle in Kintyre. Duncan and Peter Mackinnon (nephews of William) who were in charge of the Calcutta office, spent increasingly long periods at home on leave.[7] The firm was changing from its early pioneering phase, in which the first partners struggled to establish an import–export business in often difficult circumstances, sending out their assistants to seek out possible new branches in other ports. John Halliday's journey to Chittagong in 1864 was one such mission:

I arrived here this morning and have just been round having a look at the place. It is a miserable, dead & alive, tumble-down, jungly hole and looks as if a shower of rain would make it commit suicide. [Archibald] Gray is going on to Calcutta to arrange about the Agency . . . If there is one native vessel I support there is [*sic*] a hundred lying up here, all of which will doubtless get cargo to Akyab and other places. I don't see why, with an energetic agency, the steamers should not get a good deal of the cargo these people will take.[8]

By the time of Mackay's arrival in 1874 the development of the BI's services (listed in Table 2.1)[9] was such that, combined with the expansion of India's own industries, the position of shipping assistant for MM & Co. in Calcutta had great commercial potential. The export trade in indigo, tea, jute, coal, wrought iron and cotton benefited from the development of inland communications throughout the sub-continent. Subject to strong British influence from the beginning through the managing agency system, the firm enjoyed a steady and growing business.[10] The Indian coastal trade was to be the greatest source of profit to the BI, and in the second half of the 1870s, this part of their business was at its peak. Facing no sustained competition until the 1880s, the BI's sixty ships, nearly 59 000 gross registered tons in all, carried at least half the entire traffic of the Burma ports as well as half that between Bombay, Karachi and the Gulf. Figure 2.1 shows that BI steamers represented over 20 per cent of steam tonnage in Indian waters in 1880, and held its own against increased competition, which was mainly from other British and German firms, by 1895. The BI served a range of official requirements, transporting government employees, stores, specie and soldiers to relieve garrison forces. They acted as a local

TABLE 2.1 BI services 1854–1908

Main ports of call	Original service		Subsequent changes
Calcutta, Chittagong, Akyab	Fortnightly	1862	Extended to Kyouk Phyoo 1872 and to Sandoway monthly 1873 only on fair weather season. Increased to weekly and extended to Bassein 1881.
Calcutta, Akyab, Rangoon, Moulmein	Fortnightly	1856	Merged into one Line. Weekly 1881.
Calcutta, Rangoon and Moulmein	Fortnightly except Moulmein	1854	Increased to weekly 1882. Increased to weekly 1873.
Moulmein, Penang, Malacca, Singapore	Monthly	1862	Extended to Calcutta 1870. Increased to fortnightly 1879. Weekly 1884.
Calcutta Coast and Bombay	Fortnightly	1862	1875 increased to weekly. Increased to twice weekly 1884.
Madras and Rangoon	Monthly	1862	Increased to fortnightly 1875.
Bombay and Karachi	Weekly	1862	Reduced to fortnightly 1866. Increased to twice weekly 1873. Increased to three times a week 1884.
Bombay and Persian Gulf	Fortnightly	1862	Increased to weekly 1875. Karachi added 1869.
Calcutta, Port Blair, Camorta and Straits	Monthly	1870	Straits omitted. Service reduced to once every six weeks 1871. Restored to every four weeks 1873. Extended to Rangoon 1881.
Rangoon and Moulmein	Weekly	1871	Three times weekly 1894.
Calcutta, Dhamrah and Chandbali	Weekly	1873	Abandoned 1874.
Aden and Zanzibar	Monthly	1873	Extended to Mozambique. Service disappeared 1881,

This service connects with the following: Zanzibar, Comore, Mayotte, Nossi Be and Majunga	Monthly	1874	apparently substituted by service to Bombay, Aden, Mombasa, etc. Service abandoned 1876.
London, Algiers, Port Said, Suez, Yambo, Jeddah, Hodirdah, Aden, Kurrachee, Bunder Abbas, Bushire, Busreh	Monthly	1874	Increased to fortnightly 1876. Decreased to monthly 1881. Algiers, Jeddah, Hodeidah and extension to Persian Gulf discontinued 1882. Increased to fortnightly 1882. Western India added 1883. Algiers reinserted 1884.
Aden and Karachi	Monthly	1875	
Rangoon and Straits Coasting	Five weekly	1881	Service abandoned 1884, leaving service to Calcutta, Rangoon, Singapore shown above.
Bombay, Aden, Zanzibar, Mozambique and Delagoa Bay	Four weekly	1881	Discontinued 1890. Resumed 1894. Ceased 1908.
London, Columbo, Madras and Calcutta	Fortnightly	1881	
London, Batavia and Queensland	Four weekly	1881	Discontinued 1894.
Rangoon, Tavoy, Mergui	Fortnightly	1862	Increased by call at Moulmein in 1884 and to weekly service.
Negapatam, Coconada, Moulmein and Rangoon	Three services a month	1884	Extended to Madras and increased to weekly 1886. Separate service to Straits 1894 fortnightly.
Calcutta, Colombo, Mauritius	Monthly	1894	Seychelles and Aden included 1900 and increased to fortnightly. Seychelles and Aden omitted 1902 and decreased to monthly.
London, Aden, Mombasa, Zanzibar	Monthly	1890	
Calcutta, Australia	Monthly	1894	

SOURCE *Inchcape Archives*, MM & Co., E. J. Pakes private file.

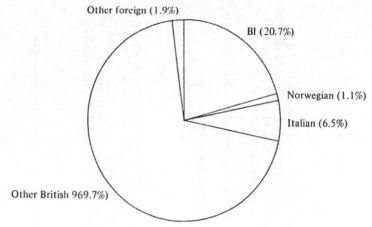

Other foreign (1.9%)

BI (20.7%)

Norwegian (1.1%)

Italian (6.5%)

Other British 969.7%)

SOURCE As source for Figure 2.5

FIGURE 2.1 Tonnage of steamers calling at Indian ports, 1880

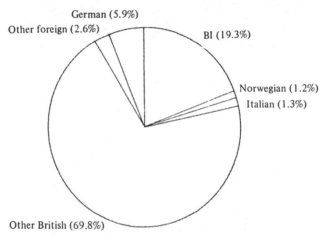

German (5.9%)

Other foreign (2.6%)

BI (19.3%)

Norwegian (1.2%)

Italian (1.3%)

Other British (69.8%)

SOURCE As source for Figure 2.5

FIGURE 2.2 Tonnage of steamers calling at Indian ports, 1895

mercantile marine whose ships could be employed on behalf of India in wartime. MM & Co.'s founders, who had a financial stake of nearly 30 per cent, were by far the largest shareholders in the BI. MM & Co. received a 5 per cent commission in the shipping line's gross annual earnings. These profits were such that it has been suggested that the BI found it necessary to hide from the Government of India the full extent of their profitability, in order to avoid the risk of losing their subsidy.[11] Thus, in terms of the commercial climate, Mackay found himself in the right place at the right time.

II

A second development favourable to Mackay's progress was the changing leadership of MM & Co. With the return to Scotland and retirement of many of the first and second generation of partners, a new corpus of non-Mackinnon (but definitely still Scottish) assistants was being recruited. In 1860, 1861 and 1871 respectively, T. M. Russell, W. P. Alexander and E. D. Wylie were appointed, who were to serve for 25, 19 and 14 years respectively. They provided new blood and smoothed the path for Mackay's future admission as a partner. This enabled him, in due course, to succeed to the overall leadership of the firm, the shipping line, and the whole commercial complex. A useful indication of a shipping agent's duties at the time of Mackay's arrival is provided by an outline of the BI's services, given in their earliest handbook.[12] In addition to the carriage of mails, the BI steamers offered a passenger and cargo service. Cabin passage cost approximately £20 per head for the complete journey from Bombay to Basra with a reduced fare to intermediate ports. This included food, but not wines, and the provision of bedding, linen and furniture by the company. Quarterdeck passengers, travelling at just over half the cabin fare, were allowed space for a bed on the poop and a trunk of 5 cubic feet. All native servants were classed as ordinary-deck passengers, although European servants travelled at half the first-class fare, and European maidservants with a berth in their mistress's cabin were charged at two-thirds the cabin rate. All berths were booked through the BI's agents, who ensured that passengers gave up any weapons on embarkation and that freight on excess luggage was paid at double rates. No indication is given in the handbook of who the passengers were, or their reasons for travelling. The BI certainly enjoyed a share of the Moslem pilgrim traffic to Jeddah from 1869. Besides persons travelling on official business already mentioned, presumably the greater part of the trade was the carriage of local merchants and labour in search of work.

A custom-house pass was required for all packages shipped, the freight being prepaid at the port of shipment. The BI's agents had to supervise the landing of cargo at the ports of delivery in their own or hired boats. They were responsible for the deposit of goods on wharves, or in receiving vessels such as lighters, emphasising that they could not guarantee against delays. They had to check that the bills of lading accurately described the contents of packages carried, especially to enforce the ban on dangerous cargoes, such as gunpowder or sulphuric acid. The agents required that goods for shipment should be alongside at least twenty-four hours before departure: the handbook warned that 'most of the mistakes arise through shippers sending their goods at the last moment'. The agents were liable to be paid in a great variety of coinage, and thus had to provide their own banking service. By the mid-1860s, the trade in horses, ponies, bullocks, sheep and goats was increasing in importance. Shippers had to provide fodder for their animals, but the charge included the passage of a 'syce' or groom in attendance on each horse. Horses were required to have their shoes removed, and coir matting was provided to prevent them slipping. Finally, the BI's agents were also responsible for organising the carriage of specie on the company's steamers. Such were the dangers of loss or theft, however, that they refused to undertake to land valuables; instead, they were delivered only by the presentation of the appropriate bills of lading on board.

By the mid-1870s, the expansion of the BI's services, as shown in Table 2.1, necessitated a geographically more widespread network of agents. The establishment of Gray Paul & Co. at Bushire and Gray Mackenzie & Co. at Basra, with Smith Mackenzie & Co. at Zanzibar, are discussed in Chapters 3 and 4 respectively. Close liaison between these partnerships and the Calcutta Head Office was essential. One of Mackay's first tasks, in 1877, after three years based solely at the Calcutta office, learning the ropes as a young shipping assistant, was to handle the operation of the Gulf mail service; his detailed and regular correspondence dominates the BI's records of this area of their operations.[13] He visited, among others, the ports of Karachi, Gwadur, Muscat, Lingah, Bahrain, Bushire, Kuwait, Abadan and Basra. These were no brief social calls just to show the locals that Head Office had not forgotten them; they were time-consuming, uncomfortable expeditions to primitive open roadsteads dealing with intractable Arab and Turkish officials and hardened BI captains resentful of a young clerk, even if a fellow Scot.

Ironically, a disaster for the BI gave Mackay his first break. The suspension of the City of Glasgow Bank in 1878, which reverberated even throughout the East – Mackinnon had been able to disentangle himself in the nick of time – led to the collapse of the BI's Bombay agents, Nichol and Co. Mackay volunteered immediately, leaving

Calcutta within a few hours, even without time to pack, and rapidly restored order at the new branch. He revealed a particular flair for delegating work to well-chosen European and local assistants. Within two years, aged only 26, he was rewarded by a partnership in the Bombay firm, with a 10 per cent share in the profits. By 1884, this had risen to 15 per cent, with an additional 3 per cent interest in the Calcutta office.[15] This growing prosperity and importance at this relatively young age is shown by his life-style in Bombay which also indicates the obsession with maintaining British customs beloved by many expatriates. He lived in an elegant 'chummery' in the city with William Bell of Messrs Wm Bell & Co., a fellow Scottish commercial house and Mr Curwen, the editor of the *Times of India*.

Life in Bombay [he later recalled] was extremely agreeable. I was elected a member of the Royal Bombay Yacht Club. I built a small yacht, which I named the *Pinafore* and had many delightful cruises in Bombay harbour. I became a member of the Bombay Hunt . . . we had glorious hunts every Sunday in the cold weather, a pack of hounds being brought out every season from home, together with a huntsman . . . I had a bungalow out at Bandra and here I used to go for the week-ends, all the year round.[16]

This position of authority at Bombay at great distance from his seniors in Calcutta allowed him to indulge in amusing personal idiosyncracies, such as one recalled by Shivram Ramchandra, a devoted Indian clerk:

Mr Mackay rode much on his favourite chestnut horse and occasionally rode up the stairs into the office to frighten us. After dismounting he would give the horse a biscuit or so to eat and order it to get down, which it obeyed.[17]

It is, however, beyond dispute that Mackay's dedication and professionalism were beyond question, and he was soon indispensable to his employers. As early as 1878 the senior partner in Calcutta, needing another young clerk, cabled to William Mackinnon in London 'send us another assistant like Mackay'. Although home leave was often taken after five years overseas, Mackay remained in India for seven, and was persuaded to go home only to recover from a violent attack of typhoid fever. He was so weakened by the illness that he had to be carried on board ship at Bombay. Even before he reached Aden, the senior partners, already missing his expertise, telegraphed 'if convalescent, please return'. He lived frugally and was thus able to save a large proportion of his growing income. Even as a young clerk in Calcutta, he lived well within his salary of 300 rupees a month (about £20), never having to draw on the income from his patrimony which was left to accumulate back in Scotland.[18]

A private letter-book kept by the Calcutta partners for the period from 1884 to 1900 shows not only the activities and profits of the firm, but the fact that the partners made several large investments in growing local industries, ventures which also attracted Mackay's increasing savings. As well as owning ships and properties in India (worth nearly 100 000 rupees or over £7000), the senior partners made substantial investments in the India Jute Co., the Equitable Coal Co., the Kondoti Coffee Estates, tea estates all over Assam and the Rivers Steam Navigation Co., not to mention enterprises outside India which will be discussed in later chapters. In the Assam Tea properties, for example, Sir William Mackinnon alone held shares worth over £15 000 of an overall total interest of his firm in this business which exceeded £47 000.[19] This was made possible by the relatively small capital inputs required to run the Mackinnon commercial business, which mainly depended on commission earnings. Besides rent on offices and godowns, the wages of native assistants made up most of the remaining expenses. That the pay of these workers was low was occasionally recognised by their employers. In the case of Tacoordoss Mookerjie, who only received 45 rupees [about £3] notwithstanding very long and faithful service, it was agreed that 'this be increased to 60 rupees per month'.[20] In that same year (1885), profits exceeded £35 000.[21] The partners were thus able to withdraw large amounts from the business, and invest in various local enterprises, in addition to remitting handsome returns back to Britain.

Mackay's own early investments, in the merchant partnerships discussed in Chapter 1, led to what ultimately was to become the Inchcape Group. The oldest and one of the most important of these companies was Binny's of Madras, well-known as a thriving import–export business. By 1876 they had established an important subsidiary, the Buckingham Mill Co. Ltd, with a paid-up capital equivalent of £35 000. By 1880 this cotton mill was producing over 6000 lb of yarn per day and paying an annual dividend to shareholders of 10 per cent. A large proportion of this output was exported to China, and the closing of this market in 1900 by the Boxer Rebellion was a great blow to the company. Meanwhile, a second subsidiary, the Carnatic Mill Co. Ltd was launched in 1881 with the equivalent of nearly £50 000 capital, invested in a large composite unit with 16 500 spindles and 129 looms. Although

2.3 Binny's: pay day at the Buckingham and Carnatic Mills at Madras in the early twentieth century

2.4 Binny's: a scene at work in the Buckingham and Carnatic Mills

2.5 Binny's: the company health service at work in the 1950s

Binny's were also in the forefront of the development of mechanised dyeing and finishing, especially of khaki cloth, they suffered heavy competition from the USA. Dividend payments became intermittent. Meanwhile, the parent company took over several cotton presses, the Bangalore Steam Woollen Mills and the Bangalore Woollen, Cotton & Silk Mills Ltd. By the mid-1880s, these enterprises were beginning to justify their existence, enabling Binny's to diversify further into the ownership of tramways, and coffee plantations, and also to begin dealing in aerated waters and salt. The business resources were widely stretched and when, in 1906, the Madras banking and agency house of Arbuthnot, with whom Binny's were closely associated and which was a branch of the partnerships later to form the Anglo-Thai Corporation failed, Binny's was severely shaken.

Itself forced to suspend payments and go into voluntary liquidation, Binny's was thus available at a bargain price. A printed schedule of its immoveable property shows that it owned office premises, godowns and stables in two locations in Madras, the three textile mills, the Lion Works containing oil mills and coffee-curing works also in Madras, and nine wholly-owned coffee estates, with an additional eight in which the partners had a private interest. Mackay saw immediately that the enterprise was well worth the equivalent of nearly £50 000 that was being asked for it. He persuaded fellow BI/Mackinnon partners Duncan Mackinnon and George Mackenzie also to take a substantial stake. They were the preferred bidders, as Binny's faced the unwelcome alternative of being taken over by an Indian firm, thereby losing its identity, name, reputation and goodwill which had taken a century to build up.[22] The new concern was then known as Binny & Co. Ltd.

A description of Binny's on the eve of the First World War shows that Mackay's initiative in 1906 benefited both rescued and rescuer. By 1910 they had gained the BI agency at the port, earning 4 per cent commission on freight and passage money and a further 4 per cent on trans-shipment freight. In connection with this work, the company acquired a flotilla of boats including 'steam and petrol launches, and a fleet of some thirty-five barges and thirty lighters' operated by '400 bargemen and about the same number of stevedores'. They handled 'a very considerable proportion' of the imports of Madras, and acted as agents to the Madras Port Trust, trans-shipping immigrants from the Straits and Rangoon. As well as their cotton and woollen mills, the company's coffee estates became profitable again, with 3500 acres under crop; between 500 and 700 tons of coffee were exported in a good season. They represented four important banks in Madras, including Baring's of London, together with textile manufacturers in Glasgow and Manchester, and fourteen insurance companies. A half-yearly dividend of 10 per cent was paid in the second half of 1906.[23]

Mackay also took substantial interests in several tea estates and the two river steamer companies, the India General and the RSN, discussed in Chapter 1, as well as their respective managing agents. These holdings formed the basis for the future Inchcape Group's Indian businesses, shown in map 2.1. The rivalry between the two steamer lines during the 1870s and the 1880s had reduced their earnings, despite increasing traffic with the growth in tea exports, the introduction of a mail service to Cachar and the reopening of the Ganges line for passengers and cargo. Pooling their resources in 1889 as the Joint Steamer Companies, they were able to fend off competition from steamers owned by the Bengal Railway, and by the Assam Railways and Trading Company. Except for the cyclone of 1909 which destroyed much of their property, the firms enjoyed steady prosperity and paid handsome dividends from the beginning of the century to 1914.[24]

III

In 1894 Mackay (who that same year was created Knight Commander of the Indian Empire) returned to Britain. His commercial life as a merchant and employee of MM & Co. was at an end, and his work now became dominated by his many directorships and involvement in several government committees. Appendix 2.1 summarises his principal contributions, both in India and Britain. Immediately on his return, he joined the Board of the BI, pioneering more new routes with the aid of Government subsidies, as shown in Table 2.1. Mackay's old employers, Gellatly's, who acted as the BI's cargo-brokers, also shared in the growing business which the new subsidies brought. The British shipping industry was buoyant in the mid- to late 1890s, with over a million tons of new shipping launched in 1894 alone. The Sino-Japanese War gave profitable work to steamers, and low grain stocks in India and Australia led to a need for large grain imports into those countries. Meanwhile, the nitrate trade of South America offered profitable cargoes, as did cattle at ports throughout the American continent.[25] Gellatly's ensured steady earnings for the BI by employing its vessels in tramp cargo trades and using their resources to make short-term profitable time-charters as an adjunct to its assured income from subsidised lines.

The BI's regular passenger services and associated business were handled by its London agents, GD & Co., who, as discussed in Chapter 1, worked in close contact with the other offices throughout the world. This merchant partnership, which remained a private firm for nearly 100 years (from 1865 to 1952) became a key company in the ultimate formation of the Group, as well as supervising and supplying business to many of its constituent parts. It was established by William Mackinnon to provide business opportunities for his nephew, Archibald Gray and a favoured young P & O officer, Edwyn Sandys Dawes, both of whom had already experienced commercial life in India but had been forced home through ill-health and family responsibilities. When Dawes wrote to Mackinnon for advice on his future career, he received this reply:

It has occurred to me that perhaps an arrangement might be made whereby you and my nephew Archd. Gray (who is also most unwilling to return to India) should endeavour to work up a quiet business in Ship Agency & Chartering & in Insurance. We could give large insurances on Steamers & Ships, which would help as a start and many of our coal charters might be thrown in your way.[26]

An Out Letter Book of GD & Co. in the years before the First World War shows the importance and variety of its business. It also reveals the nature of the relationships between the different BI agents, which despite family ties and common origins, were not always as cordial as they might have been. For example, in 1907, MM & Co. in Bombay, who had unwisely guaranteed a specific arrival date of a shipment to local merchants, had wired GD & Co. to despatch the SS *Coloba* as soon as possible, raising her speed to 12½ knots. This entailed an increase in coal consumption of 50 per cent which, the London agents pointed out, the freights received would not bear, describing the whole business as 'a very objectionable thing to do'.[27] The need to keep at least one jump ahead of other shipping lines to obtain higher freights, especially at a time of intense competition and small profit margins, was appreciated to the extent of coding all messages to Head Office, especially those which could affect the confidence of the London merchant community. For example, in 1911 GD & Co. tentatively enquired in code, 'does crop outlook indicate any doubts as to Karachi to Bombay steamers being able to load homewards during ensuing season?' and received the worrying coded reply 'crop outlook bad but if rains come within the next ten days or fortnight position will be saved we shall wire later'. Suspense at the London office was short-lived though, as dated seven days later a further wire was received informing them of the arrival of the welcome

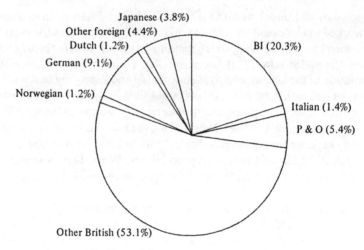

Japanese (3.8%)
Other foreign (4.4%)
Dutch (1.2%)
German (9.1%)
Norwegian (1.2%)
BI (20.3%)
Italian (1.4%)
P & O (5.4%)
Other British (53.1%)

SOURCE As source for Figure 2.5

FIGURE 2.3 Tonnage of steamers calling at Indian ports, 1914

rains and the resultant improvement in outlook and freight prospects.[28]
Despite this secrecy, GD & Co. enjoyed friendly relations with rival lines, such as the Deutsche-Ost Afrika, Union Castle and the Messageries Maritimes. On the eve of the First World War, the BI had sustained its prominence, as can be seen in Figure 2.1, and thus GD & Co. did not feel that their earnings were threatened by these competitors. Their shipments included such diverse cargoes as a body in a coffin from Calcutta to Plymouth on behalf of Thomas Cook,[29] and ground-nuts from Madras to Marseilles for Ellerman's.[30] Like MM & Co., they enjoyed a large commission from the BI and from other lines whom they represented, but their running costs were somewhat higher than their opposite number in India; they paid their dock and office staff between £2 and £3 per week.[31]

Another firm which operated in the shipping business of the port of London in this period, and was to later join the Inchcape Group, was that founded by Caleb Brett in 1885. Now, with Gellatlys, it forms part of Specialist Services International [SSI], one of the Group's most recently-acquired subsidiaries. In the 1880s the firm was based at the London docks, offering an independent cargo inspection and testing service for the benefit of importers and shippers alike, attempting to prevent malpractice in the shipping trade. Caleb Brett & Co. concentrated on cargoes from the Baltic countries, weighing and sampling bales of hemp and jute, together with more specialised goods such as rare oils and copra. Also stimulated by the boom in British shipping and trade before the First World War, Caleb Brett himself frequently visited St Petersburg to protect shippers' interests on deliveries of copra, and new offices were opened in Liverpool and Hull. Caleb Brett & Co. then expanded their business to Germany, Belgium and Holland, testing such diverse cargoes as Manchurian soya beans and bulk whale oil from the South Atlantic fleets.[32]

Although GD & Co. represented BI interests in London, before the First World War it was not the most influential base for BI business in Britain. Since the early 1860s, William Mackinnon, who had left India to concentrate on raising capital to float the BI and negotiate the various mail subsidies, conducted his affairs from his Glasgow firm, W. Mackinnon & Co. He left matters in Calcutta to his trusted nephew Peter, writing letters rarely less than 1000 words long and often exceeding 2000, as often as twice a week, always ending with enquiries of domestic trifles and always signed 'your affectionate uncle'.[33] Mutual business collaboration between Glasgow and the East is shown, for example, in the senior Mackinnon's anxious enquiries, at the end of the first half of 1861, whether the India business would repatriate gross profits of at least £25 000, required by the heavy commitments and large stocks at Glasgow. At that time, with the beginnings of the American Civil War, large supplies of cotton from Manchester had been bought up through justified fears of an interruption in this source of supply.[34] Some of his uncle's advice was probably seen as rather obvious back in Calcutta. 'Don't push large sales unless at prices covering everything and leaving a fair profit besides' was one such gem.[35] Intelligence, on the other hand, of demand for goods such as sugar, cotton and indigo in London and Glasgow, would have been invaluable to the company's India offices. Above all, William Mackinnon's most important role was in proposing and costing new services for the BI. As he wrote to his nephew from London in October 1861, describing five possible routes and the necessary subsidiaries:

These roughly are my ideas – if we could get them carried out! I got our introduction to Lord Elgin and had a very pleasant interview with him *alone* for about half an hour on Monday last. He leaves for India in December and he may have the arranging of our new Steamer Contracts . . . he is a Scotchman of very great and very varied experience . . . I spoke of our steamers and he made various enquiries about them and the traffic existing. I think he'll take some interest in them. We must try to get the contracts all in one and for 5 to 7 years.[36]

Mackinnon criticised other partners and discussed the personalities of the men at the branches, but by the later nineteenth century he became strongly involved in his East African adventures, neglecting his Calcutta business, and slowly began to lose his grip, dying in 1893 of a recurrence of an early lung infection contracted as a young man in India. Mackay, by then, not only experienced and holding large shares in the firm and its associated businesses in India and elsewhere, but also prominent on the BI Board and GD & Co. in London, was in a powerful position to assume the leadership of the Mackinnon complex of firms. Although Duncan Mackinnon succeeded to the chairmanship of the BI, Mackay was the real power behind the throne. As Blake wrote, Duncan Mackinnon 'remained Chairman of the BI until March 1913, no doubt wincing from time to time as the brilliant Mackay proposed and carried through his bold schemes of expansion'.[37] This expansion culminated in the master-stroke of merging the BI with the P & O, its natural ally, and through its long-established commercial relationship, a natural business partner. With the retirement of Sir Thomas Sutherland of the P & O, Lord Inchcape (as Mackay had then become), in a transaction involving £15m, became the head of the largest shipping combine in the world, dominating the main passenger and cargo lines from the UK through the Mediterranean to the East and Australia.

IV

The First World War gave Lord Inchcape and the firms he controlled many new demands but also even greater opportunities for profit. MM & Co's branches in India handled much of the BI's wartime operations, such as the large convoys that took British and Indian troops to Marseilles from Bombay in 1914; the carriage of thousands of horses from Australia; the supply of men and material for the Mesopotamia campaign and the fitting out of the *Karapara* as a hospital ship with accommodation for 500 patients and a medical and nursing staff of 200. Bombay became the centre for all Indian trooping, sending forces to East Africa, Egypt and Palestine as well as Mesopotamia and France. During the four years of the war, more than 2000 ships of an aggregate gross tonnage of over 9 million sailed from Bombay on war service, of which nearly three quarters were BI vessels, sailing as transports. In all, of the BI's 126 vessels, of 570 243 gross registered tons in 1914, 25 were lost during the hostilities,[38] but the shipping line had established a vital precedent in making itself indispensable to the British and Indian governments. The possible need of large passenger vessels for naval

2.6 J. S. Hulbert, who became Company Secretary of the Upper Assam Tea Company, with his bungalow and ponies at Maijan in 1891

service in times of national emergency meant that continued subsidies and government favours could be relied upon, which benefited not only the combined BI and P & O but also their agents overseas and at home.

Meanwhile, the value of Lord Inchcape's holdings in Indian companies were boosted by the war. Binny's practically clothed the entire Allied Armies in the Middle East – by 1917 they were supplying over a million yards of khaki drill a month from their Madras mills. This achievement, for which Binny's received official commendation from the President of the Indian Munitions Board, was gained despite the difficulty in obtaining dyestuffs, until then largely a German monopoly, as well as other raw materials. Bangalore had to discontinue the manufacture of dyed twist during the war for the same reason and their hosiery department was virtually closed because of a lack of needles. Woollens, however, prospered with the steady demand for blankets. Meanwhile, the war stimulated technical advances in the mills. Power-driven machines, such as looms, were installed in the weaving sheds at the Madras mills for the first time in 1915; many of them were still in use over fifty years later. During the Industrial Exhibition of Madras in December 1915 and January 1916, Binny's was able to exhibit no fewer than 6000–7000 patterns and varieties of cloth, in addition to carpets, hosiery, rope, yarn, dyestuffs, linseed products, woods, cement, asbestos sheets and tiles, together with flooring slabs. Their sugar and coffee business also continued and prospered. The activities of the House of Binny, by the end of the First World War, involved nearly every aspect of Indian life.

After 1918 the company faced new stresses and demands, including large price rises and serious strikes. Political movements were particularly directed at British-owned firms. In 1920 an opportunity was taken to reorganise these holdings, increasing the capital and concentrating on textiles, trading, services and agencies rather than branching out into mining, construction and railways, activities which had been of great interest to them in the pre-war years. Dividends, 20 per cent in the years 1922 to 1924, declined to 10 per cent by 1928. Coffee planting was abandoned. The company survived the world crisis of the early 1930s by expanding into engineering, and its diversified holdings enabled it to emerge from the depression and face the challenges of the Second World War from a position of strength.[39]

The tea estates and river steamers in which Lord Inchcape personally held substantial shareholdings (see map 2.1) also survived the First World War with enhanced reputations. The river steamers in particular proved themselves. They supplied a large flotilla to serve on the Tigris and Euphrates and benefited from the large increase in trade brought by

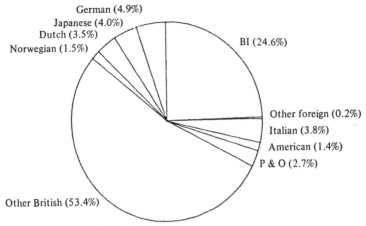

German (4.9%)
Japanese (4.0%)
Dutch (3.5%)
Norwegian (1.5%)
BI (24.6%)
Other foreign (0.2%)
Italian (3.8%)
American (1.4%)
P & O (2.7%)
Other British (53.4%)

SOURCE As source for Figure 2.5

FIGURE 2.4 Tonnage of steamers calling at Indian ports, 1928

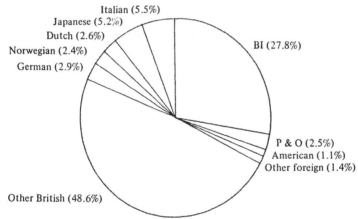

Italian (5.5%)
Japanese (5.2%)
Dutch (2.6%)
Norwegian (2.4%)
German (2.9%)
BI (27.8%)
P & O (2.5%)
American (1.1%)
Other foreign (1.4%)
Other British (48.6%)

SOURCE *Lloyd's Weekly Shipping Index*, 2 January 1880; 5 July 1895; 1 January 1914; 5 January 1928; 7 July 1938.

The companies owning steamers are not given in 1880 and 1895: BI ships were identified from the fleet list in George Blake, *BI Centenary: 1856–1956* (London, 1956) pp.253–64. Prominent British steamer companies in the India trade by 1914 included Ellerman's, Wilson's, Runciman's, Weir's, Bucknall's, the Nourse Line, the City Line, Harrison's and Binny's. In 1928 Henderson's, the Anchor Line and the Burmah Company were also important, in addition to Brocklebank's by 1938. The Bombay and Persian Steam Navigation Company was a local firm operating steamers under the British flag: three of 6170 tons were listed on 1 January 1914, seven of 29 586 on 5 January 1928 and five of 22 798 on 7 July 1938. The Scindia Company was also described as British. On 5 January 1928, eight steamers belonging to this company, each of 34 499 tons were recorded in Indian waters, and on 7 July 1938, fourteen of 62 551 tons each.

FIGURE 2.5 Tonnage of steamers calling at Indian ports in 1938

2.7 Tea bushes planted on the valley slopes near Sylhet in the late 1860s

2.8 River steamers: the RSN Dockyard at Garden Reach, Calcutta, *c*.1905. (From left to right) the vessels are the Khulna–Narayanganj mail steamer *Islay* (built 1898), the sternwheel feeder steamer *Mercury* (1895), Macneill & Co.'s Chandbali service steamer *Jattra* (*c*.1890) and the Assam mail steamer *Brahmin* (1888).

62

2.9 River steamers: the steamer *Condor* (built 1897) and the *Afghan* (built 1896) at Goalundo ghat, with a small local craft in the foreground. The steamers, designed for the Puddha Mail Service which was taken over by companies in 1895, could each carry 640 passengers.

2.10 River steamers: the steamer *Vulture*, wrecked after a cyclone at Goalundo in 1909

the war, despite severe losses: three steamers were burnt and seventeen were sunk *en route* to Mesopotamia. In 1915, Lord Inchcape acquired full control of the UK and India interests in the two partnerships of Barry and Macneill, which (with Kilburn's) not only represented the Joint Steamer Companies but also acted as agents for tea estates, coal-mines and jute mills.[40] These interests were developed and encouraged under Lord Inchcape's direction, and became among the most well-known of the British managing agency houses which prospered in India before independence.

After the First World War, Lord Inchcape faced growing local rivalry to the BI's services, such as the formation of the Scindia Company in 1919 by a consortium of Bombay merchants. Yet as Figure 2.4 shows, the BI's position was not seriously threatened. It expanded by acquiring the sizeable fleets of the New Zealand Steamship Company, the Union Steamship Company of New Zealand, the Hain line and the Nourse line, which enabled it to resume many of the old services which had had to be abandoned before and during the First World War.[41] Lord Inchcape kept a close grip on his vast commercial empire despite old age and the conduct of his business affairs from his yacht *Rover* moored in Monte

Carlo Bay. Still receiving copies of cables between London and Calcutta daily, he died on 23 May 1932 in his eightieth year.[42]

*   *   *

His son Kenneth briefly took over the leadership of the family until the outbreak of the Second World War, when the then young Third Earl took over control of the Inchcape commercial empire, as will be discussed in Chapters 8 and 9. By this date, immense changes had taken place since the formation of a trading partnership by William Mackinnon and his colleagues in Calcutta back in the 1840s. Yet, although technical change and the economic, political and social transformation of the world during these hundred years made the family portfolio of shareholdings inherited by the Third Earl in many ways different from that created by his grandfather, several important features were still the same. The family shareholdings were based in solid, old-established merchant, trading and shipping houses, and revolved around managing the profitable BI and P&O services, together with many associated businesses such as banking, insurance and import–export enterprises. Although by the time that the Third Earl took over, the family shareholdings included significant investments not only in India and also in Australia, the Middle East and East Africa, all these companies were linked to the core of the empire – India. This long association in place and activity provided the backdrop of Group expansion into modern times.

NOTES

1. Hector Bolitho, *James Lyle Mackay: First Earl of Inchcape* (London, 1936) p.13.
2. Ibid., p.14.
3. See George Blake, *Gellatly's 1862–1962* (London, 1962) and *Inchcape Magazine* 17 (Spring 1984) pp.4–5.
4. P&O Pocket Book 1870, *National Maritime Museum [NMM]* BI/P&O Archives. The impact of the opening of the Canal and the expansion of the India trade generally in this period and up to 1904 are described in detail in *The Imperial Gazetteer of India: The Indian Empire*, vol. III, Economic (Oxford, 1907) chap. 5, pp.268–315. See also the references under 'Industry, Trade, Transport and Communications' in Margaret H. Case, *South Asian History, 1750–1950: A Guide to Periodicals, Dissertations and Newspapers*, (Princeton, 1968).
5. For further information on Mackay's early life and his career generally, see

the relevant entry in the *Dictionary of Business Biography* (London, 1984–6) and the obituary in *The Times*, 24 May 1932.

6. Bolitho, *James Lyle Mackay*, quoting Mackay's own account of his voyage to the East, p.21.
7. George Blake, unpublished ms. History of Mackinnon Mackenzie & Co., p.51.
8. Ibid, p.38.
9. *Inchcape Archives [IA]* MM & Co., E. J. Pakes Private File.
10. P. J. Griffiths, *The British Impact of India* (London, 1952) chap. 45, The Development of Communications; chap. 46, The Growth of Industry; chap. 47, The Growth of the Major Industries and chap. 48, The Managing Agency System. By 1880 India had nearly 9000 miles of railways; by 1890 240 000 acres were given over to indigo cultivation in Bihar alone; by 1900 525 000 acres were given over to tea; by 1875 nearly 65 000 looms were producing jute; coal production had increased by the late 1860s to the extent that imports from England were no longer required; the wrought iron trade was flourishing through the enterprise of Tatas with a capital of £1 630 000 provided by some 8000 Indians; and the cotton textile industry was progressing to the extent that Bombay alone had eight-four mills.
11. J. Forbes Munro, 'Scottish Business Imperialism: Sir William Mackinnon and the Development of Trade and Shipping in the Indian Ocean', ESRC Report BOO/23/0049, pp.3, 7–8.
12. *NMM*, BI/P & O Archives, BI Handbook 1866.
13. *NMM*, BI/P & O Archives (see Chapter 3).
14. Blake, unpub. ms, History of MM & Co., p.89 and Bolitho, *James Lyle Mackay*, pp.32–3.
15. *IA*, MM & Co., Private Letter Book, 1884–1900 (1363), William Mackinnon, London to MM & Co., Calcutta, 27 March 1884 and ditto, 28 March 1884.
16. Quoted by Bolitho, *James Lyle Mackay*, p.33.
17. Ibid, pp.34–5.
18. Ibid, pp.23, 32.
19. *IA*, MM & Co., Private Letter Book, 1884–1900 (1363), MM & Co. Calcutta to Mackinnon, Frew & Co. in Liverpool, 6 February 1885; memo showing division of interest in tea properties, April 1885.
20. Ibid, William Mackinnon to MM & Co., Calcutta, 17 April 1885.
21. Ibid, William Mackinnon to MM & Co., Calcutta, 24 June 1886.
22. Binny & Co. Ltd, *The House of Binny* (London, 1969) pp. 71–150.
23. Arnold Wright (ed.) *Southern India: Its History, Peoples, Commerce and Industrial Resources* (London, 1914–15) pp.135–41, 212, 590.
24. See P. J. Griffiths, *A History of the Joint Steamer Companies* (London, 1979) pp.35–50; Alfred Brame, *The India General Steam Navigation Company Ltd* (London, 1900) pp.100–229; and an ms history of the India General by C. Johnson. For histories of the companies involved in the Indian tea industry, see H. A. Antrobus, *The History of the Assam Company, 1839–1953* (Edinburgh, 1957); P. J. Griffiths, *A History of the Indian Tea Industry* (London, 1967); C. A. Bruce, 'Report on the Manufacture of Tea, and the Extent and Produce of Tea Plantations in Assam', *Asiatic Society of Bengal Journal*, 8 (June 1839) pp. 497–526; B. B. Chakrabarti, 'Introduction of Tea

Plantation in India', *Proceedings of the Indian Historical Records Commission*, 18 (January 1942) pp.44–52; E. M. Clarke, 'Assam and the Indian Tea Trade', *Asian Review*, 5 (April 1888) pp.362–83; and Sunil K. Sharma, 'The Origin and Growth of the Tea Industry in Assam', *Contributions to Indian Economic History*, 2 (1963) pp.119–43. That the Indian tea business was profitable and a sound investment in this period is shown by the 25 per cent dividend paid to shareholders of the Assam Company in 1881. During the war, profits were maintained to the extent that over £78 000 was received by the Company as a refund from Excess Profits Duty in 1919. (Antrobus, *History of the Assam Company*, pp.171, 198). Agency Houses are discussed in N. Das, 'The Old Agency Houses of Calcutta', *Calcutta Review*, 46 (March 1933) pp.317–26 and Amales Tripathi, 'The Agency Houses in Bengal', *Bengal: Past and Present*, 73 (July–December 1954) pp.119–26 and 74 (1955) pp.22–27.

25. E. A. V. Angier (of J. C. Gould, Angier & Co. Ltd of London) 'Fifty Years' Freights', published annually in *Fairplay*, 1869–1919, see 1894–7.
26. Blake, unpub. ms., History of MM & Co., pp.25–6.
27. *IA*, GD & Co., Private Letter Book, 1907–20, GD & Co. London to MM & Co., Bombay, 13 June 1907.
28. Ibid, GD & Co. London to MM & Co. Bombay 26 July 1911 and MM & Co. Bombay to GD & Co. London, 3 August 1911.
29. Ibid, GD & Co. London to Thomas Cook, London, 30 January 1908.
30. Ibid, GD & Co., London to MM & Co., Calcutta, 16 January 1914.
31. *IA*, GD & Co. London memo, 25 January 1916.
32. *Inchcape Magazine*, 19 (Spring 1985) pp.3–4.
33. *IA*, MM & Co., letters of William Mackinnon to Peter Mackinnon.
34. Ibid, 17 July 1861.
35. Ibid, 10 October 1861.
36. Ibid, 10 October 1861.
37. George Blake, *BI Centenary 1856–1956* (London, 1956) pp.173–7 and unpub. ms., History of MM & Co., pp.94, 111–13.
38. Ibid, pp.178–98 and pp.113–23 respectively.
39. See note 22, *The House of Binny*, pp.175–252.
40. See note 24.
41. Blake, unpub. ms., History of MM & Co., pp.123–6. The growth of rival Indian shipping companies is discussed in Frank Broeze, 'Underdevelopment and Dependency: Maritime India during the Raj', *Modern Asian Studies*, 18, 3 (1984) pp.429–57.
42. See note 5.

APPENDIX 2.1 THE CHIEF SERVICES AND HONOURS OF THE FIRST EARL OF INCHCAPE

1852	James Lyle Mackay born, Arbroath
1864	A scrivener in a lawyer's office in Arbroath
1865	A clerk in the office of a rope and canvas maker
1874	Sailed for India as a clerk to Messrs Mackinnon Mackenzie and Co.

1889–93	President of Bengal Chamber of Commerce
1891	Sheriff of Calcutta
1891	Invested with CIE 'in recognition of extension of commercial relations between England and India'
1891–3	Member of Legislative Council of Viceroy
1892	Chairman of Indian Currency Association
1894	Created KCIE (Currency Reform)
1897–1911	Member of Council of India, Whitehall
1898–9	Served on Committee for increasing commercial intelligence provided by the Board of Trade
1901–2	Special Commissioner and Plenipotentiary for commercial treaty with China
1902	Created GCMG (China treaty)
1903	President of Chamber of Shipping of the UK
1903	Served on Committee for improving consular service
1903	Served on Secretary of State for India's Committee to inquire into the expediency or otherwise of retaining Cooper's Hill College, a seminary originally instituted by the Hon. East India Company for the training of recruits for its staff in India
1903	A representative of the Government in Conference with Governments of USA and Mexico re introducing gold standard into China and Mexico
1903–4	Served on Lord Jersey's Committee re Board of Trade
1906	Member of Committee of Board of Agriculture to inquire whether preference was given by English railways to produce from abroad conveyed over English lines
1905–7	Member of Committee appointed by Treasury re Government workshops
1906–7	Member of Committee appointed by Treasury to consider advisability of National Indemnity for ships in time of war (see 1914)
1907–8	Chairman of Secretary of State for India's Committee re Indian railways
1910	Created KCSI; member of Secretary of State for India's Committee re Military Family Pension Fund
1911	Went to India to settle disputes for the Secretary of State between railway board and railway companies
1911	Created Baron Inchcape of Strathnaver, on his retirement from India Council after just under fifteen years' service
1912	Appointed member of Committee to inquire into organisation of Department of the Controller of the Navy
1913	Became Vice-President of Institute of Shipbrokers
1914	Member of War Risks Advisory Committee
1914–19	Chairman of Committee re rates of hire for government vessels
1915	Member of Committee on Food Production
1915	Chairman of Port and Transit Committee (to expedite unloading of vessels in British ports)

1917	Member of the Imperial Defence Committee
1917	Through companies, friends and himself, subscribed £9 279 330 to National War Loan
1918	Member of Lord Cunliffe's Committee on currency question
1918	Chairman of Contracts Committee
1918	President of Imperial Association of Commerce
1918	Again elected President of Chamber of Shipping of the UK
1918–21	Chairman of Government's Committee of Inquiry into banking amalgamations as affecting public policy
1918	Member of Casual Labour Committee
1918	Chairman of Treasury's Committee re purchasing gold direct from mines
1918–23	Chairman of Treasury's Committee to control bank amalgamations
1919	Re-elected President Chamber of Shipping (1903, 1918–20)
1919	Member of Air Ministry's Advisory Committee on Aviation
1919	Member of Commercial Intelligence Committee
1919	Sold Government standard ships; realised £35 000 000 for Exchequer, at sales cost of £850
1920	Disposed of ex-enemy ships; realised £20 076 216 at sales cost of 2s 7¼d per £100
1920–1	West to India to sell Mesopotamian war craft; realised £1 080 000
1921	Made a member of the Royal Yacht Squadron
1921	President of Income Tax Payers' Society
1921–2	Member of Sir Eric Geddes' Economy Committee
1921–3	Sold prize vessels for Government; realised £657 519 at sales cost of 6d per £100
1922	Made Chairman of London Committee of Suez Canal Company of Paris
1922	Received Freedom of Arbroath. Gave £26 500 to Arbroath Council for seamen's dependants
1922–3	Went to India at the invitation of the Indian Government to preside over deliberations of Indian Retrenchment Committee (bore his own expenses); as a result budget deficits were replaced by surpluses during the succeeding four years
1923	Member of Shipowners' Parliamentary Committee
1924	Created Viscount (War and public service); GCSI
1924	Invested with Hon. LL.D. at St Andrew's University
1926	Elected President of General Council of International Shipping Federation
1927	Sold prize vessels for Government; realised £75 000
1927	Made Hon. Captain, RNR
1929	Created Earl of Inchcape
1932	Died on Yacht *Rover* at Monaco, 23 May

SOURCE Hector Bolitho, *James Lyle Mackay: First Lord Inchcape* (London, 1936) pp.255–8, and Burke's *Peerage* (London, 1984).

APPENDIX 2.2   MANN EGERTON & CO. LTD

A home-based Group company, Mann Egerton & Co Ltd, whose origins also date back to the late nineteenth century but which, based neither in London or Glasgow and not associated with shipping and overseas trading, seemed out of place in the main text of Chapter 2, is discussed in this appendix. Today, the largest single product element in the Inchcape Group turnover and profit comes from the distribution of motor cars.[1] Mann Egerton plays a vital part in these activities, having been involved in the motor business from its earliest days, which has given it a sound reputation and considerable prestige. What was its contribution to this industry? How did it survive and prosper during its many fluctuations?

When Gerard Noel Cornwallis Mann, with his electrical engineering business in Norwich, first went into partnership with Hubert Wingfield Egerton,[2] the early motoring pioneer in 1900, there were only about 5 000 motor vehicles on British roads.[3] Their first sale of a motor car, a locomobile steam car to a Dr Burton Fanning,[4] took place that same year (the firm distributed many throughout Norfolk) and they kept a detailed record of all their sales from 1907 in a special registration book.[5] Their customers came from far and wide: not only from Norwich and its environs but from London, the West Country, the North, Scotland and Ireland. At a time when the mobility of the population as a whole was less than it is now, and communications more decentralised, Mann Egerton had thus a remarkable national reputation even in its early days of trading.

In the first four years of this register alone (1907–10), the firm sold 334 motors. At an average price of between £200 and £300, these early hand-made cars were relatively very expensive, and represented a sizeable investment to their owners. With middle-class salaries then starting at about £100 per year, it was therefore to purchasers well within the middle classes and above that manufacturers and distributors sold their cars. Prominent among them were people such as doctors, who used these vehicles for professional purposes as suggested by the firm's first customer.[6]

Many of these cars were imported from France and elsewhere. De Dion, Renault, and other French makes accounted for nearly a quarter of Mann Egerton's sales in this sample from the register. The firm employed specialists to deal with the sale, after-sales service and repair of each particular make of car, who were known as 'De Dion Men', 'Napier men' and 'Daimler men'.[7] At the sale of each one, Mann Egerton would 'give one week's personal tuition in the mechanism and driving of the car, free of charge', and the customer's groom or coachman would be given 'every opportunity of gaining experience in the mechanism and management of all makes of cars'.[8]

A further insight into the running of a motor distribution and garage business is provided by the records of the Wimbledon Motor Works (later to become a subsidiary of Mann Egerton) whose letter book of 1905–6 shows that the firm would overhaul motors (at a cost of 6 guineas), totally repair and rebuild vehicles (charging £200 in the case of a 'car in a very bad state of repair throughout'), supply petrol (at 10d a gallon) and accept used cars in part exchange. Its problems included difficulties in obtaining regular supplies of lubricants and fuels for the customers, and mild steel for coachbuilding activities.[9] This small firm, which sold its first car in 1904 (a Clement for £324), was already supplying vehicles as far afield as Australia by the following year.[10] In the years before the First World War, Mann Egerton's high level of sales continued. It opened new branches in Ipswich, Lowestoft, London (88 Victoria Street) and Bury, and established coachbuilding and woodworking departments. It dealt in an increasing range of cars, including recently-developed British models such as Austin, Rover, Riley, Rolls Royce, Armstrong and Siddeley,[11] and developed an important second-hand business which also extended to the Australian market. The capital employed (share capital, loans and free reserves) rose from £66 176 in 1911 to £90 754 in 1914. Profits declared in these two years were £8 405 and £9 136 respectively.[12] Although the percentage discount allowed to Mann Egerton by the manufacturers is not known, these profits suggest that it was generous, and that the firm also ensured large profit margins on its coachbuilding, repair and used-car business. Its overheads, as a distributing rather than manufacturing enterprise, would have been low. Various dilapidated warehouses were purchased to convert to showrooms rather than renting premises,[13] and relatively few staff employed – only ten in the first few years of the company's operations.[14] Wages were kept to a minimum by the engagement of a number of apprentices, who were eager to learn about this new and rapidly growing industry. An indenture between Mann Egerton and George Robert Westry of Norwich in 1905 shows that not only was an apprentice paid just 3/- a week (rising to a maximum of 8/-), but that the trustees of the charity school from which he came paid the firm £10 to train him 'as a motor engineer'. Thus, for the four years of his indenture, during which the young man was expected to work hard, remain living at home, not marry and not frequent alehouses, Mann Egerton paid out a total of only £40.[15]

The response of the firm to the First World War showed its willingness to adapt. This flexibility was the key to Gerard Mann's continuing success as an entrepreneur. During the hostilities, he supervised the manufacture of some 400 tractors to help increase much-needed food supplies, special coachwork for ambulances and vehicles for the War Office, and repairs to military and official cars. He eagerly accepted an order from the Admiralty to build seaplanes, the first of many (the firm was to build over 800 planes in this period), thus diversifying into aircraft body construction.[16] Mann Egerton's electrical department, from which the firm originally sprang, provided new light and power installations all over the country, including the Royal Navy's cordite factory at Poole (in a contract valued at £100 000) and their torpedo ranges at Weymouth. Wiring work included government offices at Whitehall, and the firm provided a variety of central heating, sewage disposal, water-softening and refrigeration services.[17] A Ford depot run by the firm was opened in Ipswich, and a supplies department of the Norwich head office was established.

By the end of the war, the firm had literally doubled in size. Its assets of £349 366 exceeded its liabilities by £154 108 and the value of its unexecuted contracts in December 1919 was a staggering £550 000. The number of employees had meanwhile risen from 450 to 1800. Declared profits in 1918 were £32 250, on a capital employed of £159 459. Envisaging even further expansion, Gerard Mann launched his firm as a public company in 1919, one of the first in the retail motor trade to do so. He issued 104 885 8 per cent cumulative preference shares of £1 each out of a total authorised £250 000, and 60 000 ordinary £1 shares out of a total authorised £150 000. Wartime contracts played an important part in the successful flotation of the company: it is significant that Mann's eleven fellow Board directors included two naval captains, a colonel, a lieutenant-colonel, a major and a brigadier-general, all of whom had subscribed at least the qualifying shareholding of £2 500.[18] Mann Egerton & Co. Ltd then made a significant acquisition, Botswoods, the first in a series of many, followed by the opening of another Ford depot, in Bury, and the establishment of 'The Norwich School of Motoring'.

Thus the company was able to face the challenges of the inter-war years with confidence. Meanwhile, great changes were taking place in the motor business. The post-war system of lower taxation on vehicles of a low horse-power increased the popularity of small cars, which were sold by Mann Egerton in addition to its more up-market models. This, combined with rising real earnings in the 1930s, brought the ownership of motor cars to a much wider range of people. By 1934, 1.3 million cars were registered, and only five years later there were over 2 million cars of all makes on British roads.[19] The company achieved annual profits of between £25 000 and £35 000 throughout the 1920s and 1930s. In addition to car sales and garage services, it had now branched out to school and office furniture production, skilfully redeploying the resources of the woodworking department when wartime aeroplane demand abruptly ceased. The electrical and coachbuilding departments remained prosperous.[20]

Although it is not possible to separate the profits earned by the motor and non-motor activities of Mann Egerton, it appears that the former remained its primary concern. A brochure of 1936 boasted of its 300 000 square feet of showroom space, 1000 employees and carefully guarded independence, handling over thirty makes of cars: 'our enormous turnover with various manufactures', the company argued, 'enables us to exert influence when required'. In its five branches, the brochure shows, the firm sold cars varying in price from £97 10s. (for the most basic Ford Popular) to £2560 (for a 50h.p. Rolls Royce Phantom III limousine with two forward-facing occasional seats, an interior telephone and triplex glass).[21] It offered a servicing facility covering twenty-five points of the car, and a unique arrangement for persons on extended leave from abroad: it was possible for them to buy a vehicle with a guarantee that Mann Egerton would repurchase it at a pre-agreed sum. For example, an Austin 12h.p. touring five-seater costing £255 could be bought from the company (on generous credit terms of a deposit of £65 15s followed by twelve monthly instalments of £16 14s 8d, representing interest charges of only £10) and sold back to the company a year later for £190.[22] Among Mann Egerton's most wealthy and prestigious customers at this time were the British, Spanish, German and Russian royal families. It also supplied coachwork for the Harrods and Daimler hire fleets, the latter of which, in a single order, requested delivery of sixty-five large enclosed limousines.[23]

Its substantial contribution to retail motor distribution in Britain when this business was developing gave Mann Egerton the strength to survive and prosper during the Second World War, which will be discussed in Chapter 8. Its subsequent acquisition by the Inchcape Group and modern-day prominence will be one of the subjects of Chapter 10.

2.11 Mann Egerton: Hubert Egerton, filling up his De Dion locomobile during his epic Land's End to John O'Groats trial in 1900

73

2.12 Mann Egerton: the firm's war effort in 1914–18 on land: one of their 400 tractors

2.13 Mann Egerton: the firm's war effort 1914–18 in the air: one of their 800 aeroplanes

2.14 Mann Egerton: learning to drive, 1919 style. Note the two steering wheels

NOTES TO APPENDIX 2.2

1. See Chapter 10, Table 10.5. Group profit from motor vehicle distribution reached 40 per cent in 1980.
2. Egerton was employed by De Dion in the years 1897–1900. In this latter year, he successfully completed a 1000-mile trial from Land's End to John O'Groats in four days and nine hours. He left the partnership in 1911.
3. T. C. Barker, 'The Economic and Social Effects of the Spread of Motor Vehicles', a paper prepared for the 16th International Congress of Historical Sciences, August 1985, which is to form part of a forthcoming volume on the subject.
4. Mann Egerton & Co. Ltd, *Anniversary Souvenir* (Norwich, 1973) p. 8.
5. *Mann Egerton Archives [MEA]*, Registration Book 1907–20. For each vehicle sold, the ledger records the name and address of the purchaser, the registration number and date of sale, the colour and type of car, its weight and its intended use, as a private vehicle, for trade, or as a public conveyance. The legal requirements to register cars means that details (which include the occupation of the purchaser) are also kept at local record offices. The Mann Egerton Archives were consulted with the kind permission of Mrs M. Lee at the Head Office, 5 Prince of Wales Road, Norwich NR1 1BB.
6. The number of doctors purchasing cars from the firm in the years 1907 to 1910 was eighteen, representing 5.4 per cent.
7. *Anniversary Souvenir*, p. 2.
8. MEA, company history, undated, for internal circulation.
9. *MEA*, Wimbledon Motor Works, Letter Book, 1905–6, letters dated 10, 18, 29 and 30 November, and 1 and 20 December 1905.
10. *MEA*, history of Mann Egerton (Southern) Ltd, dated 1966.
11. The production of these early British cars is discussed in, for example, S. B. Saul, 'The Motor Industry in Britain to 1914', *Business History* (December, 1962); Ian Lloyd, *Rolls Royce* (London, 1978, 3 vols); R. J. Overy, *William Morris, Viscount Nuffield* (London, 1976) and Roy Church, *Herbert Austin: The British Motor Car Industry to 1941* (London, 1979). A general survey is given in Kenneth Richardson, *The British Motor Industry 1896–1939* (London, 1977). Early marketing is discussed by Roy Church in his article 'Markets and Marketing in the British Motor Industry before 1914 with some French Comparisons', *Journal of Transport History* 3rd series 3 (1982).
12. *MEA*, Prospectus of Mann Egerton & Co. Ltd, issued 6 December 1919.
13. *Anniversary Souvenir*, p.2.
14. *MEA*, Brochure, 1936, 'Cars at a Glance'.
15. *MEA*, Indenture between George Robert Westry and Messrs Mann Egerton, dated Norwich 4 August 1905.
16. *MEA*, 'Twenty Years' Progress in Pictures', Souvenir for Employees, c.1919. The Archives include several albums of photographs of the aeroplanes produced. An account of the firm's contribution to this wartime activity is given in *Aeronautical Engineering*, 6 June 1917. Ten different

models were produced by the firm, including 'Short' biplanes, 'Spad' fighters, Handley Page bombers, 'Seaboard Scouts' and Sopwith 'planes.

17. *Anniversary Souvenir*, p.3.
18. *MEA*, Prospectus. See the entry on Mann in the *Dictionary of Business Biography* (forthcoming, 1985).
19. T. C. Barker, 'The International History of Motor Transport', *Journal of Contemporary History* (London, Beverly Hills and New Delhi, 1985) vol. 20, p. 6.
20. *Anniversary Souvenir*, pp. 3–4.
21. *MEA*, Brochure, 1936, 'Cars at a Glance'.
22. *MEA*, 'On Leave with a Car', c.1930.
23. *MEA, News Bulletin* no. 1, vol. 1 (March, 1930). This was a quarterly publication, summarising Mann Egerton's activities for the benefit of employees, which continued until 1939. It was replaced by *The Link*, which has only recently ceased publication.

NOTES Original branches shown in boxes. At the end of 1984, the Group operates in
Bahrain, Dubai, Kuwait, Oman, Ras Al Khaimah and Saudi Arabia only.

MAP 3.1 The Persian Gulf, showing the location of Gray Mackenzie & Co.'s
branches at the time of the formation of the Group.

3 Shipping and Trading in the Persian Gulf: Gray Paul & Co. and Gray Mackenzie & Co., c.1870–1939[1]

شركة كري مكـزي المحـدودة
Gray Mackenzie
& COMPANY LIMITED
A member of the Inchcape Group of Companies

The economic and political significance of the Persian/Arabian Gulf has increased dramatically since the Second World War. Yet in the mid-nineteenth century, before the discovery of oil, the region was comparatively unknown and unexplored by Europeans, a backwater in the expanding network of world trade. Why then did Sir William Mackinnon, the founder of the British India Steam Navigation company [BI], in 1862 extend his established service between Calcutta, Bombay and Karachi to Basra and intermediate ports?[2] What impact did the BI steamers have on the development of the Gulf until 1939? The representatives of the BI at the principal Gulf ports were originally Gray Paul & Co. and Gray Mackenzie & Co., two merchant partnerships who, after an interlude of acting jointly with others as the Mesopotamia Persia Corporation Ltd from 1919 to 1936, formed Gray Mackenzie & Co. Limited.

The BI's India service, as we discussed in Chapter 1, was originally established as the Calcutta and Burmah Steam Navigation Company in 1856 (it became the BI in 1861), and owed much to Sir Henry Bartle Frere, a member of the Council of India and subsequently Governor of Bombay from 1862–7. The BI received a subsidy, provided by the Government of India, which had been awarded at Frere's behest, and it thereby achieved a dominant position in the coasting trade of India in the late 1850s and early 1960s.

In 1861 approval had been received from the India Office to subsidise a steamer service to the Gulf, by way of a mail contract. A subsidy was needed because the steamers of the early 1860s, with their low-pressure engines and large consumption of coal, not to mention their technical unreliability, were frequently uneconomic to operate, even with full cargoes. In fact, full cargoes, particularly on this route, were a vision for the future.

In a broader context, Frere was also interested in the possibility of developing the Gulf to provide alternative overland and maritime routes between Britain and India. Before the opening of the Suez Canal in 1869, trade went via the Cape or overland across Suez and then by the Red Sea. Another concern of Frere's was the development of an 'Indian' mercantile marine which the Government of India could employ in an emergency.[3]

In advancing the case for a formal, subsidised British presence in the Gulf, Frere was also responding to the fears expressed in England and India of the 'dangerously ambitious projects of Russia'. As early as 1839, a political pamphlet maintained that:

> If Russia had never crossed the Caucasus, the intercourse of England with Persia would now have been purely commercial; it is the ambition of Russia that forces upon us the necessity of endeavouring to preserve that which is obviously necessary to our own protection . . . The integrity and independence of Persia is necessary to the security of India and of Europe; and any attempt to subvert the one is a blow struck at the other – an unequivocal act of hostility to England.[4]

The BI mail contract was seen as a way of upholding British commercial interests, and reinforcing existing British political representation in the Gulf against the Russian threat.

One of three tenderers for the Gulf contract, the BI was in a particularly advantageous position for the award. Mackinnon had carefully cultivated his aquaintance with Frere, making it clear that his company was keen to expand its Indian coastal connections. In the report and assessment of the tenders, it was agreed that the BI offered 'a decided superiority as respects the class of vessels', 'a fixed rate of speed', and with 'no interruption to the present efficient service to Karachi'. The two local firms attempting to compete complained that the BI was gaining a monopoly in Indian waters, but the Bombay Government pointed to the poor performance of the local shipping services and maintained that 'the Government and the Public may expect a more efficient service from the Burmah Company [the BI] than from either of the other tenderers'. By choosing the BI rather than a local company, the Government of Bombay was ensuring not only the provision of a reliable shipping line, but the representation of British commercial interests. The BI in the Gulf may be seen as an example of how the state assisted private enterprise in opening up new areas to British trade and to British political influence, in the same way that the P & O vessels may be seen as 'flagships of imperialism'.[5]

Thus the establishment of the BI and Mackinnon's interest in expanding its subsidised network of services coincided with the Government of India's long-term plans to safeguard Indian coastal communications and ultimately its links with Europe via the P & O service. Two short-term factors which may have prompted the Indian Government, and Mackinnon, to take such an interest in the Gulf were, first, the disruption in the supplies of cotton to Britain and India as a result of the American Civil War, which acted as a stimulus to the growing of cotton in Iran; and second, the recent construction of telegraph and cable lines through the area. It is unlikely however, that Mackinnon would have been prepared to inaugurate a costly steamer service in the interests of extending Indian coastal communications and to exploit a short-lived cotton boom: undoubtedly the subsidy, and the prospect of its frequent renewal and possible increase was the deciding factor. It has been suggested that Mackinnon gained the contract because he happened to be passing through Bombay at the time when the mail contracts were being put out to tender. Certainly he knew, from his Calcutta–Burmah experience, what an edge a mail contract gave to the firm holding it over competing steamer concerns. Table 3.1 shows that Mackinnon's confidence was justified.

I

The BI's coastal services were managed by Mackinnon's merchant partnership in Calcutta, Mackinnon Mackenzie & Company [MM &

TABLE 3.1 The British India SN Co. Gulf service and its competitors, 1862–1904

Date begun	Company	Registry	Subsidy	Service	Home port
1862	BI	UK	Rs 80 000	8 voyages. p.a.	Bombay
1866	BI	UK	Rs 1 60 000	Fortnightly	Bombay
1869	Persian Mail	UK	—	irregular	Bombay
1870	BI	UK	Rs 7 666 per trip	Fortnightly	Bombay
1870	Bombay and Persian	UK	—	irregular	Bombay
1870	Oman and Ottoman	Ottoman	?	irregular	Istanbul
1870	Persian Gulf SN Co.	UK	—	monthly by 1879	London
1874****	BI	UK	Rs 7 25 000 (total incl. Gulf)	weekly	Bombay
1883	Messageries Maritimes	French	'Heavy'*	irregular	Marseilles
1884	BI	UK	Rs 4 39 000** (total incl. Gulf)	weekly	Bombay
1901	Russian, Gulf and Persian	R.	£4000 per trip***	monthly	Odessa
1904	BI	UK	Rs 4 26 124 (incl. Rs 3 00 000 for fast line)	2 services fast and slow	Bombay

* George Curzon, *Persia and the Persia Question* (London, 1892) vol. 2 p.557.
** This was increased to Rs 5 05 500 overall total subsidy including the Gulf service in 1894.
*** The Russian Government also refunded the Suez Canal dues this company paid.
**** By 1874 a 'home line' had been established direct from London to the Gulf by the BI, a four-weekly service via Aden and Karachi. George Blake, *BI Centenary 1856–1956* (London, 1956) Introduction.

SOURCES J. G. Lorimer, *Gazetteer of the Persian Gulf, Oman and Central Arabia* (Calcutta, 1908, 1915) p.2467; *Report on the Administration of the Persian Gulf and Muscat Political Agency* (Calcutta, annual, 1873–1905).

Co.], which he had founded as his first trading venture in India in 1847. With the expansion of the activities of the BI the operation of a large network of shipping lines was seen as possible only through the parallel provisions of shipping agents at each strategic port. In this context, many of the merchant partnerships that were eventually to form the Inchcape Group of Companies played a vital role in the day-to-day running of the BI. In selecting his representatives, Mackinnon gave priority to trusted friends and relations. In 1865, he appointed Gray Dawes & Company [GD & Co.] as his London agents.

As we have seen, Gray and Dawes were responsible for the formation of the two partnerships which managed the greater part of the BI's Gulf interests. The creation of these partnerships was necessary as there were virtually no British mercantile houses already in the Gulf which might undertake the work. Consequently, by contrast with the situation in India, where established firms took up the agencies, MM & Co. and the BI had to set up their own agency firms in the Gulf from scratch. Men formerly employed by the parent firms were obvious candidates. To join the new partnership and manage it at Bushire, Robert Paul (who originally left Scotland to avoid recriminations after jilting his fiancée), was sent out from Calcutta, where he had worked as an assistant in MM & Co. in charge of their piece goods sales, from c.1860. Grey Paul & Company was officially founded in 1865. Recruited as an assistant to Paul in Bushire in 1866 was George Mackenzie, who in 1869 helped to found the associated partnership of Gray Mackenzie & Company in Basra.[6] GD & Co. acted as their London agents. The two partnerships in effect acted as one company, keeping one set of accounts and maintaining a close correspondence.

In assessing the impact of the BI steamers on the life of the Gulf ports, it is important to consider the nature of the services they provided. These are comprehensively described in the BI handbooks,[7] referred to in Chapter 2, which also reveal the vital role played in the service by its shipping agents. The earliest surviving handbook, that of 1866, shows that the BI's fortnightly service between Bombay and the Persian Gulf, called at the ports of Bombay, Muscat, Bander Abbas, Bushire and Basra, with additional stops at Lingah and Bahrain.[8] Despite the navigational difficulties and dangers of the Gulf,[9] an attempt was made from the beginning of this liner-, rather than tramp-service, to keep sailings to specific dates. Thus a connection was made with the other mail services at Calcutta, and after 1869 the BI timetable was co-ordinated with the P & O Suez route. Also, the Persian Gulf service in effect terminated at Baghdad, as it connected with the river steamers of the Euphrates and Tigris Steam Navigation Company. Managed by another British firm, Lynch Brothers – who were first established in Baghdad in 1841 – this service provided eight trips per year, receiving a mail subsidy of £2400, compared with the BI's subsidy of approximately £6000.[10]

The BI handbook of 1866 clearly shows that this service to the Gulf ports was only one of eight BI services already in operation in that year: the BI's role in this region must be considered in the context of their shipping services as a whole. This included four routes from Calcutta: monthly to Rangoon, Moulmein and the Straits, and fortnightly to Moulmein, Akyab and Bombay coasting. BI also operated two monthly lines between Madras and Rangoon, and to China, and a fortnightly service between Bombay and Karachi.

The operation of the Gulf service and the further services shown in Table 3.1, which covers the period up to 1914, may be considered through an analysis of the impact of the BI presence at each of the major Gulf ports, in three respects. First, did the service lead to an increase in the entrances and clearances of shipping tonnage? Second, did the advent of the BI steamers result in an increase in the value of imports and exports at each port, particularly in regard to their trade with the Britain via re-exports from India and through the on-carriage of cargoes by the P & O? Finally, how important were Gray Mackenzie and Gray Paul in the merchant communities of the ports, and what were the problems of managing this service? This leads to the larger question of how British shipping in the Gulf sheds light upon the expansion of British commerce into hitherto remote and little-known corners of the world in the latter half of the nineteenth century, thereby staving off the rise of foreign competition for British industries.

II

Bushire in the late nineteenth and early twentieth centuries was the most prominent of the growing steamer ports in the Gulf, the gateway to the interior of Iran, and the home of the British Persian Gulf Residency.[11] An essential port of call of the service, Table 3.2 shows that the number and tonnage of BI steamers entering and clearing Bushire increased by over 300 per cent in just over ten years,[12] from 1873 to 1885. The inauguration of the BI service, and the opening of the Suez canal, encouraged the entry of other steamer companies into the Gulf trade, as outlined in Table 3.1. This led to a reduction in the prominence of BI shipping at this port from over 70 per cent to 44 per cent. By 1885, the BI steamers were competing with the British-registered, but locally-run, Bombay and Persian Steam Navigation Company with 21 360 tons of steam shipping entering Bushire; the Persian Gulf Steam Navigation Company, similarly British-registered with 24 640 tons; the French steamers with 12 240 tons; and another 61 000 tons of miscellaneous steam tonnage. After 1885, the statistics available do not separate BI vessels from other British steamers which, by 1904, represented 96.7 per cent of all steamers trading at Bushire. It is thus clear that the arrival of the BI service at this port played a particularly significant part by inaugurating the sustained and dramatic growth in the use of the port by steamers. Although it faced increasing competition, by the turn of the century it was still by far the largest single company operating from the port and offered the most regular and frequent service.[13] Only in the years immediately preceding the First World War did other major British steamer lines make headway in the Persian Gulf trade. Stricks, the Bucknall Steamship Lines and J. E. Guthe & Co. (the West Hartlepool Steam Navigation Company) came to a joint agreement in this trade in 1903 from which Guthe withdrew on its expiry in 1909. The previous year, Bucknalls was purchased by Ellermans who continued to provide, with Stricks, a rival UK to Gulf service until the outbreak of war.

What influence did this increase in shipping tonnage have on the trade of Bushire and its importance as a trans-shipment centre? The value of its imports increased by over 300 per cent from 1873 to 1903. This reflects the development of Bushire and especially its hinterland as a market for British goods, so far as this may be deduced from the statistics available. Table 3.3 shows that whereas only 16 per cent of the value of imports into Bushire in 1873 was accounted for by goods from Britain, by 1897 the proportion had increased to 68 per cent. Indian imports had exceeded 51 per cent in 1873 which was accounted for by goods from Britain, by 1897 the proportion had increased to 68 per cent. Indian imports had exceeded 51 per cent in 1873; by 1897, they represented only 18 per cent. Bushire's exports by value nearly doubled from 1873 to 1898; in 1873 8 per cent were shipped to the UK and 33 per cent to India. By 1898, the proportions were 27 per cent and 17 per cent respectively. Other variables, besides the impact of the BI steamers, need to be taken into account in this shift in the direction of Bushire's overseas commerce, such as changes in other trade routes, the harvest fluctuations in Persia and the fact that a plague epidemic at Bombay virtually closed it as a port in the years 1896–9. However, the BI's role in the expansion of commercial links between Bushire and Britain was vital.[14]

Imports into Bushire in 1873, which numbered over 150 separate items, included cattle, drugs, fruit and vegetables, glass, grains, hides, metals, oils, seeds, tobacco, timber and wool. By the late 1890s, the most important items (by value) imported into Bushire were cotton piece

TABLE 3.2 BI steamers entering the Gulf ports, 1873–85 and British steamers entering the Gulf ports, 1886–1904

Year	Bushire Number and tons BI (% total ss)	Bahrain Number and tons BI (% total ss)	Bander Abbas Number and tons BI (% total ss)	Lingah Number and tons BI (% total ss)	Basra Tons Br. (% total)
1873	26–26 000 (62%)	?	26–26 000 (84%)	26–26 000 (85%)	
1874	36–36 000 (61%)	15–9600 (?)	37–34 611 (66%)	?	
1875	53–37 000 (71%)	13–7540 (?)	? ?	53–37 100 (89%)	
1876	47–37 600 (68%)	13–10 400 (?)	47–37 600 (68%)	47–37 600 (70%)	
1877	52–55 952 (49%)	?	?	?	
1878	52–49 400 (56%)	16–20 368 (85%)	?	52–49 400 (82%)	
1879	52–32 240 (42%)	45–46 260 (88%)	?	48–52 800 (64%)	
1880	52–36 816 (44%)	?	52–36 816 (53%)	53–58 300 (58%)	
1881	104–67 080 (47%)	34–23 460 (91%)	104–67 080 (67%)	104–67 080 (54%)	
1882	100–67 000 (39%)	29–30 479 (87%)	?	105–115 500 (73%)	
1883	105–83 710 (38%)	31–24 025 (85%)	105–83 710 (72%)	105–83 710 (80%)	
1884	104–85 346 (42%)	37–50 727 (99%)	104–85 346 (69%)	104–85 346 (74%)	
1885	104–95 000 (44%)	33–41 394 (97%)	104–95 000 (61%)	103–94 456 (65%)	
1886	108–96 611 (93%)	49–39 139 (100%)	107–95 511 (95%)	78–62 799 (100%)	
1887	94–87 817 (97%)	53–74 969 (100%)	94–87 817 (96%)	80–70 510 (99%)	

Year					
1889	112–113 172 (100%)	38–35 281 (93%)	77–100 896 (98%)	77–92 400 (100%)	
1890	110–106 396 (98%)	38–35 568 (100%)	65–60 207 (96%)	81–162 000 (100%)	
1891	142–145 801 (100%)	36–54 272 (100%)	75–82 500 (93%)	84–168 000 (99%)	
1892	126–131 590 (100%)	56–61 327 (100%)	79–70 362 (98%)	80–160 000 (98%)	
1893	107–114 535 (99%)	43–41 514 (99%)	82–90 200 (97%)	75–142 500 (98%)	
1894	111–129 638 (96%)	77–78 112 (97%)	84–92 400 (99%)	75–82 500 (98%)	138 129 (86%)
1895	132–170 434 (92%)	84–82 440 (99%)	83–91 300 (98%)	77–84 700 (95%)	172 765 (82%)
1896	112–133 277 (96%)	88–89 195 (98%)	76–83 600 (94%)	77–84 700 (88%)	136 693 (80%)
1897	90–98 494 (86%)	59–56 230 (99%)	76–83 600 (86%)	73–80 300 (88%)	109 180 (83%)
1898	96–97 255 (97%)	107–1 150 69 (98%)	67–73 70 (100%)	83–91 300 (99%)	104 500 (83%)
1899	101–118 928 (97%)	53–89 963 (99%)	64–70 400 (99%)	78–85 800 (98%)	134 401 (81%)
1900	111–132 787 (94%)	29–28 713 (99%)	101–135 139 (100%)	78–85 800 (98%)	172 938 (86%)
1901	109–125 760 (98%)	37–37 038 (100%)	159–143 100 (96%)	81–89 100 (98%)	142 243 (79%)
1902	133–148 229 (97%)	66–72 771 (100%)	193–156 330 (96%)	95–104 500 (98%)	164 341 (82%)
1903	154–188 352 (95%)	73–104 717 (99%)	171–215 000 (91%)	74–81 400 (98%)	167 479 (86%)
1904	154–174 655 (97%)	72–97 085 (98%)	144–216 000 (93%)	64–70 400 (97%)	

SOURCE (Basra) J. A. Saldanha, *Précis of Commerce and Communication in the Persian Gulf, 1801–1905* (Calcutta, 1906) app. H. (Other ports) *Report on the Administration of the Persian Gulf and Muscat Political Agency* (Calcutta, annual, 1873–1905).

TABLE 3.3   Value of imports and exports between the United Kingdom and selected gulf ports, 1873 and 1897–9

Ports	Imports from UK to Gulf							
	1873		1897		1898		1899	
	From (UK	(UK as % of total)	From UK	(UK as % of total)	From UK	(UK as % of total)	From UK	(UK as % of total)
Bushire (lakhs of rupees or 100 000)	7 57	(16%)	1 23 82	(68%)	64 26	(48%)	66 28	(48%)
Lingah (lakhs of rupees)			9 35	(0.1%)	6 56	(0.06%)		
Bander Abbas (lakhs of rupees)	52	(3%)	10 32	(17%)	13 33	(19%)	12 92	(16%)
Bahrain (lakhs of rupees)			3 73	(5%)				
Mohommerah (£)	?	?	29 616	(24%)	53 869	(34%)	74 189	(37%)

Ports	Exports to UK from Gulf							
	1873		1897		1898		1899	
	To UK	(UK as % of total)	To UK	(UK as % of total)	To UK	(UK as % of total)	To UK	(UK as % of total)
Bushire (lakhs of rupees)	3 18	(8%)	15 49	(25%)	18 47	(27%)	11 74	(15%)
Lingah (lakhs of rupees)			48	(0.6%)	46	(0.5%)	54	(0.7%)
Bander Abbas (lakhs of rupees)	17	(1%)	23	(0.6%)	11	(0.4%)	20	(0.7%)
Bahrain (lakhs of rupees)								
Mohommerah (£)	?	?	19 443	(47%)	8 394	(25%)	11 073	(19%)

SOURCES 1873, J. A. Saldanha, *Précis of Commerce and Communication in the Persian Gulf, 1801–1905* (Calcutta, 1906), App. F. 1897–9, *Report on the Administration of the Persian Gulf and Muscat Political Agency* (Calcutta, annual, 1873–1905).

goods, shirtings, copper, and guns, cartridges and other arms from Britain, with cotton goods, rice and sugar from India. By the late 1890s Bushire's export trade included guns (imported from Britain and re-exported to Muscat), almonds, gum, hides and specie to India, and tobacco to Egypt. The third of its exports which were despatched to the UK comprised wool, carpets, mother-of-pearl shells and opium. Evidence of a shift from primary to secondary production at Bushire was slight.

Bushire's imports almost always exceeded the value of exports from the port, where local manufacturing, besides crafts for immediate use, was limited to the production of a small number of copper coffee pots only. The BI and their agents thus became interested in the development of local trades to pay for the imports, especially because the balance-of-payments difficulties of the Gulf ports were exacerbated by the scarcity of coin: gold had practically disappeared, silver was rare and even copper hard to obtain. The opium trade in particular helped to solve this problem: the ready market for the drug for the opium dens in Hong Kong and Singapore initially encouraged its cultivation in Persia, and with the rise in poppy-seed prices in Europe in the mid-1870s, it was also shipped to England and the USA. By 1879, the price of a case of opium (of 140lb each) had risen from 280 to 615 Maria Theresa dollars, this latter sum equivalent to nearly £70.[15] The BI then decided to enter the trade, employing three brand new steamers, the *Culna*, *Ellora* and *Chindwara*, all over 1900 tons gross, which carried a total of 215 cases to Hong Kong.[16] As the production of Persian opium increased – from 1560 chests in 1868–9 to over 5000 chests per year in the 1880s and 1890s, the importance of the BI in this trade grew. By 1888, when steamers of the BI carried 886 chests of opium to Hong Kong, their share of the trade reached 40 per cent, exceeded only by the Bombay and Persian Steam Navigation Company which shipped 1175 chests. The Persian Gulf Steam Navigation Company carried fifty chests to London and a further thirty-six to Hong Kong. In 1894, the 1493 chests (worth over £100 000) carried by the BI to Hong Kong represented 44 per cent of the total opium exports from Bushire. In 1901, when the new BI services which began in 1904 were first discussed, it was hoped that the employment of more vessels in the carriage of cargoes (in addition to the fast mail line) would lead to an even larger share of the opium trade.[17]

The imports of firearms into Bushire from Britain were substantial, and although the bulk of the trade was carried by smugglers in local craft, it is likely that BI vessels played some part in it. Flourishing after the third Afghan War of the late 1870s, the British and Indian Governments succeeded in persuading the Persian authorities to prohibit arms sales by the 1880s and 1890s, and the firms which carried out the import and export of arms were warned to stop by the Political Resident. These firms usually enjoyed the benefits of British protection – for example a Persian-Armenian firm, A. & T. S. Malcolm, had enjoyed close links with Gray Paul at Bushire since the latter's beginnings, despite their role in supplying British arms to the enemy. The illegal nature of this trade has necessarily precluded its contemporary documentation, but occasional seizures were reported, including one of 30 000 rifles landed at Bushire in 1897, for which the local Governor was receiving a 10 per cent commission.[18]

According to a GD & Co. notebook already mentioned, by the 1880s and 1890s, Gray Paul also became involved in the forward shipment of goods from Bushire to Teheran. In reply to enquiries from French and German merchants, Gray Paul outlined its services, for which the charge was 5 kerans (34 kerans equalling £1) per load-forwarding commission. Donkeys (which could carry up to 240lbs) were employed to Shiraz, where camels could be hired which could carry two donkey loads. The carriage of 100 maunds (or 750lb) of cargo would cost about 200 kerans from Bushire to Tehran, a journey of between two and three months' duration. By 1914, seven other European firms were established at Bushire and the British residents now numbered thirty-four. Gray Paul acquired substantial local property: it owned a large house and garden with outlying land including stables, another piece of land named Chahar Sabute, the company's office and adjoining land, together with a house and land at Bagh-i-Shiekh Ahol.[19] Meanwhile the local population of Bushire, estimated at 15 000, were crowded into 1400 densely grouped houses.

Managing the BI service at Bushire was fraught with problems, as is shown in an analysis of the arrivals of BI steamers at the port between October 1896 and December 1897, compiled by the Political Resident. The steamers then in the trade, the *Kilwa*, the *Assyria*, the *Simla*, the *Purnlia*, the *Pacumba*, the *Pemba*, the *Khandalla*, the *Kapurthala*, the *Culna*, the *Chanda* and the *Patna*, which among them made sixty-four calls at the port in this period, were on average at least two days behind their scheduled time of arrival on each voyage. By supplementing their mail subsidy with the carriage of cargo, the BI steamers caused considerable delays in the collection and delivery of mails. In the BI contract, it was stipulated that the Political Resident at a port was entitled to detain a steamer if necessary for the preparation of despatches, which further disrupted attempts to keep to the timetable. Gray Paul, in replying to the Political Resident's complaints, admitted that the delays were due to the time taken in unloading cargoes; the latter suggested that as the BI was benefiting from an increase in the cargoes carried, it should allow more time and provide more vessels to keep the Post Office contract punctually. The new service of 1904 in effect took up these suggestions, but this was only a partial solution, as the discharge of goods suffered principally from the inadequate boat and lighterage arrangements rather than just an excess of cargo. An annual contract was given to a Persian official known as the *Hamal Bashi*, whose interest in personal gain far outweighed any concern for the efficient running of the Gulf steamer service. Above all, the uncertain, disorganised and lawless nature of local conditions in Bushire in the late nineteenth century made Gray Paul's job as the BI agents a difficult one: in 1898, writing to MM & Co. in Calcutta, the company warned that 'the town iself is in a most disturbed condition and at any moment there may be a complete breakdown of (all port) arrangements'.[20]

III

Lingah, where Gray Paul established an office in 1875, developed and prospered as a trans-shipment centre for traffic to and from Bahrain and the ports of the Trucial coast. The traffic of this port declined considerably after 1902 as a result of the imposition of heavy custom restrictions by the Persian Government.[21] Table 3.2 shows that for a number of years, the BI steamers calling at Bushire also put in at Lingah on the way. Later, and especially from the mid-1880s when a new contract came into operation, the services did not always include Lingah.[22] Because of the withdrawal of competing steamships in the mid-1880s, despite this reduction in the BI series to Lingah, the company virtually monopolised steam-shipping at the Port.[23]

As in the case of Bushire, the value of imports into Lingah exceeded exports: by at least 15 per cent in 1876, for example. The import trade steadily inceased, often exceeding a crore (or 10 million) rupees in the 1890s. However, unlike Bushire, British goods imported into Lingah were few and far between. Table 3.3 shows that in 1873 there were none at all, and only 9350 rupees by 1897, or only 0.1 per cent of the total. Lingah was thus not exploited at all as a market for British goods. The BI and its agents preferred to concentrate on the leading ports of Bushire, Basra and Mohommerah, with their larger local populations and hinterlands. Ports with good inland connections by caravan routes were most important to the BI: Bushire had at least two, whereas Lingah had none, its trade mainly sea-based, involving trans-shipping goods to other ports.

Lingah's exports also rose in value before the crippling customs dues were imposed, increasing threefold between 1876 and 1892–4. The traditional trading areas of Lingah merchants were India and the Arab coast. They played an important part in the export of pearls from Bahrain, the import of guns from Muscat and coffee, cloth, flour and rice from India, and the export of dates to the Arab coast. Only drugs, pearls and mother-of-pearl shells were exported to the UK, which formed less than 1 per cent of the value of Lingah's exports in 1897–9. Thus Lingah was seen as a necessary port of call on the mail run rather than of importance for trade with Britain, although the BI steamers, in their predominant position in steam tonnage trading with this port, would have played a large part in the carriage of goods between Lingah and India.

Gray Paul's branch manager, who was the only British resident at the port, had to contend with considerable local problems in managing the steamer service. As at Bushire, the loading and discharge of the steamers were at the mercy of the *Hamal Bashi*. The master of the *Purnlia*, writing to Gray Paul at Bushire in 1897, complained 'I had a day extra at Lingah due to the want of boats, and had to overcarry 804 packages. The reason of delay appears to be that the *Hamal Bashi* would not supply boats, and your representative (the Gray Paul branch) complained bitterly of his lack of energy and co-operation'.[24]

IV

The Bander Abbas branch of Gray Paul was established concurrently with Bushire in 1865. The port was slowly developing as an exchange centre for goods from a large area of South-Central Asia, but it declined in the 1890s, when increasing Russian dominance of central Asian trade severely curtailed the import of British goods via Bander Abbas.[25] It was a regular port-of-call of the BI steamers where, as in the case of Lingah, the BI virtually monopolised local steamer traffic. Table 3.2 shows that in 1885–6, for example, when BI steamers represented 44 per cent of steam tonnage entering Bushire, the same vessels when calling at Bander Abbas represented over 60 per cent of steamers trading there. In 1897 and 1899 all the steamers entering were British, and the BI in particular continued to frequent the port despite the decline in its trade.

This decline is apparent when analysing the value of imports into

3.1 The Gulf: the Bander Abbas office, showing the rather primitive conditions of life there, even in the 1950s

Bander Abbas, which reached a peak in the early 1890s having increased sixfold from 1873. Although trade was halved by 1901, it was still an important port of call. Exports from Bander Abbas also increased, by more than 300 per cent from 1873 to 1895, thereafter declining sharply to its former level by 1900. Like Lingah and Bushire, imports predominated. However, unlike Lingah, a significant proportion of imports into Bander Abbas were from Britain as this port was also a forwarding station for goods. Table 3.3 shows that although they totalled only 3 per cent by value in 1873, British goods imported rose more than twentyfold to 19 per cent of the total in 1898. Exports to Britain from Bander Abbas however, remained insignificant throughout the period under review. The cargoes imported from Britain into this port were largely cotton piece goods, which were trans-shipped to many Asian cities until they came under Russian commercial and political dominance. India was the most important source of imports into Bander Abbas, supplying indigo, rice, copper, iron and tea. Exports included a small quantity of drugs to Britain, and dates, dried fruit and nuts to India.

With the port of Bushire, Bander Abbas acted as an outlet for the Persian Gulf opium crop. BI vessels, in competition with the Bombay

3.2 The Gulf: Lord Inchcape with Sheik Sulman bin Hamad al Khalifa, at the opening of the Bahrain Slipway in 1954

and Persia Steam Navigation Company, shipped approximately one third of its opium exports from here: this represented a quarter of the total opium output exported from the Gulf. BI steamers entered the Bander Abbas opium trade in 1885, later than at Bushire. 240 chests were carried to London, although Hong Kong was usually the most profitable destination. In 1892 the carriage of opium by BI vessels from Gulf ports reached a peak: 2194 chests from Bushire and 746 from Bander Abbas.

With its substantial imports of British goods, Bander Abbas was an important branch to Gray Paul, which was the only European firm represented at the port. In 1908 it was observed that 'except for Great Britain, no foreign power possesses any tangible interest here'. The Russians, however, did have a consulate at the port.[26] By the end of the period under review, the import and export business of Bander Abbas was being transferred to Bushire, which became the main place of trans-shipment of imports from Britain to the Persian coast of the Gulf. The considerable trade in importing rifles at Bander Abbas was, meanwhile, stopped effectively by the local customs authorities. Despite this, the port remained a regular, rather than optional, port of call, and the BI established their own loading and discharge arrangements here by maintaining their own fleet of boats.[27]

V

Bahrain, where Gray Paul opened an office in 1883, provided its base on the Arab side of the Gulf in this period. Agriculturally and commercially the most valuable district on the Arab coast, a direct service by the BI to Bahrain became especially important after the decline of Lingah.[28] Table 3.2 shows that it was not a regular port of call to the same extent as Bushire, Lingah and Bander Abbas, but the tonnage of steamers entering increased significantly. From under 10 000 tons a year in 1874–6 entrances exceeded 40 000 tons in 1879 and again in 1884–5. In the 1890s it was almost always considerably higher. The BI's dominance of the mail steamer traffic at Bahrain was almost complete: in 1884, for example, the only other steamer entering the port was a coaster of 270 tons. The steamer trade of this port fluctuated more dramatically than at other Gray Paul branches, as would be expected at an optional port of call, and was more dependent on local trading conditions. However, by 1904, the tonnage of British steamers entering Bahrain exceeded that of Lingah.

The value of goods imported into Bahrain increased consistently by over 300 per cent from 1873 to the early 1900s. Yet, like Lingah, it was not developed as a market for British goods: only 5 per cent of Bahrain's imports of 1897 were from the UK, and these were principally firearms. Exports from Bahrain, which increased in proportion to its imports, were mainly to India, accounting for 72 per cent in 1899 (68 per cent of Bahrain's imports were from India). As such, BI vessels carried a large proportion of these cargoes, which were principally coffee, dates, rice – and pearls.

The pearl fishery at Bahrain was its most important activity, representing one of the few sources of wealth on the Arabian side of the Gulf, and dominated its economy. 4500 boats, manned by 74 000 men, were employed there by the end of the nineteenth century. More than half of these vessels (2593) were operated under direct British protection, so Gray Paul, as the only British mercantile firm with a branch at Bahrain, were closely involved in the trade, and carried a large proportion of the pearl exports to India and other Gulf ports. In 1866, pearl exports were valued at £400 000; by 1905–6 the trade was worth nearly £1.5m.[29] For this reason, unlike other Gulf ports, the value of

Bahrain's exports kept pace with that of its imports in this period. Edward Hopkins, who was sent out as an assistant at Gray Paul's Bahrain office in 1912, emphasised the importance of pearls by that time:

> Pearls, the main export, were big business . . . in the season Bahrain took on a new aspect, and for a few weeks our little group was enhanced by a couple of dealers from Hatton Gardens, entertaining men of the world, full of the latest from London.

Gray Paul arranged with another European firm, Mallet and Company, to market the pearls overseas, providing them with a 3½ per cent commission covering risks of loss and theft. White rather than yellow pearls were most favoured, and valued at £1 per grain, four grains equalling one carat.

By the time of Hopkins' arrival, a second European firm had established a branch at Bahrain: Robert Wonckhaus, the agents for the Hamburg–Amerika line. By the 1900s, this firm was becoming a strong competitor, especially at the head of the Gulf, but the BI provided the only regular service. Even so, as Hopkins put it, 'the mail ship called once a fortnight on the way up, and on the alternate weeks on the way down. Thus we received English mail only once every two weeks, and our newspapers were always four weeks or more old'. The European community numbered only four men, who became firm friends in their enforced isolation: Hopkins, Macpherson (the junior partner at Gray Paul who was also branch manager), the Political Resident, and Holst of Robert Wonckhaus. Of the last named, Hopkins recalled:

> Like his sovereign the Kaiser, he inclined to the manners, customs and dress of Britain, speaking English fluently. Whether, like his sovereign, he also hated and envied her I do not know for he certainly never showed it then, and we were always on the friendliest terms with him.

Years later, looking back, Hopkins reflected on their conditions: 'they lacked "any cable, wireless or telegraphic communication with the outside world, telephone, electric light, motor cars, a cinema, a club, a bar and plumbing"'. Although very busy in the pearl season, Gray Paul's branch at Bahrain, which pracitally closed down for at least six months of the year, was enlivened only by the occasional visits of BI masters and 'the men-of-war on the Gulf anti-gunrunning and antislavery patrol'. Hopkins, who complained that 'the mails being so far apart, officework tended to be concentrated around midday, leaving little to do in the intervals', found himself quickly transferred to the busier branch at Basra.[30]

VI

Basra, the terminus of the BI service, was the second most important town in Mesopotamia after Baghdad. In decline in the second half of the nineteenth century, it regained importance with the stimulus of the river steamer service on the Tigris and Euphrates and BI shipping in the Gulf.[31] As the port of Basra did not come under the scrutiny of the British Resident at Bushire, no comparable body of statistics as used in Tables 3.2 and 3.3 is available. A short series from 1894 to 1903, however, shows that in terms of steamer entrances and clearances, Basra was one of the most important Gulf ports. Separate figures for mail steamers entering Basra have not been discovered, but British steam tonnage dominated the trade to the extent of over 85 per cent. As each BI vessel would have called there as a matter of course, it is likely that it retained a position of superiority comparable with other ports of call.

Statistics of Basra's import and export trade are given in sterling and, with an approximate exchange rate of 15 rupees to the pound,[32] it is clear that Basra's trade was among the most prosperous of the Gulf ports. In 1895, for example, imports into Basra were valued at £1 399 465 and exports at £1 090 734. (Bushire's totals in the same year were equivalent to about £1½m and about £600 000 respectively.) In 1900 the value of exports from Basra, which for the period 1893–1904 remained roughly in balance with imports, exceeded £1.5m. Recent research has shown that, as in the case of Bushire, the UK replaced India as the main source of trade. In 1901–4, goods worth over £1.5m principally comprising cotton goods and general cargoes, were imported into Iraq as a whole from Europe and North America, through Basra. Seaborne exports from Iraq tripled in quantity between 1880–4 and 1910–13. These included wool and cereals brought to Basra by the Lynch steamers down the Tigris and Euphrates and dates, liquorice root and horses by overland carriage.[33]

The date trade from Basra in the late nineteenth and early twentieth centuries was of particular importance to Gray Mackenzie, who arranged the loading of BI ships with dates both on its own account and for other Europeans and local firms on consignment for Gray Dawes and Co. of London and several merchants in America and Australia. For example, in 1982, shipments of dates on Gray Mackenzie's own account represented over 10 per cent of the total export of this commodity from Basra; 65 000 ½ cwt boxes out of a total of 550 000. However, Gray Mackenzie's main business was in shipping dates for others. A typical shipment, of 1890 to an American merchant customer was of 22 791 boxes of Hullawee dates (the finest quality) at cost per invoice of £5686. Packing charges amounted to £2206, insurance at 1 percent to £100 and freight per invoice to £1227, with an extra £455 for trans-shipment. Gray Mackenzie's 10 percent commission totalled £966, on the final bill totalling £10 628. The vessels carrying the dates exported from Basra were mainly BI ships; so it is clear that Gray Mackenzie played a prominent part in this trade. Other firms involved were Lynch Brothers, the Persian Gulf Transport Company and the German firm Hotz and Co., together with several local merchant houses. As in Bushire, Gray Mackenzie dealt with Indian and Arab merchants rather than the actual producers of the commodities they handled. A letter of 1891 discussed the possibility of arranging with 'native packers for the purchase of their dates on the spot, exercising a supervision over their packing', but complained that the date packers would not accept less than 10 percent profit – based on the price of dates in London – and it was impossible to keep an adequate check on quality control.

According to Hopkins, Basra was regarded as 'almost a metropolis' in comparison with Bahrain and the smaller Gulf ports. British interests predominated over those of other European countries at the port: twenty-seven British residents lived there, mainly connected with the two British firms, Lynch's and Gray Mackenzie. The latter owned extensive property at the port, including the first water closet in Mesopotamia and the land and buildings of the Basra Club. Hopkins, assigned to looking after the loading and discharging of BI vessels and ships of other companies for whom Gray Mackenzie acted as agents, described how Basra 'was unlike most ports in that it completely lacked most of the facilities associated with such places. There were no docks or wharves, no warehouses or cranes, no tugs or dredgers, no buoys, lights or other aids to navigation, and neither harbour master nor port charges'. Problems in managing the service included the fact that 'owing to the lack of any telegraphic line from down river, ships usually arrived more or less unexpectedly'. The port was especially busy during the date season, when as many as four or five steamers at once were loading dates for Britain, the USA and Australia. Gray Mackenzie owned four steel barges, but these were not sufficient for all the loading and discharge work: the remainder was done by local craft, known as *mahalas*, which 'were poled, rowed, sailed or drifted between ship and shore'. When timetables were being drawn up for the new Gulf Service, Gray Mackenzie staff wrote to MM & Co., in Bombay that although it was possible to load and discharge vessels at Basra in three days when business was slack, this was not the case in the date and horse seasons. All steamers were detained 24 hours in any case because of quarantine regulations.[34] Basra particularly suffered the effects of the lawlessness and piracy prevalent at the Gulf: for example, in 1912 Gray Mackenzie wrote to the British Consul at Basra complaining of the theft of ten bags of coffee, one bag of sugar and one case of tea from the *Barala*, and added, with some understatement, 'we would take this opportunity of drawing your attention to the insecure state of the river'. Rarely were the culprits tracked down or punished. When pirates raided a Strick, Scott and Company lighter, stealing two bags of sugar and exchanging shots with the watchmen, the agents complained that 'this is another instance to show the utter helplessness of the Turkish Government to protect British property'.[35] Hopkins had described Basra as 'a hopelessly inefficient port'. Nevertheless a high value of trade was achieved there.

VII

Finally, Gray Mackenzie also represented BI steamers at Mohommerah (later known as Khoramshahr) which was to become the most important of the Gulf ports after the First World War. Mohammerah, as well as Basra, benefited considerably from the opening of the Karun river to steamers in 1888, after which it trans-shipped cargoes to many central Persian settlements such as Ahwaz and Isfahan.[36] No record of British steamers entering Mohommerah survives.[36] It was an optional port of call for the BI from 1884 and enjoyed a regular weekly service from 1894. The value of imports into Mohommerah and the Karun ports rose from £125 115 in 1894 to £263 902 in 1904, reaching a peak of £340 764 in 1900. The value of exports rose from £28 251 in 1894 to £79 405 by 1904, reaching £151 725 in 1901. During the first six months of 1902, according to a return kept by Gray Mackenzie, BI steamers carried 326½ tons of local cargo and 97¾ tons of trans-shipped cargo from Mohommerah, making it quite clear that this was only occasionally a steamer port: it was, in fact, the main haven for the long-distance dhow fleet of the Gulf.[37] Although its trade in this period represented only a fraction of that of the nearby port of Basra, it also took an increasing interest in trading with Britain. In the five years from 1894 to 1899, Mohommerah's imports from Britain rose from 4 percent to 37 percent, and its exports to Britain from 14 percent to 19 percent, of its total trade. By the latter date imports from Britain were mainly cotton goods, and from India coffee, rice, silk and sugar and cheaper cottons. Exports from this area included wheat, dates, oilseeds and wood sent to Britain, and dates, horses, ghee, wool and specie to India.[38] The region was regarded as of great agricultural and commercial potential: for instance the production of gum from Shiraz and Isfahan was already worth £40 000 by 1904; further expansion was expected.[39]

Gray Mackenzie and Lynch Brothers dominated the foreign trade of Mohommerah which, as the capital and only important town of Southern Arabistan, had a British consular office. The growth of the Karun district's trade, through its connections with the BI service via Mohommerah, resulted in a threefold increase in its population and an improvement in their standard of living. The local labourers employed by shippers started their own smallholdings and purchased donkeys, ploughs and seeds. The opening of the Karun was seen primarily in terms of its benefit to the commercial prosperity of Britain and British India. As Curzon pointed out, the inhabitants of:

Central Persia, as far north as Isfahan, already derive the bulk of their luxuries, and almost the whole of their clothing, from Manchester or Bombay; and each fresh town, we may say each new village, that is brought into communication with the Persian Gulf, will thereby be drawn into the mesh of the Lancashire cotton spinner or the Hindu artisan.[40]

Thus, in the period up to 1914, the two merchant partnerships of Gray Paul and Gray Mackenzie were well established at the principal Gulf ports. How profitable were these enterprises? Their partners made substantial investments in these Gulf companies at the beginning. Both firms as we have seen were founded by the same individuals: Archibald Gray and E. S. Dawes. Paul and Mackenzie, when sent to Bushire and Basra respecitvely, put up their savings, as did J. A. Cunningham, a junior partner who was recruited in the mid-1870s. A ledger recording these investments from December 1880 shows a total of £35 000 held in respect of the Bushire branch of which £9500 each was invested by Gray and Dawes, with a further £7000 by Paul, £8000 by Mackenzie and the remainder by Cunningham. The shares were held in exactly the same proportions and amounts at Basra. The accounts survive for six years only, but it is interesting to note that Basra was already showing signs of its later predominance: whereas the total invested at Bushire by the partners was reduced to only £10 000 by 1886, at Basra the working capital rarely dropped below £30 000 and reached £55 000 in December 1885. Fortunately, amounts remitted home by the partners were also recorded, for the years 1886 to 1908. From the Bushire branch alone Dawes personally had sent back to Britain profits of over £5000 by 1886. In the following years to 1895, he remitted a further £1500. Thus despite withdrawing most of his original investment (leaving only £2500 in 1886) he made profits of over £6500, besides the earnings which he may have invested in property and other projects at Bushire of which no record survives. The other partners enjoyed similar returns on their investments at this branch. At Basra, earnings were even more spectacular. Both Dawes and Paul remitted over £7000 home by June 1886, and subsequent remittances by Dawes exceeded £19 000. On his death in 1904, a final sum of nearly £8000 went to his executors. Paul sent home further sums totalling nearly £17 000 between 1886 and 1900 and Mackenzie over £33 000 by 1908. Thus, an initial investment of approximately £10 000 in the Basra branch in the 1880s earned over 300 percent over a period of twenty years.[41]

VIII

In the years leading up to the First World War, the growth of German influence in the Gulf encouraged the British Government to support the commercial enterprise of its nationals in this area. Lord Inchcape, then chairman of the BI, played an important part in the negotiations between the Board of the Baghdad Railway Company and the Ottoman River Navigation Company [ORNCO], part of an agreement by which Turkey and Germany recognised Britain's position in the Gulf. This agreement reached in July 1913 laid down that at least two of the directors of the Board of the Baghdad Railway Company were to be British, and the ORNCO (which Lord Inchcape had been invited to form) was to enjoy a monopoly of the traffic on the Tigris and Euphrates, with a guaranteed minimum freight for the carriage of materials for the building of the railway. This was planned in conjunction with Lynch Brothers who, with Lord Inchcape, were to hold a 40 percent interest in the construction of railway terminal facilities at Basra and Baghdad. Lord Inchcape's insistence that the Baghdad–Kuwait stretch of the railway should be kept under British control led to the establishment of an informal protectorate over Kuwait in 1914.[42]

Although these plans were shelved with the outbreak of war, this international conflict itself stimulated the business and the partnerships to an ever greater extent than that promised by the establishment of the ORNCO. The area became a major theatre of military operations, accelerating a process of transformation ultimately changing the Gulf from a backwater to one of the world's most prominent economic regions. The war brought additional demands on the shipping and importing services of the partnerships in catering for the needs of the huge military presence. In shipping fuel, logistics and general supplies, the firms took over the barges of the Hansa lines, and many other agencies.[43] But the war brought disadvantages too. The partnerships began to appreciate their vulnerability. To escape Turkish jurisdiction, Hopkins recalled that he had to carry the firms' gold and office records to Bushire when Mohommerah was considered no longer safe. He described these developments:

> The Turks unilaterally denounced the capitulations, those treaties dating back to the sixteenth century under which we and other foreigners enjoyed our peculiar extra-territorial position. So we now come under the jurisdiction of the Turkish courts, and our premises were no longer free from search or our property from seizure.[44]

After the war, the partnerships were anxious to reconsider the joint proposals concerning the Baghdad railway which they had planned with Lynch Brothers, thinking that a more efficient pooling of resources would strengthen their position in an economy undergoing considerable upheaval. Lord Inchcape was again being pressed by the British Government to explore ways in which British Commercial interests could play a part in the development of Iraq. Discussions between Lord Inchcape, W. A. Buchanan (by then Senior Partner of Gray Mackenzie and Gray Paul) and F. W. Parry (an executive director of Lynch Brothers) culminated in January 1920, in the launch of the Mesopotamia Persia Corporation Ltd, [MPC]. With its registered office in Bussorah, this company took over the entire operations of Lynch Brothers and the two partnerships as well as the rights and interests of Lord Inchcape, with a monopoly of the navigation of the Tigris and Euphrates guaranteed by the Imperial Ottoman Government.[45]

Potentially, this new enterprise could have made a substantial conribution to the post-war expansion of the region and reaped good

returns, as trade in Iraq and Persia in 1919 was promising. Oil in Persia
had originally been discovered by the D'Arcy expedition in 1905, and the
export of crude oil was monopolised by the Anglo-Persian Company,
with whom Gray Mackenzie and Gray Paul enjoyed close links.
Exploration elsewhere in the Gulf had made only slow progress before,
but the war considerably stimulated further efforts in developing this
industry. Details of the remittances of the partners discussed earlier end
in 1908, and the accounts of MPC, as a company registered in
Mesopotamia, were not transmitted to London. However a brief
unpublished history of Gray Mackenzie & Co. Ltd, from its origins to
recent times, written by a retired managing director with experience of
the Gulf at that time, maintained that in the immediate post-war years,
the firms as individual entities were making handsome profits.[46] Yet the
amalgamation not only failed to achieve the expected economies in
office staff and the elimination of duplication, but through the lack of
co-operation between Gray Mackenzie and Lynch Brothers and the
resultant management difficulties, actually incurred heavy losses which
might have been avoided had the firms remained separate. The friction
between the two firms was due to two principal reasons. First, although
the agency businesses of Gray Mackenzie and Lynch Brothers were
complementary, in trading they were traditionally competitive and as
there was practically no change in the personnel at the branches after the
merger, rivalry inevitably continued. It soon became clear that the co-
operation between the senior partners which was necessary for the
proper control of the corporation's affairs was lacking. Second, an
important distinction between the two firms lay in the fact that Lynch
Brothers conducted their business in the UK through their own Head
Office in London, whereas Gray Mackenzie managed theirs through
their brokers, Gray Dawes and Co. (the London agents of the BI and a
firm with which they shared many partners). Lynch Brothers, London,
and Gray Dawes were both appointed buying and selling agents for the
MPC, their informal and loose association leading to confusion and
duplication of resources. The firms never became accustomed to
working with each other. This was also the case in Mohommerah and
Basra, where both companies had maintained separate branches. An
attempt was made to merge the offices without success.

This lack of co-operation meant that there was no adequate stock
control. The slump in world markets in early 1922 resulted in heavy
losses, and efforts to tighten control on all aspects of the corporation's
business in 1923 proved abortive. Large losses continued. Profits
distributed in 1924 and 1925 had to be reduced considerably because of

excessive stocks and bad debts which had been mounting because of management inefficiency. The corporation's problems were aggravated by personality clashes between directors. John Lynch, of the London office of Lynch Brothers, was regarded by his opposite number at Gray Mackenzie as 'a most difficult man, obstinate, and of no great business acumen'.[47] In 1924, liquidation of the MPC was discussed but abandoned. In retrospect, this proposal should have been adopted, as already over £210 000 had been written off over the years since 1920 for excessive stocks and bad debts. In an attempt to shake up the MPC, John Lynch brought his nephews Malcolm, Colin and Hector Campbell home from Australia to work in the London office, and when their uncle died in 1926, they inherited the business. No noticeable improvement took place. A particularly revealing indication of the lack of confidence of others in the corporation was the fact that the Euphrates and Tigris Steam Navigation Company, for whom Lynch Brothers, London, had acted as agents for over seventy years, were now expressing great dissatisfaction at the handling of their affairs. They opened their own London office in 1927. The ultimate demise of the MPC in 1936 was the result of the suspension of dividends from 1930 onwards and demands by Gray Dawes for the settlement of £25 000 loan.

IX

In 1936, when the firms reverted to their separate entities, the opportunity was taken to transform the two merchant partnerships of Gray Mackenzie & Co. and Gray Paul & Co. into one limited liability company registered in the United Kingdom: Gray Mackenzie & Co. Ltd. The first minute book of the new company records the inaugural meeting of its directors, who were W. A. Buchanan (originally a partner since 1888 and who had survived the troubled times of the MPC); G. P. Hotblack (a close legal and business adviser to Lord Inchcape) and John Herbert Fyfe, connected with Gray Dawes. Their registered office was shared with Gray Dawes and the BI–P & O complex at 122 Leadenhall Street. Their work as agents for the shipping line was to dominate their activities, which earned the healthy pre-tax profit of nearly £26 500 in their first half year, up to June 1937.[48] The new company's growing activities in the years immediately before the Second World War were even more closely linked to the development of the oil industry in this region. For example, Gray Mackenzie and the Bahrain Oil Co. worked closely together and jointly sank an artesian well. The

Company's Khoromshahr Branch acted as agents for the Italian Government tankers on behalf of Lloyd Trestino 'taking oil for the Anglo-Iranian Oil Co. of Abadan, the quantity of oil to be loaded between now and the end of the year being in the region of 120 000 tons'. Gray Mackenzie took over new offices and land and developed their branches, gaining the Strick Line agency at Bandar Shahpour and the Hansa Line and Silver Line agencies at Dubai. The increase in tonnage of shipping calling at Basra, much of which was handled by the company, was impressive; from twelve vessels totalling 20 000 tons in January 1914 to seven of 36 000 tons in the same month in 1927 to seventeeen (mostly tankers) aggregating over 112 000 tons by January 1938.[49] Gray Mackenzie continued their dealings in local produce, such as grain and dates, and were in a strong position to take advantage of the growth in British overseas trade with the expanding economy of the Middle East. This was accelerated in the Second World War as in the First.

*   *   *

In considering the activities and achievements of the BI and their agents over a period of nearly a century, it is striking that when an observer in the 1890s maintained that 'the mail steamers of the BI literally created the trade of the Persian Gulf', this was no hollow boast.[50] In the context of the BI services as a whole, however, the Gulf run was in its infancy and its trade before 1914 not yet on a large scale. For example, British goods imported into the Gulf were valued at nearly £2.5m in 1901–2,[52] whilst British goods imported into India exceeded £32m.[52] The subsidy received by the BI for its mail service was not large: in 1904, less than £30 000 was received for providing two services employing up to eight costly, well-appointed steamers. Profits earned from freight and passengers were not substantial: between July 1901 and July 1902 traffic from Karachi to the Gulf was worth less than £15 000 in earnings to the BI.[53] The tonnage of cargoes for export was small: from January to August 1902 only 10 703 tons was shipped by BI steamers from Mohommerah, Basra and Baghdad. Although the Gulf service was not the most important of the BI's activities,[54] it was of the greatest significance to the economic life of the Gulf. Before 1862, only a small British naval presence existed there. By 1914, the BI and its shipping agents had provided the necessary infrastructure for British commercial development in this region, providing a stepping-stone for future expansion during the exploitation of the Gulf's oil resources. By 1945, Gray

Mackenzie was playing a vital role in the growth of this trade. In the mid-nineteenth century, small local sailing vessels traded from the Gulf to East Africa, Aden and India. By the mid-twentieth century, the steamers of the BI had brought the Gulf ports into a much wider commercial network, and successfully found yet another outlet for British products.

NOTES

1. A version of this chapter was presented to a conference on 'The Gulf Region during the first half of the Twentieth Century' at the Centre for Middle Eastern and Islamic Studies, University of Durham, 19–20 April 1985.
2. *National Maritime Museum* [*NMM*], BI Archives, BI Handbooks 1866–85, BIS/36/1.
3. See Penelope Tuson, *A Brief Guide to Sources for Middle East Studies in the India Office Records* (London, 1982) p. 3. The spellings of place names in the Gulf used in this chapter correspond to those employed in this guide. See also: J. Forbes Munro, 'Sir William Mackinnon', *Dictionary of Scottish Business Biography* (Aberdeen, forthcoming); Robert Geran Landen, *Oman since 1856* (Princeton, 1967); H. Hoskins, *British Routes to India* (New York, 1928); Roger Owen, *The Middle East in the World Economy, 1800–1914* (London, 1981). Charles Issawi, *The Economic History of Iran, 1800–1914* (Chicago, 1971) and *The Economic History of the Middle East, 1800–1914* (Chicago, 1966), are two useful books of annotated readings and documents. Recent research on the Persian Gulf has concentrated on political rather than economic aspects of its history. Discussions of British shipping in the Gulf include George Blake, *B.I. Centenary 1856–1956* (London, 1956) pp. 99–108 and James Taylor, *Ellermans; a Wealth of Shipping* (London, 1976) pp. 58–62: these references are brief and lacking in detail.
4. *The Progress and Present Position of Russia in the East* (London, 1839) 2nd edn pp. 150–1.
5. This concept is employed by Freda Harcourt in her article, 'The P. & O. Company: Flagships of Imperialism', in Sarah Palmer and Glyndwr Williams (eds) *Charted and Uncharted Waters: Proceedings of a Conference on the Study of Maritime History* (London, 1982) pp. 6–28.
6. *Inchcape Archives* [*IA*]. Gray Mackenzie correspondence relating to the Wills of Gray, Dawes and Paul. I am grateful to Dr J. Forbes Munro for information about Robert Paul. Mackenzie, who was the son of William Mackenzie (then Inspector General of the Madras Medical Department), was aged only 25 in 1869.
7. See note 2. The firms' banking services were particularly important in this region, where modern banks were slow to develop, beginning with the Eastern bank in Bahrain in 1920. See Geoffrey Jones, 'Banking in the Gulf before 1960', a paper presented to the Durham Conference (see note 1). Publication of all the conference papers is planned.
8. See Map 3.1.

9. These problems are graphically described, together with British achievements in effecting improvements to the conditions experienced by shipping in the Gulf, in Valentine Chirol, *The Middle Eastern Question, or some Problems of Indian Defence* (London, 1903) p. 241. See also *Public Record Office (PRO)* FO 602/15 Piracy at Persian Gulf Ports, 1900–1906 and FO 602/24 Lights and Buoys, 1913–1914.
10. J. G. Lorimer, *Gazetteer of the Persian Gulf, Oman and Central Arabia* (Calcutta, 1908–15) App. K. p. 2439, consulted in the British Library.
11. Landen, *Oman since 1856*, p. 101.
12. With cargoes and ballast.
13. Goods were also carried by local craft; in 1874 at Bushire, for example, small native vessels plying in the trade of the port numbered 210 with an aggregate tonnage of 10 295, compared with sixty-three steamers of 59 100 tons. The trade between the Gulf and India, and through India with Britain, was not an altogether new trade: it had been carried on by these local sailing ships in the earlier years of the nineteenth century. The advent of the BI steamers diverted much of the trade away from them.
14. J. A. Saldanha, *Precis of Commerce and Communication in the Persian Gulf, 1801–1905* (Calcutta, 1906) consulted in the India Office library. The improvement in the trade of Bushire as a result of the BI steamers is highlighted by the fact that freight rates fell dramatically. In 1870, for example, the freight on iron bars from London to Bushire was 69s 6d; by 1883 it was 30s and by the 1890s even less. See George Curzon, *Persia and the Persia Question* (London, 1892) pp. 554–84.
15. *Report on the Administration of the Persian Gulf and the Muscat Political Agency* (Calcutta, annual, 1873–1905) has many references to this trade. They include: vol. 1874–5, Table 23; vol. 1877–8, Table 12; vol. 1879–80, Table 7 and vol. 1881–2, Table 3; with statistics for the period 1886–97. This source was consulted in the British Library and India Office Library. 1879 marks the entry of the BI in the direct shipping of opium to Hong Kong; it had been involved in the indirect shipping of opium via Bombay from the start.
16. Specifications of BI ships may be checked in George Blake, *BI Centenary: 1856–1956* (London, 1956) Appendix, pp. 253–64.
17. *NMM*, BIS/7/46, Persian Gulf Mail Timetables, 1883–1902, letters between captains of BI ships and Mackinnon Mackenzie at Calcutta.
18. Lorimer, *Gazetteer of the Persian Gulf*, p. 2556.
19. *IA*, Gray Mackenzie Title Deeds of Bushire Properties, 1896–7.
20. *NMM*, BIS/7/47, letters between the Political Resident at Bushire, Gray Paul and Mackinnon Mackenzie at Bombay and Calcutta, 1898.
21. Lorimer, *Gazetteer of the Persian Gulf, entry on Lingah;* Landen, *Oman since 1856*, p. 101.
22. From 1874 the BI mail service called at Lingah at least once a fortnight. See Lorimer, *Gazetteer of the Persian Gulf*, p. 2467.
23. The BI met with less competition at the smaller ports, which were ports of call for the purposes of the mail contract rather than for cargoes. Irregular traders mainly called at the largest, most prosperous ports.
24. *NMM*, BIS/7/47, quoted by Gray Paul to the Bushire Political Resident, 1897.
25. Landen, *Oman Since 1856*, p. 101. Threatened Russian imperial expansion

108   *Two Centuries of Overseas Trading*

in the Gulf was one of the main reasons of the supporters of British trade in this region: by the end of the nineteenth century, the Russians dominated the trade of northern Persia with the British in the south. See Curzon, *Persia and the Persia Question*, pp. 554–84.

26. Lorimer, *Gazetteer of the Persian Gulf*, entry on Bander Abbas. The Russian consul here reflected Russia's attempt to break into the Gulf trade in the early 1900s, an attempt which failed.

27. *NMM*, BIS/7/47, letter from Bushire Political Resident to Mackinnon Mackenzie at Calcutta, 1898.

28. Lorimer, *Gazetteer of the Persian Gulf*, entry on Bahrain.

29. Ibid, App. C, p. 2220.

30. *IA*, Gray Mackenzie, memoirs of Edward Hopkins, unpublished ms. 'Bahrain'.

31. Lorimer, *Gazetteer of the Persian Gulf*, entry on Basra; Landen, *Oman Since 1856*, p. 101. Gray Mackenzie also acted for the BI at Baghdad, but only for the years 1876–83. Lynch Brothers dominated British interests at this city.

32. Calculated from *The Imperial Gazetteer of India: the Indian Empire, Vol. III, Economic* (Oxford, 1907) p. 277. See note 21.

33. Roger Owen, *The Middle East*, pp. 183, 273; Lorimer, *Gazetteer of the Persian Gulf*, entry on Basra, in which he states that in 1908 goods valued at £1.3m were imported into Basra by sea, nearly half of which were cotton goods from the UK. By 1914, the import and export trade of Iraq was 'still mainly in the hands of the British', S. H. Longrigg, *Iraq 1900–1950* (Oxford, 1953) p. 54. Information on the date trade is to be found in *IA*, Gray Dawes, Notebook 1891–1909 (1372).

34. *NMM*, BIS/7/47, letter from Gray Mackenzie at Basra to Mackinnon Mackenzie at Bombay, 1897.

35. *Public Record Office*, FO 602/27 Robberies on British ships and lighters at Bastra, 1909–1914. The India Office Library also contains claims by Gray Paul against robbers, e.g., R/15/5/54 19/6, Gray Paul's claim against Muhammad Ibrahim ibn Saif, 1917–18.

36. Landen, *Oman Since 1856*, p. 102. The opening of the Karun River to British trade was seen as a counter to Russian influence in the area, *PRO* FO 60/414 Memorandum by R. M. Smith, 1 June 1878.

37. *NMM*, BIS/7/46, Persian Gulf Traffic, January–August 1902. The trade deficit was largely financed by specie exports, as in the case of many of the Gulf ports, and as was true of early British trade with China.

38. W. F. Ainsworth, *The River Karun: An Opening to British Commerce* (London, 1890) p. 187, quoting Col. Champlain, a contemporary observer.

39. Cutting from the Board of Trade Journal, c.1904, from Gray Dawes Archives at Inchcape, uncatalogued notebook, 1886–1926, p. 121.

40. George Curzon, 'The Karun River and the Commercial Geography of South West Persia', *Proceedings of the Royal Geographical Society* (1890) pp. 514–8. George Mackenzie played a prominent part in making surveys of the commercial potential of the Karun area and the costing of the river steamer service for Gray Mackenzie. See Ainsworth, *The River Karun*, preface and pp. 132–3 and 205.

41. *IA*, Gray Dawes, Ledger 1877–1908 (1411).

42. See Noble, unpub. ms, pp. 2–8.

43. Ibid, p. 8.
44. *IA*, Gray Mackenzie, memoirs of Edward Hopkins unpub. ms. (To Bushire and Back to Basra).
45. *IA*, Gray Mackenzie, Articles of Association of the Mesopotamia Persia Corporation Ltd, 1920.
46. Noble, unpublished ms., pp. 9–10. For a discussion of the early oil industry, see R. W. Ferrier, *The History of British Petroleum* vol. 1, 1901–1932 (Cambridge, 1982) and Geoffrey Jones, *The State and the Emergence of the British Oil Industry* (London, 1981).
47. Noble, unpublished ms, p. 10.
48. *IA*, Gray Mackenzie, Minute Book, 1936–45.
49. Lloyd's Collection, Guildhall Library: Lloyd's *Weekly Shipping Index* January 1914; *Lloyd's List*, 1 January 1927; Lloyd's *Weekly Shipping Index*, 1 January 1938.
50. Curzon, *Persia and the Persia Question*, preface.
51. Ibid, p. 63.
52. *Imperial Gazetteer of India*, p. 311, Table IV. For further discussion of British goods in world trade see A. G. Kenwood and A. L. Lougheed, *The Growth of the International Economy 1820–1960* (London, 1971) and James Foreman-Peck, *A History of the World Economy* (Brighton, 1983). The export of British cotton manufactures is examined in D. A. Farnie, *The English Cotton Industry and the World Market, 1815–1895* (London, 1979).
53. *NMM*, BIS/7/46, letter from Karachi branch to Mackinnon Mackenzie at Bombay, July 1902. Freight earnings were approximately £11 500 and passenger earnings £1750.
54. The eight steamers employed by the BI for the Gulf Service accounted for only 13 per cent of the total fleet of sixty-one vessels by the early 1880s.

NOTE A version of this chapter was published in *The Great Circle*, the Journal of the Australian Association for Maritime History, Volume 7, Number 1, April 1985, pp. 23–44. It appears again with the permission of the editor.

110

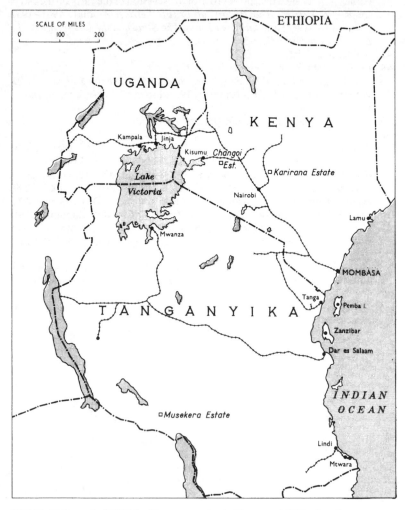

NOTE At the end of 1984 the Group operates in Kenya and Ethiopia only.

MAP 4.1 East Africa, showing tea estates and location of Smith Mackenzie & Co.'s branches at the time of the formation of the Group

4 A British Merchant Partnership in East Africa: Smith, Mackenzie & Co., 1877–1939

Until the expeditions of Livingstone, Burton and Speke in the late 1850s, Zanzibar and the mainland of East Africa were virtually unknown to the inhabitants of early Victorian Britain. The religious and humanitarian zeal of these early explorers was accompanied by an interest in the possible economic potential of this land. Reports on their discoveries were eagerly awaited by the public and government back at home. It was against this background that the British Postmaster General opened discussions in 1871, which led, in 1872, to the BI's contract for a service 'to convey mails between Aden and Zanzibar once (each way) every four weeks'.[1] This linked the East African coast to the growing network of BI services, which already included the Indian coasting trade and the Persian Gulf. A new merchant partnership was formed to manage this service and represent British commercial interests in Zanzibar and on the East African coast: Smith, Mackenzie & Co. Yet why was the British Government, notoriously cautious and hesitant in the question of making financial commitments overseas, prepared to grant a mail subsidy to aid the opening-up of an area which was out of the mainstream of European shipping traffic? Why was Sir William Mackinnon so keen to take up the challenge of providing this service? What was the impact of the BI steamers and the activities of their agents?

British mercantile interest in East Africa, as in many areas, began with the trading activities of East India Company ships, which developed when Zanzibar became linked to the Gulf State of Oman. Attempts to establish Omani control over the east coast of Africa culminated in the transfer of the Sultan of Oman's court from Muscat to Zanzibar in 1840. This encouraged considerable international interest in this island trading post: an American consulate had been established in 1837, followed by the French in 1844. The East India Company revived their agency at Muscat, which had been allowed to lapse until the appointment of Atkins Hamerton as political agent in 1840. The British already enjoyed a treaty relationship with Oman, so when the Sultan changed his official residence to Zanzibar, Hamerton became the local East India Company representative and HM Consul there. The initial opening-up of Zanzibar in international trade brought with it a large influx of Indian merchants and settlers – another reason for British interest.[2]

I

The origins of the mail contract of the 1870s may be seen in the official correspondence, which declared that it was designed 'not merely for postal purposes, but also, and to a greater extent, with a view to facilitating communication with HM Naval and Consular establishments on the east coast of Africa for the abolition of the slave trade'.[3] Britain's commitment to the eradication of this infamous traffic had grown considerably during the course of the nineteenth century, but this was not the only reasons for the grant of a £10 000 annual subsidy. Another argument was the need for the improvement in communications (there was no cable link between Aden and Zanzibar until 1877) but this was not necessarily the deciding factor.

In taking a financial interest in the Aden to Zanzibar route, the British Government was strongly influenced by the success of its grant of a subsidy from Bombay and Karachi to the ports of the Persian Gulf ten years earlier, described in Chapter 3. This service had greatly benefited from the opening of the Suez canal in 1869, a development which may have played a part in the timing of the African contract, as it shortened the route from Britain to Zanzibar by over 2000 miles. One of the aims of the Gulf subsidy had been to combat Arab piracy in the area, but it soon became clear that a strengthened British commercial presence was also required for the extension of British-Indian and British political authority in the area, against the threat of Russian ambitions. In the same way, the Zanzibar subsidy, seen officially as a weapon in the fight against slavery, was also aimed to encourage British commercial interests – and thereby political prepresentation – in a strategically important trading outpost in which the Americans and other European countries has already shown considerable interest.[4]

Chapter 1 has already shown that by the early 1870s, the international trade of Zanzibar, particularly its exports of cloves, was thriving. This must have been of considerable significance to Sir William Mackinnon when he was offered the opportunity to inaugurate his mail service. The African contract also meant a further extension to the existing range of BI routes. As in the case of the Gulf contract, however, the subsidy and prospect of its continued extension was the most attractive feature, although Mackinnon had to be content with only a 5 shillings per mile rate compared with the usual rate of 8 shillings.

From its beginnings, Smith Mackenzie a Co., the BI's agent, enjoyed strong links with Gray Dawes & Co. in London, Gray Mackenzie & Co. at Basra and Gray Paul & Co. at Bushire. Archibald Gray and Edwin Sandys Dawes invested in 5/16 and 4/16 respectively, Archibald Smith held 3/16 and E. N. Mackenzie two, with the remaining two shares held by Archibald Brown who had joined the partnership in 1876, from Calcutta. During the next decade, the partners jointly provided nearly £30 000 in original capital and ploughed-back profits for their operations in Zanzibar.[5] The initial activities of the partners, aided by a handful of native assistants, were confined to their official role as BI agents. Yet this was to become a springboard for the expansion of the firm's interests into other fields. These included the representation of other shipping lines, acting as local Lloyd's agents, and organising the supply of coal to British and German naval vessels. Coaling was to gain particular significance during the First World War. Smith Mackenzie also represented the ill-fated Imperial British East Africa Company, arranged caravan expeditions into the interior, provided goods and services for journeys of exploration and made trading agreements with local tribes. The firm was also to become involved in land-owning, coffee- and sisal- growing. They acted as agents for several insurance companies and for the international news agency, Reuters.

The early effect of the mail-steamers service was assessed in Prideaux's report, mentioned in Chapter 1, on the Zanzibar trade of 1873–4. He described how the new lines provided by the BI and Union company, to be discussed later, 'have brought a revolution in the carrying trade of Zanzibar'. They connected the island not only with Aden, but with Bombay, the Comoro Islands, Madagascar, Natal and the Cape with the

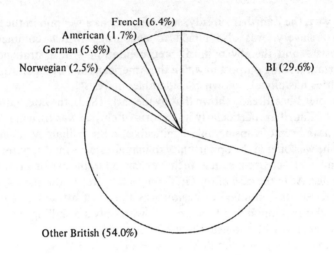

French (6.4%)
American (1.7%)
German (5.8%)
Norwegian (2.5%)
BI (29.6%)
Other British (54.0%)

SOURCES As for Figure 4.3

FIGURE 4.1 Tonnage of steamers entering Zanzibar, 1918

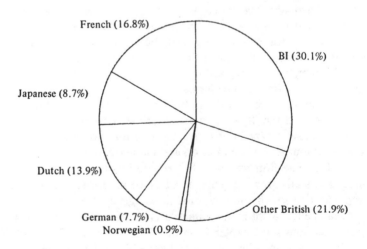

French (16.8%)
BI (30.1%)
Japanese (8.7%)
Dutch (13.9%)
German (7.7%)
Norwegian (0.9%)
Other British (21.9%)

SOURCES As for Figure 4.3

FIGURE 4.2 Tonnage of steamers entering Zanzibar, 1927

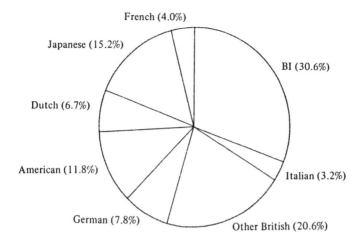

French (4.0%)

Japanese (15.2%)

BI (30.6%)

Dutch (6.7%)

American (11.8%)

Italian (3.2%)

German (7.8%)

Other British (20.6%)

NOTE The only rival to the British steamers at Zanzibar before the end of the nineteenth century was the German line. The percentage of British steamers declined from 88.7 per cent in 1874 to 52.6 per cent in 1896 and 40.6 per cent in 1897. In 1897, 109 612 tons of German steamers entered Zanzibar, compared with 75 013 tons of British steamers.

SOURCES: *Reports from HM Consuls on Manufacturers, Commerce, &c., of their Consular Districts including Zanzibar, PP,* 1876 LXXIV (c.1421); *Trade and Shipping of Africa, PP,* 1899 LXIII (c.9223); *Lloyd's List* and *Lloyd's Weekly Shipping Index* for 1918, 1927 and 1938.

FIGURE 4.3 Tonnage of steamers entering Zanzibar, 1938

exception of a few small vessels in the coasting trade; he concluded 'the whole of the commerce of Zanzibar is now conveyed by English tonnage'.[6] The importance of these steamers is seen in entrances at the port, shown in the note to figures 4.1 to 4.3. In 1874, British steam vessels, totalling over 30 000 aggregate tons, called at Zanzibar. Their only rivals in this period were the Germans, who sent steamers of a total of nearly 4 000 tons to the port. Otherwise sailing ships, of between 250 and 500 tons, (about 15 000 tons in all) continued in the trade, registered in England, America, Germany, France, Norway, Portugal, Holland and Denmark and over 200 Arab dhows continued to operate in East African waters.

By the late 1880s, this situation was changing. German steamers became increasingly important and by 1896 and 1897 were neck and neck with the British, as seen in the note to Figures 4.1 to 4.3. After the First World War, the British again obtained an overwhelming ascendancy, representing nearly 84 per cent of Zanzibar's steamer traffic in 1918. Although this subsequently fell to just over 50 per cent, BI tonnage entering the port rose impressively, and formed an increasingly greater proportion of British tonnage in these waters as a whole. This brought more and more business to Smith Mackenzie. The other British companies competing against the BI were largely the same as their rivals in the Indian coasting and long-haul trades and in the Persian Gulf, although by 1939 British steamer traffic at Zanzibar had declined in comparison with these areas. They included the Union Castle Line, the Anglo-Saxon Petroleum Company, the Bombay and Persian Steam Navigation Co. (using Zanzibar as a coaling- and watering-point whilst trading to the Persian Gulf), the Clan Line, Harrisons, Weirs, Bucknalls and Ellermans.[7]

II

The BI agency brought many advantages and benefits to Smith Mackenzie and to the commercial development of the port as a whole. The inauguration of the service introduced the firm not only to the BI business laid down by the contract, as discussed in Chapter 2, but to the import–export trade of Zanzibar. BI vessels carried British and British-Indian products, such as cotton piece goods *to* East Africa and local products *from* the region, including ivory, cloves, chillies, coconuts, copra and mangrove bark. The total value of imports into Zanzibar rose from £565 010 in 1873–4 to £1 399 078 by 1897, approximately equivalent to the trade of Bushire in these years. By the latter date, the value of piece goods imported was more than three times as much as any other single import, those from India being most competitive.[8] In fact, nearly half of Zanzibar's imports by the turn of the century came from India.

Rice came second among these imports and other items in demand included bags and canvas, beads, coal, coins, crockery, glassware, dried fish, flour, groceries, ghee, hardware, jewellery and ornaments, paint, oil, turpentine, petroleum, spirits, sugar, timber, tobacco, vegetables, wine, and wheat and other grains. Manchester manufacturers found a thriving market for brightly-coloured cloth made up into *kangas* to be worn by Zanzibari women, specially made to local designs. The UK was also the main source of other cloths, such as shirtings, mulls and indigo-dyed cottons known as *koniki*. Zanzibar's role was chiefly as a transshipment centre and base for supply to the interior. According to the *British and South African Export Gazette*, 'only a comparatively minor portion of the total imports into Zanzibar are consumed in the Sultan's dominions of the gross imports of 1899 . . . [45 per cent] . . . was re-exported to the mainland and to German East Africa, British East Africa . . . and the Italian Benadir Ports'. Similarly, 20 per cent of the gross exports of the port came from the mainland.[9] Through the stimulus received by the BI steamers and the subsequent expansion in shipping at the port, local production of cloves, one of the most important local export commodities, rose from 50 000 frasilas (35lb equalling 1 frasila) in 1873 to 356 877 by 1896.

Plentiful evidence of Smith Mackenzie's involvement in the carriage of locally-produced exports is to be found in their correspondence with the British Consul. For example, in 1875 the *Coconada* carried 30 tons of ebony to Calcutta and in 1896 the *Canara*'s cargo included twenty tusks of ivory. When the Imperial Institute in London requested samples of Zanzibari produce, Smith Mackenzie was quick to oblige, sending India rubber, tobacco, hippo teeth, tortoise shells, beeswax, hippo hide, coir rope, *papri* twigs, nutmegs, sugar, molasses, turmeric, white and red *sim sim* (a type of cereal), haricot beans, maize, red and white *koondi* (small beans), arrowroot, dhal, rice, manioc, *kachi* (armadillo scales), orchilla weed and gazelles' feet, besides the items already mentioned.[10] In the late 1890s the BI employed an additional BI steamer the *Pachumba*, to ply in the coasting trade. She could carry 650 tons of cargo, twenty-two first-class passengers and fourteen second-class, with at least 500 more on deck. This trade with local ports, served by dhows, German steamers and vessels owned by the Sultan, was already considerable. In 1899, for example, 29 061 packages were imported into Zanzibar and 60 877 exported from the port to Bagamoyo, Dar es Salaam, Kilwa, Lindi, Mikindani, Ibo, Tanga, Mombasa, Malindi, Lamu and Kismayu, together with 2709 passengers.[11] In 1901, the BI put on a new steamer to trade between Zanzibar and Delagoa Bay, the *Goa*, of 1902 gross tons. This was a completely new service without competition from the Germans. By 1903 two smaller steamers, the *Vasna* and the *Vita* had also entered this trade, to be joined later by the *Putiala*, *Nuddea*, *Nevasa* and *Nerbudda* when the volume of traffic required further tonnage.

After the 1890s, and indeed until the outbreak of the Second World War, the import and export trade of Zanzibar, including re-exports, continued at a high level. A healthy balance between the two was achieved during most of these years, when both totals rarely fell below

118

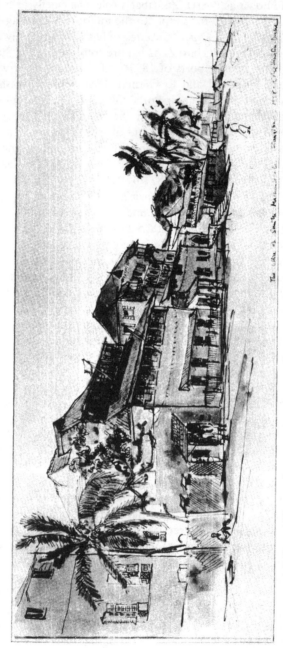

4.1 East Africa: a drawing of Smith Mackenzie's Zanzibar office, by Edward Millington Drake

4.2 East Africa: Mombasa harbour in the 1950s, packed with BI steamers, easily identifiable from their distinctive funnel markings

£1m sterling in value. The Post-war boom of 1919–20 acted as a great stimulus to the Zanzibar economy, with imports that year valued at £2 901 000 and exports £3 606 000. This high level of trade continued throughout the 1920s, reflecting the island's continuing importance as an entrepôt for that part of Africa then declined only slightly to recover again by 1939. The East Africa Protectorate's imports in 1895 were valued at only £149 000 and its exports at £62 000. This area, which became Kenya and Uganda after 1914, grew rapidly, its trade surpassing that of Zanzibar during the boom years of the First World War. By 1928, the value of goods imported into Kenya and Uganda exceeded £10m; their exports also reached this level by 1937. This far outpaced the trade of the German East African colony of Tanganyika: only Ghana and Nigeria, among other African countries, generated a more valuable trade, and then only marginally and occasionally. The BI's prominent position in the steam tonnage frequenting the East African coast, as shown in Figures 4.1 to 4.3, strongly suggests that their impact in this growth was considerable.[12]

III

Yet the management of the BI service and its operation in East African waters was not without problems for Smith Mackenzie, British trade with the port, and the economic growth of the region. A frequently recurring problem was the somewhat erratic levies of customs and trans-shipment charges. Archibald Smith, in 1875, wrote to the Consul in protest that the Sultan was charging him trans-shipment duties on cargoes transferred from the *Umballa* to the *Khediva*, and he tried to avoid payment by maintaining that he did not know the value of the cargoes and was thus unable to pay the percentage levy on them. Meanwhile, other firms, such as the German merchant house of O'swald, enjoyed complete exemption. A special notice was issued by the Sultan as late as 1891 finally clarifying the matter, whereby goods destined for a foreign port trans-shipped from one vessel to another were declared free of duty. From the beginning of the service until this date, Smith Mackenzie challenged nearly every payment they were charged. Duties on coal deliveries were similarly inconsistent.[13]

Local merchant houses to whom goods carried in BI ships were consigned often made life difficult for their agents. In June 1885, Smith Mackenzie complained to the Consul that the Custom House was particularly overcrowded, mainly because of the failure of consignees to take immediate delivery of their goods, which, after the arrival of the monthly BI steamer, together with the Sultan's SS *Merka* and the American vessel *Essex*, were mounting up alarmingly. With the depressed state of trade that year, merchants were obviously reluctant to collect their goods – and pay the appropriate duty – before they had found customers for them. Smith Mackenzie naturally resented the extra work that this entailed for BI clerks, and asked the Consul if a notice could be posted at the Custom House warning those concerned that unless they took delivery of their goods within five days of their discharge, they would be liable to an extra fee to cover the expenses of warehousing. European firms were generally exempt from these accusations. It was the British Indian merchants, with presumably less capital and greater cash-flow problems, who were the main culprits. In March 1887, the Consul received from Smith Mackenzie a specific request that Messrs Lellanie and Peera Dewjie should immediately collect their goods, as the firm had only two godowns within the Custom House, and further accommodation was needed with the approach of the rainy season.[14] Smith Mackenzie's work as BI agent was further increased by the need for frequent packing inspections, the chasing of bad debts and having to auction unclaimed goods.

BI vessels carrying goods and passengers, especially in the coasting trade, were subject to quarantine regulations, particularly concerning cholera, which entailed long and expensive delays. The *Goa*, trading between Zanzibar and Delagoa Bay, received official instructions to the effect that:

> the steamer must first discharge all her cargo, then the empty steamer must be disinfected by a Portuguese Doctor under the control of the Portuguese Consul. The steamer must remain for *twelve days* under quarantine, having no communication with the shore, but is allowed to load with cargo which has been disinfected on shore, the voyage to the next Portuguese port counting on the quarantine.[15]

In 1898, the BI steamer SS *Bhundara* from Bombay had to be washed down with a solution of corrosive sublimate after six passengers had died of plague.[16]

These delays made it difficult for Smith Mackenzie to ensure that the mail steamers kept to the BI's timetables. Moreover masters of BI vessels frequently complained that the sailing times were too ambitious, taking insufficient account of other causes of delay, in loading and discharging cargo and passengers, navigational problems, the monsoons and harbour congestion.[17] In addition consuls were empowered to hold back steamers for especially important despatches, resulting in great inconvenience for local merchants.[18] Even merely entering harbour could involve delay. In one instance an American sailing vessel was berthed in the space reserved for the BI steamers.[19] On another occasion a dispute broke out between lightermen unloading a vessel owned by the Sultan and BI employees, concerning who had precedence. As Smith Mackenzie wrote to the Consul:

the headmen discharging the Sultan's boats are putting every obstacle in our way and have, we hear, threatened to set on our man, Mohammed bin Salem, after dark. As the Mail steamer leaves tomorrow and has still a large number of packages to discharge, we should esteem it a favour if you would help us in this matter, and request his Highness to have orders given that our work is not to be interfered with and also that in case of need you will give the necessary protection to Mohammed bin Salem, being in British employ.[20]

These difficulties seemed to affect the BI particularly in the years before the First World War when, as we have seen, the rivalry of other lines, especially the Germans, was proving fierce. The subsidy the BI received was minimal: only £10 000 p.a. from 1873 to 1884, which was subsequently reduced to £7950, and a further £16 000 for the monthly service all the way from London, which lasted only from 1890 to 1893.[21] The Deutsche Ost Afrika Line, by comparison, received £67 500 by 1900.[22]. Even in the carriage of mails on behalf of the British Post Office, other lines were often preferred. In September, 1888, the Postmaster General, writing to the British Consul, noted 'the good service offered by Messageries Maritimes'. The BI contract was about to expire, and if it had not been renewed, mails would have been sent by the most efficient line, regardless of nationality.[23]

In 1905, the General Post Office at Mombasa wrote to the Consul requesting that the dates of sailing of the BI steamers should be changed, as its monthly service coincided with the German line, which gave a much quicker service. The Mombasa Postmaster considered that the contract which the British government had with the BI was practically useless, but it might gain more business if it provided sailings one week earlier or one week later. Eighty-seven per cent of mails were carried by foreign or British non-contracted steamers: of bags of letters received from London in the period July to December 1904, the BI carried only seventy-one, while other steamers carried 493; and of bags despatched to

London, the BI carried just sixteen, with foreign and other British vessels taking sixty-three,[24] The mails to Mombasa were carried from London to Aden by the P & O and then by whichever steamer was leaving first. This was rarely a BI vessel, which was usually desparately searching for cargoes to offset its expenses.

The larger subsidies enjoyed by the foreign lines enabled them to offer lower rates of freight and still make an overall profit. As an experiment, in the 1890s, Mackinnon, Mackenzie & Co. sent specie, valued at Rs 550 000 (or $258 000 or £10 000) to Zanzibar from Calcutta by three different lines – the P & O to Aden and then BI to Zanzibar, the Messageries Maritimes, and the German line. The former was by far the most expensive: Rs 639 compared with Rs 601 by the French and only Rs503 by the Germans.[25] Thus BI steamers were frequently uncompetitive and consequently lost business. Once the British Treasury withdrew its subsidy from the London–Zanzibar route in 1893, the BI effectively withdrew from competition with the German and French lines. The BI directors finally refused to take on the long distance, oceanic routes without the same kind of support which the German line enjoyed. Instead, BI concentrated on the local trades, where small, old steamers could still be employed to advantage. The local line to Delagoa Bay, for example, proved profitable for a time. In four voyages in this trade in 1901, the *Canara* earned a total of £14 316. Table 4.1, showing the results of BI steamers on the East Africa line for the years 1900–05 (unfortunately the only figures of these details available) reveals that this coasting trade was of great significance to the BI's profits. Then their passenger trade, lost to the Germans and French, declined dramatically, from over 300 000 to fewer than 118 000 persons per half year. With the exception of the second half of 1903 freight has also fallen off. This was the result of the opening of a new trade, the carrying of cattle from Ibo to Beira, in which the *Vasna* and *Vita* had earned £3696 in less than two months alone. This was based on regular monthly shipments of fifty head of cattle per ship at Rs 30 per head. However, because of the objections of the Hindu passengers, who refused on religious grounds to share accommodation with the cattle aboard the ships, BI had to abandon this lucrative trade or face losing its declining passenger traffic completely.[26] By June 1905, on the instructions of MM &Co., BI gave up managing the service to ports south of Zanzibar. The four-weekly service from Bombay, Aden, Zanzibar, Mozambique and Delagoe Bay was finally discontinued in 1908, as shown in Table 2.1

The BI steamers were unable to compete in efficiency and cheapness because their German competitors were large, modern vessels (such as,

TABLE 4.1 Results of voyages of **BI** steamers on East Africa Line, 1900–05

Half year	Number of voyages	Aggregate gross tons	Coal consumed (Tons)	Income					Rs Disburse- ments	Rs Profit/ Loss	£ eq. approx.
				Rupees							
				Freight	Passen- gers	Subsidy	Misc.	Total			
2nd half 1900	16	6476	14422	516786	336797	68394	27872	949849	714326	235523	33500
1st half 1901	9	3590	7325	176734	251744	41538	13010	483026	364650	118376	17000
2nd half 1901	9	5006	13919	297366	358312	83087	17719	756484	586721	169763	24250
1st half 1902	9	4230	11663	244647	235487	67500	22254	569888	480669	89219	12750
2nd half 1902	9	3901	10341	142080	207573	46731	17651	414035	397372	16663	2380
1st half 1903	9	4086	11306	134692	189615	67500	27528	419385	415159	4226	600
2nd half 1903	12	8908	16042	407705	192283	10384	268141	878513	655704	222809	32000
1st half 1904	9	4865	11662	286176	124280	10384	40955	461795	460389	1406	200
2nd half 1904	9	6491	17133	294622	150020	83076	16292	544010	617807	73797	10500 Loss
1st half 1905	12	6363	16586	230302	117755	83078	37541	468676	585659	116983	16700 Loss

SOURCE: *National Maritime Museum [NMM]*, BI Archives B15/7/41, Voyage Accounts of **BI** steamers.

by the early 1890s, the *Reichstag* and *Bundesrath* of 2300 tons and the *Kaiser* and *Kauzler* of 2600). The BI's East Africa service, on the other hand, was run by old, small vessels, cast-offs from the more important and prestigious Indian routes. The *Africa, Canara, Ethopia* and *Goa,* smaller than their German rivals, were built in 1874 and by the 1890s required conversion to quadruple expansion engines to use fuel more economically.[27] This was especially vital on this run where coal was more expensive. Mombasa rates often exceeded 55/– per ton, compared with 23/– at Port Said.

What Smith Mackenzie received for its considerable services on behalf of the BI is not known, but there is evidence to suggest that its rates of pay were far from generous. At Mombasa, for example, the Smith Mackenzie branch, which opened in the later 1880s, was allowed only Rs 500 per month to cover all expenses, when boat hire alone was Rs 8 per day, and ordinary trans-shipment charges Rs 2 per ton. At the Zanzibar Office, they were allowed Rs 650 per month for wages and Rs 100 – only £14 – per month as a bonus and to protect the firm against loss. In the early 1890s, the BI declared that it would no longer pay for Christmas and Ramazan presents for its most important clients, or for coolie hire or the cost of coal pumps.[28] Some indication of the BI's treatment of its agents is seen in the complaints of its Beira representative, the Rhodesia Cold Storage and Trading Co. Ltd. who maintained that not only was it doing the BI's agency work, but it was also practically financing their operations, as on nearly every steamer which arrived, the agents found themselves having to pay out more than they received. In 1903 for example, £549 was owing by the *Nevasa* and £115 on the *Vasna.* Labour was expensive at Beira, Goanese workers costing the firm £180 each per year. The agents had to employ at least two clerks at £300 p.a. each to deal with the Customs regulations. In addition, it had to pay a £40 licence fee per year just to act as shipping agent. Between January and June 1903, its total commission received from BI was only £219. Only its other agencies saved the Rhodesia Cold Storage and Trading Co. Ltd. from heavy loss. The BI steamer agency entailed four times the amount of work required by other lines, and the firm considerred that it was expected to work for honour alone. They even had to wait at least a month before being reimbursed.[29]

If Smith Mackenzie was not always happy about working for the BI, the BI and its Calcutta and London agents were often displeased with Smith Mackenzie. MM & Co. maintained that the East Africa firm charged excessive landing fees, and even considered changing agents and appointing a local merchant – Essa Thawur in its place.[30] GD & Co. in London also complained that Smith Mackenzie's lighterage charges were too high. However, it was inevitable that agents and the firms they represented would not agree over everything. The great advantages which the BI brought to Smith Mackenzie as a merchant house far outweighed the problems and shortcomings of the service, which were generally the result of inadequate investment and working capital. Although the BI's prominent role in the steamship services on the East African coast was challenged by the German lines particularly, it remained the most important single company on this route throughout the period under review.

IV

In any case, Smith Mackenzie's work as shipping agents in Zanzibar was not limited to acting as agent for BI. As early as 1874, Captain Fraser represented the Union Steam Navigation Co. Smith Mackenzie took over this agency from Fraser and acted for the firm when it became the Union Castle Line in 1910. Between 1873 and 1881 the line received a subsidy of £20 000 per year to provide twice-monthly sailings between the Cape and Zanzibar.[31] Smith Mackenzie earned 2 per cent commission on goods it forwarded by the Union steamers and was paid Rs 2 per ton for trans-shipping this cargo from its vessels to those of the Union SN Co.[32] The firm therefore provided agency services for the two major British shipping lines linking the UK and India with the East Africa coast. The losses it incurred from acting as BI agent when these steamers were unprofitable were largely offset by earnings from the Union vessels and other activities.

Smith Mackenzie's prominent position in the maritime trade of Zanzibar was formally recognised when it was appointed Lloyd's Agents in May 1884 for a region covering nearly the entire East African coast, from Delagoa Bay to Cape Guardafui.[33] Its principal duties in this connection involved discovering details of all wrecks and casualties in the area, and to assessing claims on Lloyd's for cargo and vessels lost or damaged. Before this appointment, the firm had already been of considerable assistance to Lloyd's, receiving a letter of thanks for its help in the wreck of the *Taitsing* in December 1883. In January 1884, when a 12-year-old wooden sailing ship of 285 tons, the *Royal Irish*, was wrecked carrying piece goods worth £12 000 from Bombay to Zanzibar, Smith Mackenzie helped to take out the stores and salvage the cargo.

As official Lloyds's Agents, however, the firm was empowered to hold courts of inquiry in cases of dispute. Thus in May 1886, after the total

loss off Pemba of the *Adria*, an iron steamer of 781 tons owned at
Bombay, Smith Mackenzie asked the Consul to authorise such a court
as, they argued:

the captain and the whole crew being present, and as there are two of
Her Majesty's ships at present in harbour, we shall feel much obliged
if you will arrange for one being held. Another reason for our desiring
the court to be held here is that we believe our London firm, Messrs
Gray Dawes & Co. were the agents by whom the ship was insured, and
it is always more satisfactory to have such an enquiry held as near
where the accident took place as possible.

The company was responsible for selling the vessel's stores, and usually
provided free passage on BI steamers for the shipwrecked crew, but in
this instance, the Sultan offered the services of his own steamer, the
Malacca, free of charge. Another example of its duties as Lloyd's Agents
is seen in the case of the *Asturia* of 1902. Her cargo of tin, worth £60 000,
was lost with the vessel; Smith Mackenzie had to trace the marks on the
cargo to establish ownership and thus rights to claims; but, by this time,
the valuable consignment was being 'salved' by local dhows, and turning
up for sale in Somaliland. Smith Mackenzie tried in vain to protect the
wreck against such pilferage.[34]

A fourth activity of the firm was the supply of coal to British and
German naval vessels stationed in East African waters. Smith Mackenzie enjoyed a long-standing contract with Cory's, who shipped the coal
from Newcastle and South Wales to Zanzibar. In a contract of 1889,
Smith Mackenzie charged 4/– per ton for shipping the coal and 4/– for
landing it free on board, to the Admiralty depot, landing up to 300 tons
in 24 hours. They earned a commission of 2½ per cent on the sale price of
the coal. This was especially valuable in view of the high price of coal on
this distant station. Similar commission and charges were levied on the
German navy, as well as on the BI steamers. Although the price of coal
fell from 65/– in 1890 to 45/6 by 1895, the coaling of steamers at
Zanzibar remained a profitable sideline to them.[35]

V

One of the most important aspects of the firm's work was less related to
maritime commerce. This was its role as agents for the Imperial British
East Africa company. The ultimate failure of this enterprise, its lack of

financial support from the British government and its over-ambitious schemes have been well documented.[36] Sir William Mackinnon and other individuals associated with his 'group' invested heavily in the concern: Sir William contributed £25 000, E. S. Dawes and G. S. Mackenzie £5000 each, with a further £5000 from Smith Mackenzie itself. The overall total raised was £240 000.[37]

Smith Mackenzie had already acted as the agent and supplier of local transport and labour to the African Lakes Corporation of Nyasaland and Rhodesia, the East African Mission, the Equatorial African Mission and the Congo Association. Its aid to the various mainland expeditions included offering its offices as a resting-place for the body of David Livingstone, brought back by his porters. In 1886 the firm recruited and fitted out 620 Zanzibari porters for the expedition to relieve Emin Pasha, via the BI steamer *Madura*.[38] J. W. Buchanan, a Smith Mackenzie employee who had previously worked for another British firm at the port, Boustead, Ridley & Co., took over the responsibility for dealing with a new account opened that same year – the Special African Mission. The results of the survey work undertaken by this mission led in May 1887 to a formal concession to the British East Africa Association (which became IBEA) to explore and administer the area. A lease of the customs administration of Zanzibar had first been offered to Mackinnon by the Sultan as early as 1877. The BI presence at this port had always been especially favoured. Just before he died, E. N. Mackenzie accepted the concession on behalf of the Association, and accompanied General Sir Lloyd Matthews, with the British military forces, on a tour of the hinterland of Mombasa to make treaties with the native chiefs.

IBEA took over the running of the new BI service direct from London at Mombasa, but the extra business that Smith Mackenzie gained from the IBEA agency well made up for this. For example, four vouchers certifying the handling of supplies for IBEA by Smith Mackenzie in 1888–9 have survived, concerning a piece goods shipment, a Masai interpreter for the projected Uganda railway survey, local porters, and two Snider rifles with ammunition.[39] From the early 1880s, Smith Mackenzie had been responsible for the import of a large quantity of guns, rifles, percussion caps and cartridges, the landing of which required the consul's permission. In 1881 alone, the firm imported over 5000 guns, over 9000 rifles, over 2 million percussion caps and nearly half a million cartridges. These were primarily for the use of naval personnel and for the Sultan, but by the late 1880s and early 1890s, they were imported for arming the caravans of porters into the interior which

IBEA organised. Smith Mackenzie also supplied IBEA with dynamite and detonators for their mining ventures, bullocks for transport, and copper, rice and other consumer goods, mainly from Bombay. They also imported the Lake steamer *Sir William Mackinnon*, in sections, for local assembly. The firm also carried locally-grown exports, the production of which IBEA helped develop, such as tobacco grown at Mombasa: 1705 lb. were shipped to Bombay on board the *Purnlia* in 1890. Although inferior tobacco, its low price produced a steady demand.[40]

Smith Mackenzie also acted as the official agent for the East Africa Protectorate on its formation in 1895, and played an important part in the winding-up and liquidation of its predecessor, IBEA. Its Mombasa branch was promptly reopened in 1895, taking over IBEA's lighters, marine equipment and other assets. It was to play an important part in the building of the Uganda Railway, importing supplies and foodstuffs for the Indian labour force as well as many of the necessary raw materials. Started at Mombasa in 1895, the railway line reached Nairobi in 1899 and was completed, terminating at Port Florence on Lake Victoria, at the end of 1901. It cost the British tax payer at least £5·5m.

In its work in organising caravans, Smith Mackenzie came under considerable criticisms in correspondence between British military personnel and the Consul: it apparently made no attempt to improve the practically impassable road between Kibwezi and Kikuyu; Pordage and Martin, the local Smith Mackenzie employees, had little experience of road transport problems; and no alternative had been found to the constantly diminishing supply of local porters. However, it would have cost at least £600 to metal the road surface – a cost which the Protectorate was not prepared to undertake – and Smith Mackenzie did try to provide local assistance by appointing an agent there. Boustead Ridley, who also covered the area, was also subject to complaints. Smith Mackenzie at least tried to improve the lot of the porters it recruited, by providing medical facilities, disciplining cruel and over-zealous headmen, and by building shelters at suitable points along the caravan routes provided with blankets and clothes for the porters.[41] The importance of the firm in the development of the East Africa mainland was to grow considerably in the first half of the twentieth century.

VI

Smith Mackenzie's activities in this region also included acting as the agents for Reuters, various insurance companies, petroleum firms and

TABLE 4.2 Cash remitted to the UK partners in Smith Mackenzie & Co. at Zanzibar, 1886–1907 (£ Sterling)

Half-year ending	E. S. Dawes	E. N. Mackenzie	G. S. Mackenzie	A. Gray	W. J. W. Nicol	J. W. Buchanan	Total
June 86	10 422	3 994	441	32			14 889
Dec. 86	1 088	661	544	363			2 656
June 87	669	586	335	223			1 813
Dec. 87	—	873	—	—			873
June 88	658	(died)	329	219			1 206
		(total 6 114)					
Dec. 88	987		200	303			1 490
June 89	1 109		942	407			2 458
Dec. 89	921		800	413			2 134
June 90	—		—	—			—
Dec. 90	553		437	175			1 165
June 91	—		—	—			—
Dec. 91	196		155	62			413
June 92	566		477	179			1 192
Dec. 92	579		457	183			1 219
June 93	532		420	168			1 120
Dec. 93	—		—	—			—
June 94	—		—	—			—
Dec. 94	547		432	173			1 152
June 95	667		527	211			1 405
Dec. 95	1 359		1 073	429			2 861
June 96	1 171		924	370			2 465
Dec. 96	1 572		1 241	496			3 309
June 97*	—		—	(died?)			—
				(total 4 406)			
Dec. 97*	—		—				—
June 98*	—		—				—
Dec. 98*	—		—				—
June 99	1 737		1 371				3 108
Dec. 99	482		380				862
June 00	536		423				959
Dec. 00	613		484		452		1 549
June 01	773		610		571		1 954
Dec. 01	1 144		903		—		2 047
June 02	1 135		896		—		2 031
Dec. 02	1 381		1 090		1 018		3 489
June 03	396		313		276		985
Dec. 03	1 115		876		758		2 749
June 04	(died ?)		—		426		426
Dec. 04			1 245		800	413	2 458
June 05			1 340		986	604	2 930
Dec. 05			543		393	199	1 135
June 06			730		568	175	1 473
Dec. 06			205				205
June 07			671		352	45	1 068
Dec. 07			738	590	670	1 998	
TOTALS	32 908		22 522		7 190	2 106	75 246

Annual total remittances

1886	17 545	1897	—*
1887	2 686	1898	—
1888	2 696	1899	3 970
1889	4 592	1900	2 508
1890	1 165	1901	4 001
1891	413	1902	5 520
1892	2 411	1903	3 734
1893	1 120	1904	2 884
1894	1 152	1905	4 065
1895	4 266	1906	1 678
1896	5 774	1907	3 066

* Smith Mackenzie & Co. were requested not to remit home until Mombasa losses were recovered.
SOURCE *Inchcape Archives*, Gray Dawes & Co., vol. 1411, Capital Accounts relating to Bushire, Busreh, Baghdad, Zanzibar, Mozambique and Mombasa, 1877–1939.

for the producers of a number of consumer items in Britain and Europe. On behalf of Reuters, the firm reported stories of the visits of distinguished people to East Africa. These included the Duke and Duchess of Connaught's visit in 1906, Winston Churchill in 1907, Theodore Roosevelt in 1909, the Duke and Duchess of York (later to become the King and Queen) in 1924, and the Prince of Wales in 1928. Like many merchant houses in Zanzibar, Smith Mackenzie represented a number of insurance companies, including the Marine Insurance Co. Ltd from 1879. An advertisement of the company's services in the *Zanzibar Gazette* of 1911 mentions its representation of the Asiatic Petroleum Co. Ltd, and its business in importing kerosene oil in bulk.[42] Earlier, in 1898, the firm had won the Shell agency contract, which it enjoyed until 1930. Smith Mackenzie was the sole importer into Zanzibar of such diverse commodities as Alexander Fergusson & Co.'s paints and oils, D. & S. McCallum's 'Perfection' Whisky, James McIllwraith and Co.'s barge covers and tarpaulins, 'Black & White' Scotch Whisky, Portland Cement, 'Bull Dog' ale and stout, not to mention the various brands of champagne and brandy.

The firm was also prepared to invest directly in the economy of Zanzibar and its hinterland rather than just concern itself with imports, exports and shipping. It ventured into coffee- and rubber-estate owning and management. In late 1895, it began planning its first coffee plantation at Kikuyu. The building of the 'Mackinnon Road' at Dar, which had been started by Sir William in 1876, brought its attention to the rubber-growing areas in that locality. When rubber prices rose to $22 (over £4) per frasila of 35lb, Smith Mackenzie advocated the opening of new plantations and a new system of tapping the rubber trees.[43]

What profits did Smith Mackenzie make upon its initial capital of £30 000? Judging by the surplus remitted home by the partners, which was additional to the profits ploughed back into the business (shown in Table 4.2), earnings must have been considerable. Although the home-based Senior Partners, Gray and Dawes, who had invested in the largest number of original shares at the formal registration of the firm, made the largest returns, employees on the spot who were admitted as Partners reaped adequate rewards. Edmund Mackenzie sent home £6114 after only two years of the firm's trading, 1886 and 1887. This may have included earnings from previous years, but even if it covered the period from 1877, these may seen as very high profits, as they were surplus to living expenses, local purchases and investments.

VII

The expansion and consolidation of Smith Mackenzie's activities before 1914 enabled the firm to survive and prosper between the wars. In 1914–18 its work in supplying coal for the British navy took on a new significance: the marine side of the firm's business became virtually a annex of the Royal Navy. The company found its resources severely stretched with the combination of the increased workload for its lightermen, stevedores and wharfingers through the movement of troops, armaments and provisions, and the depletion of its workforce with a large number of employees joining the armed services. The need for more capital to finance the company's expanding operations was partly fulfilled by hiving off its shipping activities into a separate concern, the African Wharfage Company. Its capital of £100 000 was divided into 'A' and 'B' shares, of which only the 'A' shares carried voting rights. Smith Mackenzie's shipping operations then lost much of its independence as, although it became the general manager of the new company, it held only non-voting 'B' shares. The BI and Union Castle remained a controlling interest through holding the 'A' shares, by which it aimed to ensure greater financial security for its East African agencies, but it is significant that it still wished to retain the management expertise of Smith Mackenzie. The high wartime prices for local produce aided the economic development of Kenya and Uganda, and of the former German colony of Tanganyika, which became a British mandated territory after the First World War.

Smith Mackenzie had managed to continue its trading and agency activities, and opened several new branches. Between 1916 and 1923, new offices were opened in Nairobi, Kisumu, Kampala, Dar es Salaam, Tanga and Lindi. A glimpse of life at the Lindi branch just before the Second World War has been given by an ex-African Wharfage Company employee, John Hall. He recalled that there were only twenty-seven Europeans in the town, and a further fifty in the district, that there was no electricity, and only one water closet in the whole settlement until he installed another in his flat over the office. Local water and meat were highly suspect, so the former was brought from the other side of the harbour in old petrol tins and the latter purchased from passing ships. Despite isolation and the lack of luxuries, Hall and his wife (married at the port in a ceremony attended by every European inhabitant except one), regarded life as very enjoyable. His pay was low – only £45 a month – but chickens were only 1/- each, and a local fisherman would deliver fish every day for a month for only 6/-. Hall managed the Lloyd's Agency at the port and supervised the deployment of his company's craft, nearly all of which were built at Grimsby and shipped out in parts. A relic of the First World War, an old wood-burning stern-wheeler, the *Tomondo*, was still in service, carrying produce and passengers up local rivers. The African Wharfage Co. soon established its own subsidiaries, including a branch in Tanganyika and the African Marine and General Engineering Co. in Mombasa.

Meanwhile, Smith Mackenzie's general produce trade declined, influenced by the demonetisation of British gold sovereigns and the increase in import duty to 10 per cent. Its agency business remained successful, but it soon became clear that new capital resources, and a stronger link with London rather than Calcutta, was essential to its activities, previously centred on Zanzibar, moved to Kenya. So in 1936, the firm became Smith Mackenzie and Company Limited, registered in Nairobi, with a share capital of £280 000 which had increased to £580 000 by 1937.

The original partners of the firm were all long-established Smith Mackenzie men: W. J. W. Nicol; J. W. Buchanan (See Table 4.2); W. A. M. Sim; W. F. Jenkins; W. G. D. H. Nicol; H. H. Robinson; S. H. Sayer; W. M. Buchanan and N. J. Robinson. Hall described how these men worked very closely with all the Company's employees, and that it was still very much a family firm. 'Billy' Buchanan, he recalled, drove a much-loved Bentley, and George Nicol 'was a bit of a character: he once volunteered to fly Santa Claus' to the local children's Christmas Party in his private plane, but crashed in a bunker on the golf course'. This gives a further indication of the level of wealth achieved by these men, and how the British way of life was usually reconstructed as much as possible by expatriates. Sixty European staff directed 550 subordinate employees, and shareholders in the new company were limited to fifty only. It was written into the articles that the senior Sim and Nicol intended to leave their shares to their sons when they died, and 'any invitation to the public to subscribe for any shares or debentures of the company is hereby prohibited'. The senior Sim and Jenkins both acted as London directors. The first Lord Inchcape had close links with Smith Mackenzie as a merchant partnership, and the family connection was strengthened in 1936 when his son became Chairman, and appointed three colleagues, George Finch Hotblack, Sir John William Bell and John Herbert Fyfe as co-directors. Thus Smith Mackenzie was enabled to face the Second World War with more powerful backing.[44]

*   *   *

The economic development of the region in these years, the suppression of the slave trade and the need for British commercial and political representation among the growing interests of other nations, shows that the British Government's initial aims and proposals in awarding the East African mail contract to Mackinnon were justified. Yet the contribution of Smith Mackenzie to the achievement of these objectives was much greater than might be expected from the rather miserly level of government subsidy to BI. The BI steamer service certainly gave the firm its initial *raison d'être*, but its other activities, as Union Castle representatives, as Lloyd's agents, through working for IBEA and importing and exporting a myriad of commodities, together with its investment in local agriculture, considerably increased its impact on the local community.

Few competing merchant houses, such as the German firms Widmer, Hansing and O'swald, the Americans Arnold Cheney and James Whyte, the Norway and East Africa Trading Co., the Redland and Bombay Co., Filinado of Italy, Cawasji Dinshaw (the Admiralty stores agents) and Boustead Ridleys, prospered and expanded in East Africa like Smith Mackenzie. Its initial capital of £30 000 had risen to £580 000 by 1937, and the first Report and Accounts of the new company showed a net profit of £37 797, paying a 5 per cent dividend.[45] Nowadays, the firm is still regarded with nostalgic affection, even in post-revolutionary Zanzibar.

NOTES

1. *Contract of the B. I. and Union S. S. Co. for the Conveyance of mails between Aden, Zanzibar and the Cape of Good Hope, Parliamentary papers [PP], 1873 XXXIX (62).*
   The contract was signed on 20 December 1872, to run for ten years.

2. The early history of Zanzibar and its hinterland is discussed in S. G. Ayany, *A History of Zanzibar* (1970); N. R. Bennett, *A History of the Arab State of Zanzibar* (London, 1978); R. Coupland, *The Exploitation of East Africa, 1856–1890* (London, 1939); H. B. Frere, 'Zanzibar, A Commercial Power'; *Macmillan's Magazine*, 32 (1875); W. H. Ingrams, *Zanzibar: Its History and Peoples* (London, 1931); J. Kirk, 'Agricultural Resources of Zanzibar', *Kew Bulletin* (1892) and F. B. Pearce, *Zanzibar: The Island Metropolis of Eastern Africa* (London, 1920). J. S. Galbraith, *Mackinnon and East Africa, 1878–1892: A Study in the 'New Imperialism'* (Cambridge, 1972) and J. Forbes Munro, *Africa and the International Economy, 1800–1960* (London, 1976) have proved especially useful in providing background material for this chapter. The lack of business history studies of this region is discussed by A. G. Hopkins in his article 'Imperial Business in Africa Part I: Sources', and 'Part II: Interpretations', *Journal of African History*, XVII, 1 (1976) pp.29–48 and XVII, 2 (1976) pp.267–290. He regards Smith Mackenzie & Co. as 'undoubtedly one of the most important commercial concerns in colonial East Africa' and maintains that 'a full history of this firm, which was one of the first European companies to trade directly with the interior and not just with the coast, and which has now adapted to the requirements of the post colonial era, would make a fascinating and substantial contribution to East African economic history in the twentieth century'. This present study attempts partially to fill this gap. An invaluable guide to primary sources to this region is Anne Thurston, 'Kenya and East Africa: Sources in British Official Records', Preliminary Version March 1982 (typescript).

3. *Further Correspondence Relating to the Zanzibar Mail* Contracts, *PP*, 1873 XXXIX (241). See R. J. Gavin, 'The Frere Mission to Zanzibar, 1873,' *Historical Journal* 5 (1962) pp.122–48.

4. See J. Forbes Munro, entry on Sir William Mackinnon in *Dictionary of Scottish Business Biography* (Aberdeen, forthcoming).

5. *Inchcape Archives (IA)*, Gray, Dawes & Co., vol. 1411, capital accounts relating to Bushire, Basra, Baghdad, Zanzibar, Mozambique and Mombasa, 1877–1939.

6. Reports from HM Consuls on the Manufacturers, Commerce &c. of their Consular Districts, *PP*, 1876 LXXIV (c.1421) report on the trade of Zanzibar by Captain Prideaux.

7. *Lloyd's List* and *Lloyd's Weekly Shipping Index* for 1918, 1927 and 1938.

8. *The Trade and Shipping of Africa, etc., PP*, 1899 LXIII (c.9223).

9. *British and South African Export Gazette* (1899), cutting in *Zanzibar National Archives [ZNA]* vol. B.65, 1900, containing a report of the Acting Consul, Kestell Cornish, on the commerce of Zanzibar.

10. *ZNA*, vol. E.70, 1875; vol. B.63, 1896.

11. *National Maritime Museum [NMM]*, BI Archives, B15/7/45, local steamers on the East African coast, 1899–1902, letter from MM & Co. to Smith Mackenzie and reply.

12. *NMM*, B15/7/41, Bombay to East Africa trade 1900–12; B. R. Mitchell, *International Historical Statistics: Africa and Asia* (London, 1982) pp.374–9.

13. *ZNA*, vol. E.70, 1875; vol. E.132, 1890–1.

14. *ZNA*, vol. B.1, 1885; vol. E.97, 1887. Another problem was caused by

merchants wanting to pay duty in kind; in a letter to the Sultan they maintained that this was common practice and acceptable to the Customs officer, vol. E77, 1883. At Mozambique, BI insisted on the payment of duty owing to the Sultan from local shippers. Because of the shortage of coin, local merchants preferred to use the Sultan's steamers, where barter goods were acceptable in lieu of duty, vol. E.84, 1885.

15. *NMM*, MM &Co. to Smith Mackenzie 1901. My italics.
16. *ZNA*, vol. D.26, 1899–1900.
17. *NMM*, B15/7/41–5 include many such complaints.
18. There are frequent examples of this among the consular out-letter books.
19. In January 1883 the American brig *Don Jacinto* anchored in the BI mooring space, much to the annoyance of the master of the *Oriental, ZNA*. vol. E.77, 1883.
20. *ZNA*, vol, E.104, 1888.
21. See note 1, and *Post Office Mail Contract etc.*, *PP*, 1884, XLVII (5) *Mail Contract, London and East Coast of Africa, PP*, 1890 XLI (122) and *Aden Zanzibar Mail Contract, PP*, 1893–4 L (2).
22. *IA*, Gray Dawes & Co., Notebook, 1885–1926, p.125.
23. *ZNA*, vol. E. 104, 1888; vol. E.105, 1888; vol. B.3, 1888.
24. Ibid, vol. E.30, 1905.
25. *IA*, MM & Co., Notebook, 1890–6, p.135.
26. *NMM*, B15/7/41.
27. *IA*, MM & Co., Notebook, 1890–6, p.76, p.121.
28. Ibid, p.117, p.122.
29. *NMM*, B15/7/41.
30. *IA*, MM & Co., Notebook, 1890–6, p.122.
31. *ZNA*, vol. E.73, 1877.
32. *IA*, MM & Co., Notebook, 1890–6, p.121.
33. *ZNA*, vol. B.58, 1884.
34. Ibid, vol. E.84, 1885; vol. E.235, 1903.
35. *IA*, GD & Co., Notebook, 1885–1926, pp.53–5.
36. See Galbraith, *Mackinnon and East Africa*; P. L. McDermott, *British East Africa or IBEA* (London, 1893); Marie de Kiewiet Hemphill, 'The British Sphere, 1884–94', in Roland Oliver and Gervaise Matthew (eds) *History of East Africa* (Oxford, 1963–76) vol. 1, p.391 and the same author's unpublished London Ph.D. of 1955, 'History of the Imperial British East Africa Company'; P. J. Griffiths, *A Licence to Trade: The History of English Chartered Companies* (London, 1974) chap. 17 and Cyril Ehrlich 'The Uganda Economy, 1903–1945' in Oliver and Matthew (eds) *History of East Africa*, vol. 11, p.395.
37. McDermott, *British East Africa*, Appendix 11, pp.280–1.
38. Smith Mackenzie & Co. Ltd, *The History of Smith Mackenzie and Company Limited*. The names of the porters are recorded in a muster book preserved at the Nairobi office.
39. *ZNA*, vol. E.103, 1888–9. Arms imports are recorded in vol. N.8, 1881.
40. *IA*, MM & Co. Notebook, 1890–6, p.122.
41. *ZNA*, vol. B.37, 1896.
42. *ZNA, Zanzibar Gazette*, 1 January 1911.
43. *ZNA*, vol. B.58, 1883.

44. *IA*, Smith Mackenzie & Co. Ltd, Articles of Association and first Minute Book, 1936–7.
45. *IA*, Smith Mackenzie & Co. Ltd, Report and Accounts, 1936–7.

NOTE The original 'Mackinnon Road' is not to be confused with the later use of the term to describe the Railway Station on the Mombasa – Nairobi line between Samburu and Voi. The reminiscences of John Hall were given in a letter to the author dated 4 January 1985.

The Zanzibar National Archives were consulted for British Consulate Miscellaneous Despatches, Outward and Inward. These archives are described in Anne Thurston, John Walford and Allyson McDermott, 'Review of the Zanzibar National Archives', January 1984 (typescript) and were made available with the kind permission and help of the Zanzibar Ministry of Education, Culture and Sport and the archives staff.

A version of this chapter was presented as a short lecture to the archives staff and members of the Zanzibar National Archives Conservation Expedition in August 1984.

138

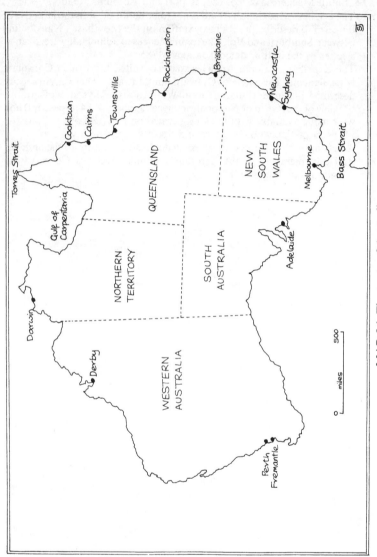

MAP 5.1 The ports of Australia

5 Maritime Enterprise in Australia: the Australasian United Steam Navigation Company [AUSN Co.] and Macdonald Hamilton & Co., 1887–1939

One of the earliest overseas trading networks established by Mackinnon Mackenzie & Co. from their Calcutta base arose from Mackenzie's visit to Australia in 1852, prompted by news of the discovery of gold there the previous year. In Chapter 1, we saw how the partners ran sailing ships from Calcutta to Sydney and Melbourne and through their associated firm in Scotland, from Glasgow to Australia. This business was ultimately to lead to the award of a mail contract, the formation of a coastal shipping company in Australia and the establishment of a merchant partnership to act as its agents. To a greater degree than in other countries in which Group businesses operated, because they were British owned, they were resented by local enterprises and accused of stifling indigenous commercial growth.[1] How justified were such assertions? What was the impact of these two companies on Australian shipping in comparison with local concerns?

The origins of the Australasian United Steam Navigation Company [AUSN] lay in the desire of Sir Thomas McIlwraith, premier of Queensland, to improve the flow of immigrants to that colony. In the late 1870s, Queensland had no regular direct shipping link with Britain. Settlers coming to Australia were usually landed in southern ports such as Adelaide, Melbourne and Sydney, and only a small proportion of them found their way north to Queensland. McIlwraith approached the BI about extending its existing services in the East Indies to Queensland via the Torres Strait, thus establishing a direct link between the colony and Britain. To encourage Mackinnon and the BI to provide this service, McIllwraith persuaded the Queensland legislature to vote an oceanic mail contract between the colony and Britian worth £55 000 p.a. Many Queenslanders had opposed the contract, but it was nevertheless awarded to the BI in 1881.[2]

From its beginning in 1881, the new shipping service was known to the public as the 'Queensland Royal Mail Line', but from 1886, the BI subsidiary running the service was called British India Associated Steamers Ltd. Initially, the flow of settlers from Britain to Queensland proved considerable and Mackinnon found himself short of ships, so from 1882 vessels of the Ducal Line were hired to assist in running the service. After a depression in the Queensland trade during 1886, the late 1880s saw a revival, only to be followed by a serious decline in the 1890s. A prolonged drought did much to damage the Queensland trade, while in 1895, the Queensland oceanic mail contract was terminated. In the early 1900s, the service was reorganised. The BI Associated Steamers Company was liquidated, and the main BI company took over responsibility for a service which by 1905 was concentrating more on cargo than on passengers.[3]

Among the most vociferous opponents of the BI's appearance in the Queensland trade were the Australian coastal steamship companies, notably the Australasian Steam Navigation Company [ASN], which had been formed in 1851 from the original Hunter River Steam Navigation Company of 1839. These companies did good business bringing settlers up to the colony from the main ports of debarkation in the south, chiefly Sydney, and they cut their passenger rates as a reply to the BI's challenge. Mackinnon answered by forming his own coastal shipping company, the Queensland Steam Shipping Company, at the end of 1881. For some years the coastal companies waged a cutthroat rates war, but during the depression of 1886 it became clear that some firms could not carry on the struggle any longer. At the end of that year, the ASN agreed to sell out to the Queensland Steam Shipping Company, and the new firm produced by the merger emerged in 1887 as the AUSN itself.[4] Now, with its involvement in the AUSN, the Mackinnon group of enterprises reached a peak with five companies which owned a total of 181 steamers with a book value of nearly £3m.[5] Many Queenslanders now felt they were in the grip of a BI monopoly, covering both coastal and oceanic routes. The local press reported that the BI and the Queensland Steam Shipping Company were identical, and that the BI was the sole purchaser of the ailing ASN. The BI's agent at Townsville, James Burns, hotly denied these reports.[6]

Presumably these denials were made to accentuate the supposedly increased participation of local Australian interests as a result of the merger, but in fact, of the original eight shareholders of the AUSN in 1887, five were BI men. They comprised Sir William Mackinnon, the chairman of the BI; Alexander Monteath and Duncan Mackinnon, BI directors; Anthony Norris, a director of the Netherlands India Steam Navigation Company, a BI subsidiary and Edwin Sandys Dawes, a partner in Gray Dawes & Co., the BI agent in London. The other three shareholders were Thomas Sutherland, MP, the Chairman of the Peninsular and Oriental Steam Navigation Company [P & O], which had close links with the BI and important interests in the Australian trade; Peter Denny, the Dumbarton shipbuilder, and Charles Lees, an Oldham manufacturer who had links with Mackinnon through the textile trade with India. Each of these original shareholders took fifty £50 shares, and in an attempt to stress the Australasian links of the management of the new firm, Dawes and Denny were described in the prospectus as chairman of the Queensland Steam Shipping Company and a director of the Union Steamship Company of New Zealand respectively.[7]

With eight such notable figures as original shareholders and directors, the AUSN had no difficulty in attracting a further 181 investors, including four companies, in its first five years of existence. The largest shareholders were the BI Associated Steamers Company, the British India and Queensland Agency Company, and the original eight shareholders, Sir William Mackinnon alone having an investment of £57 425. The average investment was £2000, and so the backgrounds of the investors were mainly professional and often aristocratic. Nearly 32 per cent were merchants in the City of London and 24.5 per cent were ladies and gentlemen of independent means. Nearly 12 per cent of investment in the AUSN in the years 1887 to 1892 came from other companies, usually associated with the BI, and over 10 per cent came from military and naval officers and the nobility. Members of

Parliament and civil servants contributed 5.2 per cent, professional persons, such as barristers, bankers and stockbrokers, some 4.9 per cent, while nearly 7 per cent of investment came from shipbuilders and marine engineers, with other manufacturers accounting for 3.5 per cent. Only 0.4 per cent, representing £1640, was invested by master mariners.[8]

The wealth of many of the investors, several of whom must have had large portfolios of many investments, may be seen in the AUSN probate records. Of those shareholders who died between 1917 (when the AUSN probate book begins) and 1940, forty-five left over £100 000 gross. Sir William Mackinnon's personal estate was valued at £514 843 at his death, Duncan Mackinnon left £1 522 012, Sir Thomas Sutherland left £723 075 and Alexander Monteath left £126 087. The value of the estate of the First Lord Inchcape was published, at his death in 1932, at £552 809, and the Second Earl, who died in 1939, left £701 230. One of the wealthiest investors in the AUSN was Sir John Reeves Ellerman, Bart, of the Ellerman Shipping Lines, who left £17 224 425[9].

The occupational structure of shareholding in the AUSN was in marked contrast to investment in steam shipping at many British ports, where a much wider range of persons, including many shopkeepers, those in service industries, and many small manufacturers, were attracted to shipowning, especially through buying 64th shares in individual ships. The small investors in the AUSN, a limited liability company, were rarely from maritime backgrounds, and may be regarded as passive rather than active investors.

Of the 12 000 £50 shares which made up the £600 000 authorised capital of the AUSN, 10 000 were allocated to British investors and only 2000 were made available to potential investors in Australia. Of these, however, only 259 fully-paid shares were taken up, representing an investment of only £12 970. This would suggest an unwillingness on the part of Australian businessmen to invest in their own maritime industry, especially as the ASN had found it difficult to raise capital on several occasions before the merger which produced the AUSN. Yet the reluctance to invest in a still obviously British company was probably the explanation.

I

Native Australian shipping companies had emerged in the second half of the nineteenth century and these were preferred by Australian investors. Burns, Philp and Company, the Adelaide Steamship Company, the

Melbourne Steamship Company and the Union Steamship Company were already plying in the Australian coastal trade by the time that the AUSN was formed. McIlwraith McEacharn and Company had been formed in London in 1875, twelve years before the AUSN, so that the concept of a British company operating in Australian coastal shipping was not unknown: but McIlwraiths soon established a separate Australian company to manage its business. The two remaining of the larger companies in the Australian coastal trade were Howard Smith & Co. and Huddart, Parker & Co., both formed by British merchant ship captains during the gold rush years of the early 1850s. Two smaller locally-formed companies were James Paterson & Company and the Tasmanian Steamship Company. On the eve of the foundation of the AUSN, twenty-five companies and individual owners operated 170 vessels in Australia's coasting trade, owning nearly 400 000 aggregate tons of shipping, nearly all of which was steam-propelled.[10]

How did the AUSN expect to make large profits in a trade in which so many other companies were already established? The merger of the ASN and Queensland Steam Shipping Company to form the AUSN made it one of the largest Australian coasting companies with 27 per cent of the ships and 22.6 per cent of the aggregate tonnage. It had a large range of vessels suitable for a variety of traders and cargoes. Of the forty-six vessels of an aggregate tonnage over 31 000 tons owned in 1887 (see figure 5.1) five exceeded 1500 tons, seven were over 1000, and thirteen vessels were 500 tons or over. The carriage of coal, sugar and general cargoes occupied the smaller vessels, but the operation of liner services carrying passengers and mails was seen as the principal source of revenue. The major railway lines of Australia were only being built, and the Sydney – Brisbane line was not opened until 1888, so the demand for passengers and mail space was heavy. The Company secured the Queensland Government coastal mail contract, providing a regular income, and some stability in general trading was ensured by agreements reached with other coastal companies to delimit 'spheres of influence'. Thus the directors and shareholders were optimistic at the time of the first meeting held at 13 Austin Friars in the City of London when it was reported that:

> advices from the company's agents in Australia indicate that traffic on the coast, both in passengers and cargo, is increasing, and information has recently been received by telegraph that the Queensland Government have renewed their coastal mail contracts with this Company for a further period of five years from 1st July 1888.[11]

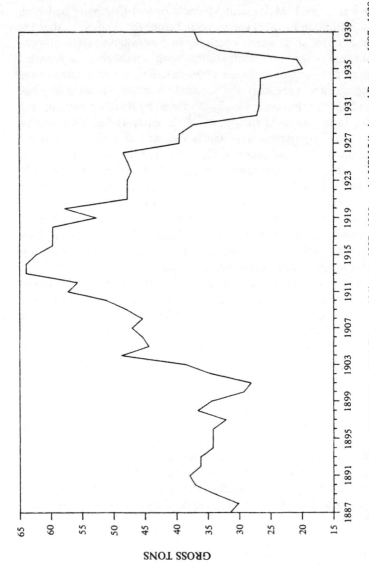

FIGURE 5.1 The AUSN fleet 1887–1939: gross tonnage

SOURCE *Inchcape Archives*, AUSN 1/3 and 1/4, Directors' Minutes, 1887–1939, and AUSN 2/1, Annual Reports, 1887–1939

145

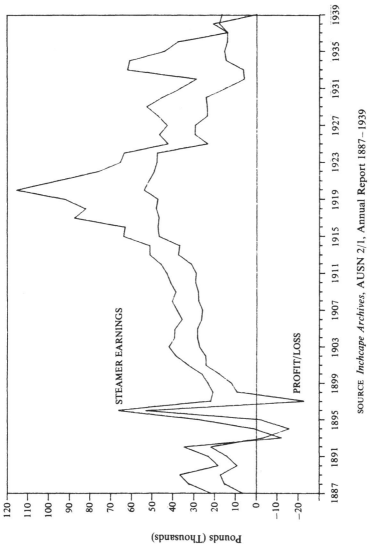

SOURCE *Inchcape Archives*, AUSN 2/1, Annual Report 1887–1939

FIGURE 5.2 The AUSN fleet 1887–1939: steamer earnings and profit and loss

In analysing the performance of the AUSN in its first fifty-two years, Figure 5.1 shows that the increase in the Company's tonnage reached a peak in 1914 and then steadily declined, especially after 1926. Before this turning-point, the earnings of the Company's steamers and its overall profits had steadily grown. From 1903 to 1924, a dividend of between 7 and 10 per cent had been paid annually. From 1925, profits fluctuated considerably, allowing only a small dividend.

Thus, in the first phase of the Company's activities, from its inception until 1925, a good return on investment was achieved. Losses in the early 1890s were partly the result of the breakdown of the 'spheres of influence' in trading areas that had been established in 1887. The Adelaide Steamship Company won contracts for the carriage of flour in 1892–3 which were not obtained until 1894 by the AUSN, and the former also gained a monopoly of the transportation of the sugar output of the entire Queensland coast. All the principal companies were engaged in vigorous rivalry in the coal trade at Melbourne, Adelaide and Western Australia. Meanwhile, the Union Steamship Company and Huddart Parker competing with the AUSN on the Melbourne to Sydney passenger run had caused a significant drop in fares.[12]

The importance of the passenger trade to the AUSN is seen in the survival of one of the *Handbooks of Information*, dated 1899–1900, the twelfth edition.[13] This also provided details of the services of the BI and BI Associated Steamers Company, with a description of the tourist attractions of Australia, entitled 'Five Thousand Miles on the Australian Coast'. It listed its eight services which covered the coast of Australia from Geraldton, north of Perth, to the Torres Strait and the Gulf of Carpentaria, excluding only the north-west coast, as yet only sparsely populated. The AUSN also ran monthly services to New Caledonia and Fiji. According to its fleet list, its entire fleet of thirty-two steamers (reduced to twenty-eight by 1899) were engaged in the carriage of passengers and included those which acted as tenders, lighters and hulks, of which twelve ships were 'fitted throughout with the electric light'. This publication shows the continued links which the AUSN maintained with the P & O and BI by supplementing their services. Tickets for the passenger services of the three companies were sold at the same location: a plan of the Melbourne offices of the AUSN's agents shows three adjacent counters for bookings.[14]

The poor returns and losses of the 1890s were principally the result of a depression in Australian shipping and the declining efficiency and increasing age of the AUSN fleet – from 1887 to 1898 twenty-four of the Company's vessels had left the fleet: eleven vessels had been lost or converted to hulks, and thirteen mainly small vessels had been sold. Meanwhile only nine vessels had been acquired averaging less than 3000 tons each. The visit of the first Lord Inchcape to Australia in 1900–1, when he toured all the ships, workshops, wharves and offices, resulted in a long overdue shake-up of the Company. The Earl of Inchcape, who

5.1 Australia: the first class dining saloon of the AUSN steamer *Wyreema*, a large twin screw steamer of 6338 gross tons, built by Alexander Stephen & Sons of Glasgow in 1908

5.2 Australia: the AUSN steamer *Arrawatta* discharging bananas at Melbourne, c. 1899.

has been described as 'the man who put the AUSN on its feet',[15] when James Lyle Mackay, had invested in the AUSN from its beginning and joined the London Board of Directors in 1894. In 1913 he became the Chairman and Managing Director of the AUSN and, as discussed in Chapter 2, in 1914 he chaired the merged BI and P & O, thereby controlling the largest shipping enterprise in the world. When in Australia, he recommended the sale of the AUSN's most outdated tonnage and the purchase of a series of large modern liners. Between 1899 and 1903 nine vessels were purchased, costing nearly £600 000,[16] which increased the earning capacity of the fleet and raised overall profits.

The reorganisation of the AUSN confirmed its principal commitment to passenger traffic, but the reorganisation of the BI's service to Australia at about the same time showed a greater emphasis on carrying cargo. Certainly two vessels ordered by the BI for the Queensland trade and delivered in 1904–5 still offered limited passenger accommodation, but their principal task was carrying cargo. Ironically, one of the chief loads carried by these vessels in the years up to 1914 was material for the construction of the North Queensland railway, whose completion in the 1920s was to spell the end of much of the AUSN's passenger traffic.

In their annual reports, the directors of the AUSN maintained that the outbreak of war in 1914 had an injurious effect on the volume of trade on the Australian coast, but earnings were maintained by Government work. For example, the *Kyarra* served as a hospital ship, the *Kanowna* as a troop ship, and the *Mallina* carried coal for Government purposes. By April 1917, all the AUSN steamers were in the hire of the Government. The war ended in 1918, but it was soon clear that there would be no return to pre-1914 normality for the AUSN. Strikes among the crews in 1919–20 did some damage, but the worst blow came in 1924. In that year the Townsville–Cairns railway was opened, completing the railway that linked all the main centres on the Queensland coast. In future, the mails and many passengers would go by rail rather than sea, so the Queensland coastal mail contract, held by the AUSN, was terminated. This blow to the earnings of the AUSN, together with the decline in the passenger trade on all its other routes, was reflected in the profits of 1925, which were less than half those declared in 1924.

Unfortunately it has proved impossible to discover the reaction of the management to this watershed in its history – an AUSN minute book baldly records that:

it was reported that the Brisbane/Townsville section of the mail contract terminated on 7th. January 1924 owing to the completion of the Railway and on the further extension of the Railway through to Cairns the Townsville/Cooktown section of the mail service was terminated by the Authorities on 5th. December 1924.[17]

The response of the AUSN directors was to spread their investments more widely. When the loss of the mail contract became a possibility, when the decline in the passenger trade was alrady apparent, the AUSN invested in the Eastern & Australian Steamship Co. Ltd, [E & A] gaining a strategic 25 per cent holding in 1920. In contrast with the parent company's involvement in the coasting trades, the E & A vessels traded from Australian ports to Manila, Hong Kong, Shanghai, Yokohama, Singapore and Java. The E & A acquisition was beneficial to the AUSN in the wider context of BI – P & O interests as a whole, by forming a connection between the BI – P & O Far Eastern routes and the AUSN's Australian services.[18]

Another example of the widening of AUSN investments was the formation of Kuranda Hotels Ltd, a property venture additional to the Company's wharf and harbour interests. With a minimal capital of £20 000, of which £9450 was paid up, the decision to invest in the hotel chain was taken immediately after the news of the loss of the mail contract was announced.[19]

II

The second phase of the shipping activities of the company marks its total change of function and *raison d'être*: from dominating the Queensland outport trade and mail services as the second largest Australian coastal fleet, the AUSN, without its mail subsidy and passenger trade, was left to glean earnings from carrying general cargoes, coal, sugar, bananas and chartering its vessels to other companies. A fresh 6 per cent debenture issue in 1927 helped to maintain a dividend of 5 per cent, by raising £300 000. The minute book gives no clue to the reasoning behind the issue but it would appear to be in response to the downturn in the Company's fortunes in the mid-1920s.[20]

By 1930 the annual report of the directors described the conditions of trade in Australia as 'deplorable', worsened by problems in remitting profits home. Of each £1000 earned in Australia and allocated to the shareholders, only £770 was actually received in London, because of the Australian Government levy on profits leaving the country. From 1934, income was deducted at source from shareholders' dividends. In 1931, when a 2½ per cent dividend was declared, £11 130, tax free, was allocated to shareholders. In 1936, the 2½ per cent dividend for the same number of shares taken up meant that only £8 348 after tax, was paid out. Continuing waterside industrial unrest, heavy depreciation on the Company's fleet and properties with a contraction of trade made a return to the high dividends of the immediate post-war period impossible.

The survival of a voyage ledger of 1937 to 1946 shows the attempts of the AUSN local managers to employ their fleet profitably.[21] By 1937, only three AUSN vessels still carried passengers, including the *Ormiston* and *Orungal* which had been purchased from the Khedivial Mail Steamship Company in 1936 to try to win back some of the diminished seaborne passenger traffic which now faced competition from air travel. The other AUSN vessels tramped the coast, carrying general cargoes, coal, ironstone, sugar and timber. The slackness of the passenger trade is seen in the accounts of the *Ormiston* and *Orungal* – in 1937 they made losses of £565 and £3363 respectively. The coal and ironstone trades were most profitable, whilst carrying general cargoes and sugar could not be relied upon. Losses were reduced in 1938 and the five vessels then carrying passengers made small profits. The most profitable vessels in these years were those prepared to carry any goods requiring shipment – the *Mareeba*, 3663 gross tons, carried sugar, ironstone, coal and passengers in 1938, earning £4319. On the eve of the Second World War earnings had improved, but depreciation on the fleet, to which only two large vessels had been added in the previous ten years, was so high as to erode profits heavily.

However, from Figure 5.2 it is clear that the overall profit or loss was not solely dependent on the earnings or losses of the steamers. This figure, the profit or loss, refers to the amount left for distribution to shareholders and the balance for the next year, if any. The overall profit exceeded the earnings of the steamers in 1937 and 1939. The continued payment of a dividend was only achieved by investing AUSN funds in other Australian companies and British and Australian Government securities. After 1932, the Annual Report and Accounts show the value of the AUSN ships and investments separately, although it is clear that this trend of substantial investments in non-shipping fields by the AUSN began in the 1920s.

Thus, it is possible to regard the AUSN by the eve of the Second World War as an investment company as much as a shipping company. This conclusion, drawn from the published reports and accounts of the company, contradicts the statement of N. L. McKellar, the author of a lengthy history of the AUSN, that it 'did not diversify in other directions on its own account . . . it had no substantial outside sources of income to see it through lean periods'.[22] By 1940, the value of the AUSN's investments and the earnings they made exceeded those of its ships, so it was precisely the investment income of the AUSN which tided it over when shipping profits were low and helped to reduce heavy losses. This determination to continue the operation of the AUSN fleet despite low profits and overall losses, supplemented by investment earnings, was largely due to the insistence of the shareholders. The bulk of the capital was still held by BI men, members of the Inchcape family and persons associated with the Gray Dawes and Mackinnon Mackenzie partnerships who were not prepared to give up the Australian coastal service even though it may have been one of the least profitable of the network of routes covered by the BI and P & O ships. Many of these shareholders would have had many other investment interests besides the AUSN,[23] and so long as the Company maintained a respectable rate of dividend they were content that it should continue.[24]

III

Meanwhile, the management of the AUSN, in addition to a host of other activities, was the concern of the second company to be considered in this chapter, Macdonald Hamilton & Co. Through its primary role as a shipping agency firm, it may be seen as a more typical Group Company. The interest of the first Lord Inchcape in the AUSN was channelled through this partnership, which became the means whereby he maintained a close degree of control over the shipping line's activities. Although its managing agency functions could have been carried out by the AUSN itself, as in the case of the river steamers and tea estates in India, it relied on these outside managers. McKellar has suggested that 'the First Earl had absorbed the principles of shipping management from those masters of agency work, Mackinnon Mackenzie & Co., and doubtless he was steeped in the tradition of managing agencies instead of direct management'.[25] This practice certainly helped the AUSN, as we shall see.

Originally, the British India and Queensland Agency Company [BI & QA] had acted as the AUSN's agents. Set up as an arm of the BI in Australia in 1885 soon after the award of the mail contract, its capital of £120 000 was subscribed by MM & Co., GD & Co. and a local company, all with equal shares. Two prominent branch managers of this company were to play an important part in the subsequent formation of Macdonald Hamilton & Co. Benjamin Wickham Macdonald, yet another Scottish exile, had originally joined MM & Co's Karachi branch after working for a shipbuilding firm in his native land. Transferred to Brisbane in 1884 on health grounds, he was soon promoted from a clerical post in the Queensland Steamship Company to be the AUSN's Rockhampton agent by 1887.

Mackay, during his tour of AUSN holdings in 1900–1, became aware of Macdonald's considerable abilities and asked him to take charge of the BI & QA in addition to acting as General Manager of the AUSN on Mackay's behalf. When he returned to England in 1894, Mackay maintained his interest in the day-to-day minutae of AUSN affairs, at least until 1906–7 when the pressure of his other activities forced him to reduce his involvement in the shipping line. His letters to Macdonald gradually became shorter and his replies to his manager's decisions tended to be confined to phrases as 'I note what you say' or 'I approve of your recommendation'.

Meanwhile, the other half of the future partnership also attracted Mackay's attention. David Hamilton had been born in Queensland of Scottish parents, and joined the BI & QA on its formation as a bookkeeper. His promotion was slower than Macdonald's; he became Melbourne branch manager in 1903. Increasingly trusting Hamilton to share the burden of responsibility with Macdonald, Mackay wished formally to acknowledge his obligation to them.

In 1915 (by then Lord Inchcape) he wound up the BI & QA and established a new firm, Macdonald Hamilton & Co.[26] Regarded as a compliment by both the partners as well as by the local business community, the creation of this partnership reinforced Lord Inchcape's dependence on these men to manage the AUSN. He also wanted to make it plain to the partners that he expected them to devote themselves to the interests of the shipping line, and insisted that 'the AUSN will be your mainstay; on its success depends the success of Macdonald Hamilton & Co'. He realised that the agents might be tempted to claim extravangant expenses from the shipping line, and encouraged the firm to conduct the shipping line's affairs as economically as possible, suggesting that 'should the AUSN experience lean years, it may well be necessary for you to manage its affairs at lower fees than in normal times'. Macdonald Hamilton were able to aid the ailing AUSN with a large rebate from commissions received and other income, equalling more than £200 000 in the period 1927–31. Through Macdonald Hamilton, Lord Inchcape was able personally to direct funds to the AUSN; as the largest shareholder in Macdonald Hamilton, this rebate meant that he was using his personal income for the benefit of AUSN shareholders, to keep the latter in business. Thus he ensured that the managing agents could not take advantage of their powerful position *vis à vis* the AUSN, by always putting the Company's interests ahead of the Firm.[27]

IV

What were the other activities of Macdonald Hamilton in the years before the Second World War? With Lord Inchcape's chairmanship of the combined P & O/BI from 1914, it was a natural progression for Macdonald Hamilton to take over the P & O agencies in Australian ports: at Sydney, Melbourne and Fremantle in 1917, and Brisbane in 1920. This added considerably to the firm's income, but did not exceed earnings from AUSN commissions until after 1945. They also managed the E & A fleet, already referred to as a subsidiary of the AUSN.

   Much of the AUSN's stevedoring was organised by Macdonald Hamilton. At Fremantle, the firm jointly with Elder, Smith & Co., acquired the business of Robert Laurie & Co. which had initially handled this facility. The Adelaide Stevedoring Co. Ltd, which provided services for the AUSN at that port, was owned by four local concerns, including Macdonald Hamilton. They also held a quarter share of the Newcastle Stevedoring, Tug and Lighterage Co. At Melbourne, the firm was responsible, with Gibbs Bright & Co. and Wm Crosby & Co., for the formation of the United Stevedoring Co. Ltd. Similar arrangements were ultimately made at Sydney, Brisbane and Townsville.[28]

   Beside stevedoring, other maritime activities of Macdonald Hamilton were towage and ship repairs. They were also involved in wool dumping and cold storage, and invested in non-marine local enterprises such as mining and pastoral management.[29] The firm remained dominated by directors close to the Inchcape family. After the death of Macdonald in 1920 and Hamilton in 1924, William Aberdein Mackay and David James Mackay Sim (both nephews of Lord Inchcape) achieved prominence in the firm, and Macdonald's son Rodney, who had joined it on his father's death, was subsequently to become Macdonald Hamilton's senior partner in Australia.

*　　*　　*

In conclusion: the importance of the AUSN and Macdonald Hamilton in the Australian coasting trade was thus considerable. It has been suggested that, as British enterprises, their success was achieved at the expense of local concerns, to the detriment of this region's economic development. Writing of the relationship between exporters and the owners of the transport carrying their goods, John Bach, the historian of Australian shipping, pointed out that the former are often critical of their dependence upon the latter. Bach went on to observe that the strained relationship between the two sides was particularly pronounced in Australia, for

the exporter was unable to exercise any significant influence upon the policies of an industry operated at such a great distance. The idea that malevolent British shipping industries were engaged in the ruthless and deliberate exploitation of helpless Australian producers has been perhaps the most identifiable single characteristic of such national attitude to shipping as has existed in Australia.[30]

Bach further suggested that 'it is perhaps impossible to discern a distinctively Australian category of shipping enterprise, and that in fact shipping in Australia has always been but a branch of the British [shipping] industry'.[31] However, of the seventy-five years of existence of the AUSN, it enjoyed for only half that period the predominance that might have allowed it to oppress Australian producers as Bach maintained. The AUSN had been born as a result of the BI's attempt to monopolise the Queensland trade, both oceanic and coastal, but the BI had been invited into that trade by Australians supported by Australian mail contracts. Similarly, although the investors in the AUSN were largely British, the day-to-day running of the firm was in Australian hands, and the London directors rarely overturned the decisions taken by the local managers. With the completion of the Queensland railway in the mid-1920s and the end of the coastal mail contract, the AUSN lost its special advantages. The firm's slow decline from then onwards was in part obscured by its earnings from investments. Macdonald Hamilton's survival and prosperity was also due to its diversification into investment in local enterprises to augment its shipping agency earnings, which served to stimulate rather than restrict the development of Australia's economy.

NOTES

1. John Bach, *A Maritime History of Australia* (Melbourne, 1976) pp.5–7.
2. George Blake, *BI Centenary, 1856–1956* (London, 1956) pp.109–14.
3. John M. Maber, *North Star to Southern Cross: The Story of the Australiasian Seaways* (Prescot, Lancs, 1967) pp.170–4.
4. Ibid, p.172.
5. See J. Forbes-Munro, 'Sir Willian Mackinnon', entry in the *Dictionary of Scottish Business Biography*, in preparation, edited by A. Slaven and S. G. Checkland, p.5.
6. N. L. McKellar, *From Derby Round to Burketown: The AUSN Story* (St Lucia, Queensland, 1977) p.74.
7. *Inchcape Archives [IA]*, AUSN 1/2 (838), Memorandum and Articles of Association.
8. *IA*, AUSN 1/10 (1319) Register of Members, 1887–92.
9. *IA*, AUSN 1/19, Probate Book, According to the entry in J. R. Jeremy (ed.) *The Dictionary of Business Biography* (London, 1984–6) Ellerman left an even greater sum.
10. Bach, *A Maritime History*, pp.189–91. See also B. M. Pemberton, *Australian Coastal Shipping* (Melbourne, 1979).
11. *IA*, AUSN 2/1 (717) Annual Report, 1887.
12. Bach, *A Maritime History*, pp.202–5.
13. *IA*, AUSN P/3.
14. *IA*, AUSN 3/2.
15. McKellar, *From Derby Round to Burketown*, frontispiece.
16. Hector Bolitho, *James Lyle Mackay: the First Earl of Inchcape* (London, 1936) pp.76–9. The prices of ships were taken from *IA*, AUSN 1/3 (1320) Director's Minutes, from 1887, and *IA*, AUSN 1/4 (227) Directors' Minutes, to 1942.
17. *IA*, AUSN 1/4 (227) Directors' Minutes, to 1942.
18. W. A. Laxon, 'The Eastern Mails: The Story of the Eastern and Australian Steamship Company Limited', *Sea Breezes* (October 1963) pp.269–93.
19. *IA*, AUSN 1/4 (227) Directors' Minutes, to 1942.
20. *IA*, AUSN 1/4 (227) Meeting of Directors, 2 September 1927, p.245.
21. *IA*, AUSN 2/23 (946) Ledger, B4, 1937–46.
22. McKellar, *From Derby Road to Burketown*, p.643.
23. The high level of wealth of AUSN shareholders recorded in the Probate Book suggests that this was so.
24. The AUSN dividend rate from the early 1930s maintained a level slightly above bank interest rates, such as those paid by the Hong Kong and Shanghai Bank, for example.

25. McKellar, *From Derby Round to Burketown*, p.345–6.
26. P. J. Griffiths, *A History of the Inchcape Group* (London, 1977) p.90.
27. McKellar, *From Derby Round to Burketown*, p.464.
28. Ibid, p.7.
29. P. J. Griffiths, *A History of the Inchcape Group*, p.90.
30. Bach, *A Maritime History of Australia*, p.5.
31. Ibid, p.7.
NOTE A version of this chapter was presented at Professor T. C. Barker's seminar in Modern Economic and Social History at the Institute of Historical Research, University of London, in Spring of 1983. This was subsequently published in *Business History*, vol. XXVII, no 1, March 1985, pp.59–74. It appears again with the permission of the editor.

158

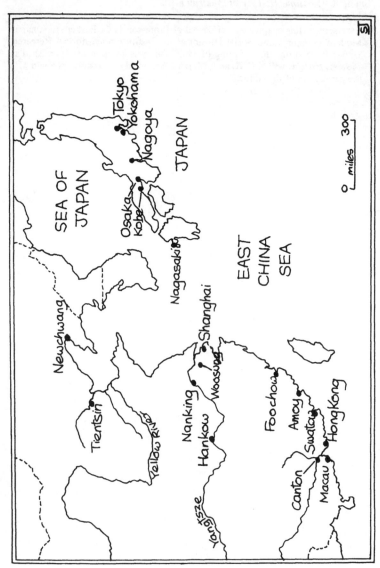

MAP 6.1 The ports of China and Japan

6 Trade in the Far East: Companies in Hong Kong, China and Japan, c1870–1939

Although the Inchcape Group has ventured into the Far East relatively recently, the companies it has acquired were among the first to be established there. As we saw in Chapter 1, in Canton, the merchant house of Gibb Livingston & Co. was founded in 1836, to be followed by the tea traders, Gilman & Co., in 1840. In Shanghai, the silk merchants, general trading and shipping agents who were ultimately to become Dodwell & Co. Ltd were established in 1858, and Caldbeck Macgregor & Co.'s wines and spirits business began in 1864.

Many previous studies of British merchant enterprise in the Far East have relied heavily upon the archives of Jardine Matheson and Swires.[1] This had given the impression that these were the most important British firms in this region. Is this the case, or may the four companies to be considered here claim equal significance?

Of the four, the most detailed documentation survives for Dodwell's. This, together with available material concerning the other three businesses, will be used to consider their contribution to the development of trade between Britain and the Far East.

The foundation of these firms has been described in Chapter 1. By the last quarter of the nineteenth century, they had expanded dramatically from their modest beginnings. For example, W. R. Adamson & Co. (the forerunners of Dodwell's), appointed a full-time shipping clerk at its Shanghai office in 1872 to manage its growing maritime agency work on behalf of British shipping companies. By this date, imports into China from Britain (40 per cent of which were cotton goods) were valued at 63 million taels or nearly £20m, representing nearly 82 per cent of all imports into China.[2] A similar proportion of China's export trade was directed to Britain. Adamson's new clerk, George Benjamin Dodwell, was to make a profound impact on this trade, to the extent that it may be argued that this firm was among the most prominent foreign enterprises in the Far East by the late century.

I

Dodwell, born in Derby, and then aged 20, was engaged at a salary of £400 for the first year, with a room, fire, light and medical attendance. His conditions of service laid down that he should devote his whole time and attention to the House (Adamson knew only too well the temptations to trade on one's own account) and he was allowed a 5 per cent interest on all the profits of the shipping business of the Shanghai office, on all profits earned above 7000 taels per annum (equivalent to £2 100 sterling), an indication of the department's income. His work as a shipping agent was interpreted in a wide sense: he was to act for the owners or charterers of vessels in securing cargoes, clearances and any other business, including insurance. Rather than acting as an agent for one specific fleet of merchant vessels, as in the case of James Kirton, who acted solely for the Henleys, primarily in the English coasting trade,[3] he managed a general shipping agency business, acting for a variety of owners and principals. He was not concerned with the buying and selling of ships, their outfits, crews and provisions, but with their profitable operation through consigning and despatching vessels entering and clearing the port of Shanghai and other ports where Adamson Bell & Co. maintained branches. Adamson Bell also allowed Dodwell to take a one-tenth interest in steamers and one-fifth in sailing ships chartered for speculative voyages on the account of the Shanghai office. These percentages of the profits were not, however, allowed on commission business (on the shipment of cargo held by the firm) which was seen as the department's main activity. The final condition of Dodwell's appointment was that he should 'not indulge in racing of horses and ponies', in contrast to the largest merchant house in China, Jardine Matheson.[4]

A detailed notebook kept by Dodwell covering the decade 1873–83 provides an insight into the vessels and owners for whom he acted as agent. This had been used to compile Figure 6.1, which summarises the profits of Adamson Bell's shipping business at Shanghai and Hankow. Dodwell clearly dealt primarily with steamers, the profits of which exceeded those of sailing ships after 1875. Steamships gained an early predominance in the Far Eastern trade, which specialised in high-value, low-bulk traffic such as tea, silk and passengers rather than high-bulk, low-value cargoes such as coal or timber, which continued to be carried by less highly capitalised sailing vessels. The profits achieved by the shipping department of Adamson Bell & Co. may be divided into two categories: those earned as a result of Dodwell's own speculative ventures in the chartering of vessels, and those of ships trading on consignment for the firm. Regular high profits were earned especially by the 'Castle' steamers (owned by T. Skinner & Co. of London) but the extension of European telegraph and cable services to all the major countries of east and south-east Asia between 1871 and 1875 soon diminished the profits of speculative trading. Success in such trading relied upon a greater knowledge of the market than that of one's competitors. When an accurate and up-to-date listing of arrivals, departures and prices of commodities was made easily available to all, this advantage was lost.

Dodwell recalled that a great deal of risk was involved in chartering, and often heavy demurrage charges were incurred through waiting for a full cargo. He regarded it as a generally unsatisfactory system, especially as he was often forced to buy his own cargo to fill the ships, 'and that is the worst thing that could happen if you were a merchant'.[5] From 1879 the profits from charters averaged a third of the total income from shipping and contributed considerably to Dodwell's earnings. For example, the profits of nearly 6000 taels on the chartering of sailing vessels in 1881 added over 1000 taels or over £300 to his salary, then £1000 p.a. and, as that same year, steamers earned over 10 000 taels, his 10 per cent share was again over £300. To this may be added his share of the overall profits, 5 per cent on his department's profits exceeding 7000

162

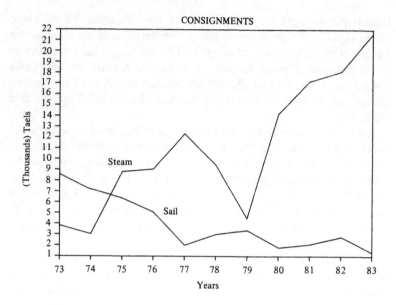

CONSIGNMENTS

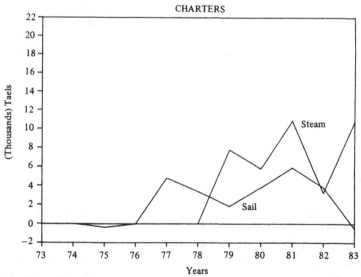

CHARTERS

Year ending 31 March
3.33 taels – £ sterling

SOURCE *Inchcape Archives*, DOD 6/3, Notebook of G. B. Dodwell, frontispiece.

FIGURE 6.1 Adamson Bell & Co. shipping agency: profits at Shanghai and Hankow, consignments and charters

taels, which equalled nearly 1500 taels or approximately £450. Thus in 1881 his gross earnings exceeded £2000, doubling his salary.

Whereas Dodwell's chartering business was based on tramp steamers, the firm also acted as agents for liners trading on consignment. The regularity of the Castle and Shire line ships in their voyages to Shanghai, for example, may be seen in the contemporary commercial press.

Dodwell's work as a shipping agent also led to an expansion of the firm's income from these vessels, too – in the case of the Castle steamers, by more than fivefold. Profits from the Castle fleet agency were derived from charging 5 per cent on homeward freights, 1 per cent of which was held on the account of each steamer. A further 5 per cent was levied on coasting cargoes obtained, and 2½ per cent was charged on payments made by Adamson Bell on the behalf of Skinners' over and above the credit which was held on the account of each steamer. A half per cent was claimed for collecting debts and one-eighth per cent on bill brokerage. Of the 5 per cent charged by Adamson Bell on rice charters, 1 per cent was put to the credit of the steamer. Similar arrangements existed with the other shipping lines with whom Adamson Bell dealt, including D. J. Jenkins & Co.'s Shire Line, Geo. Thompson Jr. & Co., Killick Martin & Co. and Alex Stephens & Sons. The results of these arrangements in terms of profits earned by Dodwell for his employers are summarised in Figure 6.1. Strangely, such detailed information has not survived for the later period.

A wide variety of cargoes was carried on consignment and by charter through Dodwell's agency work. In the early days of trading with China the export trade was dominated by tea and silk: imports were mainly raw cotton and opium. By the mid-1870s the Chinese supplied new lines of exports, such as Chinese beans, vegetable oils and bristles. Imports included cotton piece goods, kerosene for lighting, metal wares, matches, soap and cigarettes. This diversification was explained in a custom report from Shanghai in 1876:

> British merchants in China sought some other and more profitable medium than bullion in which to remit the proceeds of their imports, and a trade of greater or less magnitude . . . in consequence . . . developed in articles which a few years before were unknown among foreign exports, such as sugar, tobacco, hides, camel's wool and straw braid.[6]

Yet even by the end of the nineteenth century nearly 60 per cent of China's exports consisted of tea and silk. In order to consider the importance of Adamson Bell as a merchant house, in Table 6.1 tea has

TABLE 6.1 Number of chests of tea shipped by Adamson, Bell & Company from Shanghai and Foochow, 1874–8

Shanghai

Year	Tea type	Number of chests shipped by A, B & Co.	Total number of chests shipped from Shanghai	Number of companies shipping more chests of tea than A, B & Co. in that year	Total number of companies involved in the shipment of tea in that year
1874	black	–	–	–	–
	green	–	–	–	–
1875	black	–	–	–	–
	green	–	–	–	–
1876	black	24 045	277 949	2	35
	green	57 161	431 903	1	24
1877	black	19 130	227 669	1	33
	green	76 681	416 893	1	25
1878	black	5 614	146 465	7	28
	green	30 911	147 765	1	25

Foochow

Year	Tea type	Number of chests shipped by A, B & Co.	Total number of chests shipped from Shanghai	Number of companies shipping more chests of tea than A, B & Co. in that year	Total number of companies involved in the shipment of tea in that year
1874	black green	71 448	740 043	1	24
1875	black green	79 053	752 520	0	26
1876	black green	53 658	740 818	4	25
1877	black green	52 587	644 692	3	25
1878	black green	40 988	698 318	6	26

Overall totals

Year	Number of chests shipped by A, B & Co. at Shanghai and Foochow	Total number of chests shipped at Shanghai and Foochow	Number of chests shipped by A, B & Co. as % of total tea shipment that year
1874	71 448	740 043	9.65
1875	79 053	752 520	10.51
1876	134 864	1 450 670	9.30
1877	148 398	1 289 254	11.51
1878	77 513	992 548	7.81

SOURCE *Inchcape Archives*, DOD 6/3, notebook of G. B. Dodwell, pp.104–6.

been taken as an example of an important commodity handled by Western firms in China. If we consider exports of tea from the ports of Shanghai and Foochow for a few years in the 1870s for which statistics happen to survive, Adamson Bell appear among the leading firms. In 1875 the total number of chests of tea it shipped from Foochow exceeded that of any other Western firm, more than 10 per cent of all tea exports from that port. In the following year Adamson Bell & Co.'s tea shipments were only marginally behind those of Butterfield & Swire, Fairhurst & Reeves, Jardine Matheson and Westall Galton & Co. In 1877 the firm ranked fourth in tea shipments, and in 1878 seventh. At Shanghai, it was the second and third most important shipper of green and black teas respectively in 1876. In 1877 Adamson Bell & Co.'s totals were exceeded only by the firm of Maitland & Co. In 1878 they maintained their position in green teas but fell slightly to eighth ranking in black tea shipments.[7]

Such a prominent position in the tea trade thus ensured Dodwell's role as a leading shipping agent. His firm, unlike John Samuel Swire, Jardine Matheson and the American firm, Russel, did not actually invest in local steamers,[8] but otherwise his activities included all aspects of the maritime trade of Shanghai. His notebook is packed with *aides-mémoire* pertaining to his duties. He had to consider the varying charges made at the ports of arrival and departure of the vessels he represented. He had to note the costs of loading, discharge and storage of particular cargoes. He kept a record of all the 'correspondents' or contacts at foreign ports. He arranged the insurance of cargoes and vessels. He recorded the London credits of London firms operating in China. He made regular references

TABLE 6.2 Tons of cargo shipped by Adamson, Bell and Company from Shanghai, May 1876 to April 1877 – destinations and commodities

Commodity	London steam	sail	New York steam	sail	Lyons	Colonies	Coast (steam)	Total
Tea	7381	930	1563	1811	—	—	—	11 715
Straw goods	230	—	—	316	—	—	—	546
Sugar	483	954	—	—	—	—	—	1 437
Hides	707	—	1	—	—	—	—	708
Silk	23	—	—	—	19	—	—	42
Cotton and piece goods	—	—	—	—	—	—	536	536
Goatskins	44	—	—	13	—	5	—	62
Sundries	69	—	—	—	—	3	—	72
Totals	8937	1884	1594	2140	19	8	536	15 118

SOURCE *Inchcape Archives*, DOD 6/3, notebook of G. B. Dodwell, pp.120–1.

to the fluctuations in the exchange rates between the tael, sterling and US dollars, noting that this in itself varied between different Chinese ports.

Dodwell also noted, for the years 1876–9, the vessels for which he acted as agent and the freight rates he obtained. Table 6.2 is a summary of the shipping movements of the season 1 May 1876 to 30 April 1877.[9] In this period, he was personally responsible for arranging the shipment of over 15 000 tons of various cargoes. Tea dominated the export trade, followed by sugar and hides, with straw goods and cotton piece goods also of importance. The largest part of these cargoes was destined for London, but the supply of goods to the USA was already significant and increased rapidly.[10] The shipment of silk goods to Lyons, comprising raw silks, silkworms and silkworm eggs, was the result of the outbreak of a silkworm disease in Europe and the need to restock the industry. The cargoes analysed in Table 6.2 were carried in eighty-two shiploads, sixty-two by steamer and twenty by sailing ship. Dodwell's duties included the safe storage of cargoes. Great care had to be taken in the shipment of tea, which was liable to be tainted if placed in close proximity to hides or sugar cargoes. Silk and straw braid were also fragile and easily damaged.

In many of his tasks Dodwell was aided by the firm's compradore. It was a peculiarly Eastern custom to employ a local assistant whose knowledge of the Chinese language, customs and practices helped

Western merchant houses in the day-to-day running of their affairs. They were often disliked by other Chinese as commercial 'traitors', in the employ of foreigners, working against the interest of their fellow-countrymen, but they were often also envied for their wealth. They became an essential element of Chinese commercial life, not only because of the linguistic and cultural differences between East and West, but also because of continued government restrictions on trading by foreigners, the lack of uniformity of weights and measures used in different provinces, the unsettled nature of the national currency, and the unregulated issue and circulation of money certificates and credit bills by native banks. The establishment of the Hongkong & Shanghai Bank, which was incorporated in 1866, helped ease commercial transactions,[11] but the compradore remained a vital go-between in the native market. He brought together local buyers and sellers, settling their disputes, securing his principal against loss, and giving him advice on the condition of the market generally. In theory, employing a middleman would tend to increase the price of goods to the Chinese consumer, but in practice experienced compradores created price combinations with the compradores of other firms in the same trade, or with Chinese wholesale dealers. In this way he increased his share of the profits, and the foreign traders bore the brunt of the increase by paying more for materials for export.[12]

This formation of rings may be seen on a larger scale in Dodwell's activities as a shipping agent: obtaining the best rates for the vessels he represented and thus maximising his firm's commission brought him into contact with the first major shipping conference in the Far East trade, that of 1879. Instigated by John Swire, who founded the partnership of Butterfield & Swire, this conference helped Blue Funnel Line ships particularly, for which Swire's acted as agent. Although the Holt fleet was known for its low fuel consumption and slow passages, it required high freight rates to stay profitable, as the lengthy voyages incurred heavy overheads in terms of depreciation and interest on capital. The Castles and Shires, represented by Adamson Bell & Co., offered high-speed passages in return for higher rates: Swire's saw them as a threat to the earnings of the Blue Funnel ships.[13] However, the conference was regarded as a great success for the steamer owners and shipping agents. Arranged between Swire's, P & O, Holt's (Blue Funnel), T. Skinner (Castle), McGregor Gow (Glen), D. J. Jenkins (Shire) and Gellatly Hankey and Sewell,[14] the conference ensured that rates were kept high by offering the shipper a deferred rebate and limiting the number of departures per season.[15] Despite a clause added in 1885 which specifically stated that 'agents of conference steamers in China . . . to be prohibited from being interested . . . in opposing steamers, or in the loading of sailing vessels', Dodwell continued to load both sail and steam, as Figure 6.1 shows. He continued to represent Skinner's Castle Line, whilst his firm was employed as agent for Killick Martin & Co.'s sailing ships.

Thus in his first decade as a Far Eastern shipping agent Dodwell helped to increase the shipping tonnage handled by Adamson Bell & Co., to improve the variety and quantity of cargoes imported and exported, and to raise profits generally in the firm's Shanghai office. Despite China's great land mass and population, however, the total value of her foreign trade by the end of the nineteenth century was only £53m.[16] Meanwhile, in the late 1870s, branches of Adamson Bell & Co. were established at the ports of Kobe and Yokohama in Japan.

The *Japan Weekly Mail*, which reported shipping arrivals and departures at Yokohama, shows that at the time when the firm was setting up in business at the port, shipping activity was limited, at a weekly average of only a dozen or so vessels clearing outwards with cargoes. Adamson Bell appear as consignees of the Castle Line steamers *Glamis Castle*, *Londoun Castle* and *Braemar Castle*, a Danish steamer and two British sailing vessels. It dispatched nine shiploads of outward cargo during the 1878 season. The three named vessels traded between the ports of Shanghai, Kobe and Hong Kong, except for the *Glamis Castle*, which sailed to New York. General cargoes, tea and coal were carried; frequent voyages in ballast indicate a shortage of goods for shipment before the expansion of Japan's overseas trade in the following decades.[17] By 1883 activity at Japanese ports had markedly increased, and with it the business of Adamson Bell. Of shipments organised by Dodwell from the firm's Shanghai office in 1883, twenty-four were destined for the ports of Kobe and Nagasaki. In the same year Dodwell handled a total of eight-nine shiploads, acting as a consignee for vessels trading to Chinese ports, such as Foochow, Swatow, Hankow, Woosung, Amoy and Newchwang.

The carriage of tea, silk and sundry goods to London, New York and Marseilles was still important.[18] When Japan's ports were opened to foreign trade, imports were mainly textile yarns and piece goods, metal wares, ships, munitions and pharmaceutical chemicals. Exports were chiefly raw silk, tea, rice, as in the case of China: in the 1880s these commodities accounted for two-thirds of outward cargoes.[19] The twenty-four shipments from Japan arranged by Dodwell in 1883 increased to fifty-seven in 1889,[20] and seventy-four in 1892.[21]

II

These shipping intelligence reports demonstrate clearly that the largest share of the Japanese tea trade was in the hands of the Americans. This fact, and the large American demand for silk, convinced Dodwell of the great commercial potential of a Far East trans-Pacific service. In 1883 he himself had organised the shipment of a cargo of silk across the Pacific which had sold for more than $6m.

In 1886 the Pacific and Atlantic coasts of Canada were linked for the first time by direct rail communication, and the Canadian Pacific Railway began chartering sailing ships to import goods from China and Japan. Dodwell's 1883 consignment of silk had been carried by steamer, so he now saw a golden opportunity to introduce a regular steamship service. Meanwhile the Fairfield Shipbuilding Company on the Clyde had three ex-Cunarders available for charter. The *Parthia*, *Batavia* and *Abyssinia* had been taken over in part-payment for the new and larger tonnage which the firm had built for Cunard's Atlantic trade. A large proportion of the carrying capacity of these vessels was given over to passenger accommodation, which made them unsuitable for short trade-runs to the Far East but ideal for a trans-Pacific passenger and freight service. Having come to an agreement with Sir William Pearce, the chairman of Fairfield's and whom he already knew (through his contacts with the Scottish Oriental Steamship Company, another of Pearce's interests) Dodwell appealed direct to Canadian Pacific, offering a ready-made steamship line, and won a three-year contract to manage the ships, which were still owned by Fairfield's. To all intents and purposes, he controlled this new shipping service, the main purpose of which was to facilitate the interchange of east- and westbound freight and passenger traffic at Port Moody, the CPR terminus.

Thus Dodwell played an important part in the expansion of his firm's business throughout the Far East, and personally pioneered the steamer links between Canada and the ports of China and Japan. But his own shipping agency work and plans to expand his commercial networks were severely curtailed by his employers. Adamson had retired in 1886 and Bell, who had succeeded him as senior partner, proved inept and profligate. The company also suffered as a result of a major change that occurred in the Far Eastern shipping trade in the late 1880s: a large number of steamers not belonging to regular shipping lines entered the trade, by accepting low freights. Dodwell was later to describe how these freights, considerably lower than those ruling before, paid only very small profits but enabled new competition to enter the field.[22]

6.1 The Far East: George Benjamin Dodwell, one of the founders of Dodwell & Co. Ltd, who pioneered the first trans-Pacific steamship service

6.2 A. J. H. Carlill, the joint founder of Dodwell & Co. Ltd, who was in charge
of the firm's successful tea business

6.3 The Far East: Dodwell's Foochow branch staff in May 1906

For Adamson Bell, bankruptcy loomed on the horizon from March 1890. On a voyage from Vancouver on the *Parthia*, beginning a month later, Dodwell and A. J. H. Carlill, the tea department manager, plotted the take-over of their moribund parent company. Their letters from this period to 1 May 1891, the date when their objective was finally realised, have survived.[23] They provide further insight into the business which Dodwell helped to develop. The demand for Indian tea had caused a decline in the Foochow–London tea trade, and silk shipments from Japan were less in demand after the recovery of the European silk industry. Meanwhile the export trade in tea to America and also to Russia was still thriving. Dodwell saw a chance of success for a new firm if he could take over all his company's principals and 'chops', or trade marks; keep the arrangement with Fairfield's; keep the insurance agencies, and concentrate on his commission business. Slight improvements in tea and silk prices in London enabled Adamson Bell to survive a little longer. Dodwell had to maintain confidence among the firm's twenty European employees based at Yokohama, Kobe, Hong Kong, Shanghai and the London head office for over a year.

In setting up the new firm he had to raise some £20 000 capital from other employees whilst having to warn them that they would have to accept lower salaries until the new firm had found its feet. Thomas Dermer, at the London office, refused to accept a salary of only £300 a year, considering that he was worth £800. Also in London, Frederick D'Iffanger broke down completely under the strain of waiting for the company's impending demise and withdrew from the proposed new undertaking. Dodwell's brother, Fred, based in Hong Kong, also gave cause for concern. He was given to an enthusiasm for personal speculation and trading on his own account, to the detriment of his parent firm, and, since Hong Kong was seen as the future chief earning port in the East rather than Shanghai, he had to be brought into line. Dodwell saw the fortunes of his new company hinging on the expansion of its shipping agency work and carefully ensured that existing agencies would transfer their business from Adamson Bell's to the proposed new firm. Sealed instructions were drawn up and addressed to all constituents and agents, containing full instructions for carrying on transactions already in progress and advertising the new company, to be opened at the receipt of a single word by cable – 'Haddock'.

Carlill described how well these preparations paid off when Adamson Bell at long last expired: 'with no more delay than the time required for cablegrams to reach the chief business centres, the new firm was widely advertised, and the whole transformation was effected with a minimum of friction and disturbance'. He went on, 'never was there a more startling birth of a new firm springing full-fledged without a pause the moment the old firm closed its doors'. Rival firms were taken aback: when they cabled their branches to try to secure the late company's agencies they found they were too late. John Swire, for example, was not slow to apply for the CPR agency and was disconcerted to discover that it had already been passed to the then unknown new firm of Dodwell Carlill & Co.[24]

In setting up his new business Dodwell planned from the beginning that it should be a limited company, but this status was not achieved until 1899, partly through the loss of the supply of shipping services to the CPR. Dodwell had originally entered into a three-year contract with Sir William Van Horne of the CPR: but when the shipping line had quickly established itself and shown that the level of eastbound traffic was sufficient to ensure that it would continue to pay its way, the CPR decided to run its own fast mail line in place of the old hired Cunarders. The CPR then successfully campaigned for a £60 000 annual mail subsidy for five years (£15 000 from Canada and the remainder from Britain) and commissioned the building of the Empress Line of steamers for the then new Canadian Pacific Steamship Company. Dodwell was notified that the contract he enjoyed with the CPR would not be renewed, although as the successor to Adamson Bell he was asked to continue to manage the service at the Far Eastern end. Before the creation of his new firm Dodwell had spent four months with Sir William Van Horne and various heads of departments of the CPR and had impressed them with his knowledge of Far Eastern commerce, to the extent that in 1892 Van Horne offered him the full management of the new line if he would abandon his newly-created firm and join them as an employee. Dodwell was promised complete control of CPR shipping and the freedom to develop the service as he thought best, second only to Van Horne himself. He was offered the highest remuneration paid to anyone in the CPR, a salary of £2000 a year with commission earnings promising to equal that, totalling £4000 p.a. Dodwell declined the proposal. He thus turned down a splendid offer from one of the world's best-known railway companies, preferring the leadership of his own new and untried firm, which he had so recently rescued and rebuilt from bankruptcy. Also, by spurning the CPR, he knew he would incur that powerful company's hostility. 'It is the worst day's work you have ever done, Dodwell,' Van Horne threatened, 'I will crush you.' Shaughnessy, the CPR's vice-president, added 'Don't you attempt to start a steamship line of your own. If you do, we will run you off the Pacific'.[25]

Fairfield's, left with the redundant Cunarders, informed Dodwell that it was willing to re-enter the Pacific trade if he could find a suitable railway connection. (Almost all the Pacific steamship lines inaugurated in the late nineteenth and early twentieth centuries were controlled by railway companies.)[26] Dodwell thereupon cabled J. M. Hannaford, the traffic manager of the Northern Pacific Railroad, who jumped at the idea of forming an alternative service. Branch offices were soon established at Victoria and Tacoma. Unwilling to await the preparation of the Cunarders, Dodwell chartered the Scottish Oriental Company's largest coasters to begin his new line. The Northern Pacific Steamship Company, as it came to be known, proved ten times more profitable to Dodwell's company than the Empress Line could have been, according to the memoirs of J. P. Dowling, who acted as his personal secretary and stenographer when working at the Pacific coast branches.[27] Whereas the Empresses carried only 2580 tons deadweight and the CPR would not add extra steamers when the volume of passengers was small in the autumn and winter, the NPSS regularly chartered extra steamers when cargo was plentiful, running up to twelve vessels at any one time. This concentration on the carriage of freight rather than passengers was seen as an important element in his success.[28] The Pacific trade contributed greatly to the turnover of $20m achieved by Dodwell Carlill & Co. in the first six months of trading from May 1891.[29]

The successful expansion of Dodwell's shipping agency work was aided considerably by the political and economic events of the last decade of the nineteenth century. Throughout this period the sizeable emigrant traffic in Japanese contract labour to Hawaii profitably filled the steerage of many of the trans-Pacific vessels chartered by Dodwell's. The Sino-Japanese war of 1894 saw the firm in an unaccustomed role of shipbroking. The Japanese company Nippon Yusen Kaisha asked Dodwell to arrange the purchase of vessels for its fleet, at a commission of 5 per cent. The forty-three steamers which Dodwell purchased on their behalf brought in £80 000.[30] The gold rush to Alaska, with its demand for shipping space for gold prospectors and their stores, added yet further business. Dodwell's sponsored the incorporation of the Washington–Alaska Steamship Company, by the purchase of a two-thirds share in the SS *City of Seattle*. Making round trips between Puget Sound and Alaska in ten days, she grossed between $20 000 and $25 000 per voyage, paying a 400 per cent dividend on the initial investment over four years. This service was extended with the acquisition of an inland water steamer, the *City of Kingston* and a sternwheeler, the *State of Washington*. An associated railway venture, the Chilcoot Railway & Transport Company, designed to extend the line of communications to include the Klondike gold fields, was less successful. Dodwell Carlill & Co. invested two lots of $50 000 in the construction of a wire tramway. It took so long to build that by the time of its eventual completion, in 1899, much of the equipment and supplies had already been carried to the gold-fields by human packers. Meanwhile the construction of the White Pass Railroad twelve miles to the south threatened to put the tramway out of business. The Company's investment was recovered, however, when the tramway was sold to White Pass under the threat of reducing the rate to render the railroad uncompetitive.

Dodwell's even managed to make the best out of a crushing duty of 10 cents per lb. imposed on tea imports by the US government. Fairfield's had just added the Guion Line *Arizona* to the NPSS fleet. With luxurious passenger accommodation, she was the largest vessel then on the Pacific. The duty was imposed, effective in thirty days, whilst she was crossing the Pacific westwards; so on her arrival in Japan she discharged her entire cargo and turned round loaded to capacity with tea, arriving at Tacoma a day before the duty came into effect, and achieved record earnings of 6 cents per lb.

The supply of vessels to the US military and naval authorities proved especially profitable. The outbreak of the Spanish–American War and the destruction of the Spanish fleet in Manila Bay resulted in a frantic search by the US War Department for steamers to transport troops and supplies to capture the city of Manila which was strongly garrisoned by 50 000 Spanish troops. Dodwell hesitated to break the neutrality laws, turning down an offer of 15 cents per register ton daily (later increased to 20 cents) for the charter of the entire NPSS fleet. Dodwell's brother Fred, who had arrived at the Tacoma branch in 1898, by-passed the neutrality laws through the American embassy in London, by incorporating the North American Steamship Company, with a nominal capital bond issue of $1.5m for the purchase of the NPSS fleet. Control of the fleet was maintained, for, although aliens were limited to the ownership of only 20 per cent of stock in an American corporation, the law imposed no restriction on bond issue. All the vessels were immediately chartered to the War Department, at rates varying between $250 a day for the *Batavia* and $350 for the *Victoria*. The barge *Arizona*, which was too capacious for the Pacific trade, especially after the increase in the tea duty, was sold to the US War Department for $600 000. Dodwell's continued thereafter to cash in successfully on the changing economic fortunes at the Far East end of its trade. It took a financial interest in three steamers with James Chambers & Co. It helped in the creation of a new port for tea shipments from Japan, Keelung, which avoided the expense of transhipment to Amoy, and it acted as the exclusive agent for the chartering of ships by the Japanese government during the Russo-Japanese war of 1904–5. Its Japanese trading business continued to expand, with the export of coal from Japan to Singapore and Shanghai, and the shipment of Japanese straw braid from Kobe for Europe. Dodwell's also helped with the opening of a new port, Yokkaichi, for the export of Japanese porcelain. This became a direct port of call, saving trans-shipment from Nagoya.[31]

III

George Benjamin Dodwell retired from the East in 1899, to return to London and complete successfully his plan for the transformation of his business into a limited liability company. This reorganisation provides a detailed insight into the sources and nature of its capital structure and a consolidated picture of its earnings. The first register of members of Dodwell & Co. Ltd records the names, addresses and occupations of the first group of shareholders investing in the company on 17 January 1899, the first day of issue. It is clear that from the beginning existing employees of the company were responsible for a substantial amount of the capital. Of the thirty-two persons listed, twenty-two were directly associated with Dodwell's. The senior partners of the old firm became the majority shareholders: A. J. H. Carlill, Frederick D'Iffanger, Dodwell himself, Fred Dodwell, G. S. Melhuish, E. A. Whealler and G. S. Thomson, who were mainly branch managers, invested over 80 per cent of the total paid-up capital on that day. Mercantile assistants, clerks and bookkeepers of the firm also availed themselves of the £25 shares. The firm's compradore at Hong Kong, Lim Pong Poo, purchased 100 shares, and his opposite number at Shanghai, Tong Chung Lane, bought twenty. Investors not already associated with Dodwell's were accountants, merchants and married women, who invested a total of £183. Of these initial investors, 47 per cent of the capital was derived from London, 11 per cent came from Hong Kong, 27 per cent from Shanghai, 11 per cent from Kobe and Yokohama, and the remainder from the American ports of Tacoma and Seattle. Further investments followed, so that by 23 March 1899 £47 650 of the total nominal capital of £100 000 had been paid up. The high proportion of investments from within the company itself remained. In opting for limited liability the original founders were thus not necessarily seeking to gain outside investment. The advantage of the new arrangement lay in the fact that each shareholder's liability in the event of bankruptcy was limited to his or her original investment, however large or small.

Dodwell immediately put down £1067 and Carlill £554, giving an indication of their personal wealth, their confidence in the new firm, and their expectation of future growth and diversification.[32] This confidence was justified: that Dodwell's achieved a turnover of $90m in its first six months has already been noted. The first year of trading of the limited company resulted in a profit of over £25 000, from which a dividend of 10 per cent was paid to shareholders.[33] This profit is especially remarkable in view of the fact that the company's branches were often run by only one or two persons, sometimes sharing an office with another firm, and helped by a few loyal compradores and other local labour. On its foundation in 1891 Dodwell's had similarly had only twenty full-time European employees.

The performance of the company's branches over its first decade is analysed in Table 6.3. The Russo-Japanese war stimulated profits at Shanghai, Hong Kong, Yokohama and Kobe: the former two ports achieved the highest totals for the decade, equalling 68 per cent of total profits. At Shanghai the main preoccupation of the branch was the export of tea and other produce, the import of Manchester piece goods, and ships' agency business, before it began, in the 1920s, dealing with machinery and electrical goods. Shipping was the principal activity of the Hong Kong office, which entered trading and agency business on a large scale in the early decades of the twentieth century, investing in local electrical and dock companies. The war with Russia doubled the profits of the Yokohama branch and increased the Kobe office's profits fivefold, especially on account of the Japanese navy's need to lay in large reserves of Cardiff coal. When hostilities ceased, these branches supplied and fitted out several tramp ships to return Russian prisoners from Japan to Odessa. The engineering concern of Mosle & Co. was acquired in 1906 as part of an unsuccessful policy of expansion, resulting in heavy losses, but these branches flourished again with the advent of the First World War.

At Foochow, where Dodwell & Co. held its only agency in the Far East for the Blue Funnel line, the export of tea was the main preoccupation: profits were accordingly reduced when public taste increasingly switched to Indian teas. The Colombo branch concentrated on the sale of Ceylon teas to Russia, and the export of cinnamon, cocoa beans and coconut products. The losses of 1905 were the result of heavy investment in the Malacca Rubber Plantation Co. Ltd of which Dodwell

TABLE 6.3 Declared profit per year before payment of dividend of Dodwell & Co. Ltd – earnings per branch in £ sterling

Branch	1899	1900	1901	1902	1903	1904	1905	1906	1907	1908	Totals
Shanghai	7 391	7 677	4 987	4 459	12 187	12 375	5 729	7 092	12 187	4 010	78 094
Hong Kong	6 398	18 553	12 249	3 408	6 410	7 020	8 238	9 360	7 769	4 795	84 200
Yokohama	124*	251	3 246	6 927	5 520	14 482	8 089	5 140	2 754*	2 297*	38 480
Kobe	2 312	7 059	2 906	1 328	2 404	12 056	6 184	1 036	1 349*	4 735*	29 201
Tacoma	4 505	8 122	3 138	289	2 072	2 373	4 946	3 294	3 647	3 419	35 805
Portland	1 655	3 601	355*								4 901
Seattle	859	1 164	836*								1 187
Victoria	77*	2 821*	546*	235*	554	338	788	1 665	1 808	1 857	3 331
Vancouver	292*		300							1 395*	1 387
Foochow				500		294*	3 596*	1 746	1 359	1 855*	2 140
Colombo				444	173	563	7 021*	2 039	1 861	2 312	371
London	2 692	7 872*	11 718	10 600*	12 582*	6 801*	2 511*	13 781*	4 075	1 944	33 718
Totals	25 319	35 734	36 807	6 520	16 738	42 112	20 846	17 591	28 603	8 055	238 325
Dividend	10%	10%	10%	10%	10%	10%**	10%	15%	20%	5%	
Balance for next year	5 319	8 592	10 400	11 920	12 159	16 272	16 938	19 779	22 233	23 790	

*Losses
**In addition, shareholders received a bonus of £2 10s per share
SOURCE *Inchcape Archives*, DOD 3/1, Reports and Accounts, frontispiece.

himself was chairman: but the branch soon recovered and its profits rose.

In the Far East trade generally the expansion of Dodwell & Co.'s business was based mainly on the homeward-bound trades, a distinction which emerged in the discussions of the Royal Commission on Shipping Rings of 1909. The outward trade of manufactured goods from the UK employed regular liners for high-value, low-bulk goods. These items were usually sent in many small packages requiring a speedy passage. Liner services had only a limited need for the work of the shipping agent, as their lines and departures were well advertised and merchants could thus approach them direct. The greatest scope for profits for shipping agents was derived from organising whole shiploads of bulky, seasonal goods on board tramp steamers, which relied on the agent for local knowledge of commodities and merchants, for the shipment of homeward cargoes from the East.[34]

Of the Pacific branches, Tacoma made steady profits as the base of the steamship line, and especially through its association with a successful flour-milling business. The Seattle office became fully established only through a huge demand for timber after the Yokohama earthquake of 1923. The Vancouver office did relatively little business in the first decade of the firm, but was to gain important shipping agencies, such as Norddeutscher/Lloyd and services to South America. The Victoria branch recovered from early losses and developed a solid shipping-agency business. The profits of the London branch fluctuated according to the demand for UK goods all over the world. In 1901 it reaped the benefits of the Underwood typewriter agency, which gave it exclusive marketing rights throughout China and Japan. The personnel of the London branch were well known at the Baltic Exchange, where their main occupation was to arrange tonnage to fill Dodwell & Co.'s runs on the New York berth, mainly with vessels owned by James Warrack & Co., James Chambers & Co., Barber Steamship Lines and Gellatly, Hankey, Sewell & Co., all companies with which Dodwell's had had a long and close association.[35] It must be emphasised that Dodwell's profits were largely derived from its function as agent only, although, as stated earlier, it did occasionally take a financial interest in a venture.

IV

Figure 6.2 shows the performance of Dodwell & Co. Ltd from its formation into a limited company until the outbreak of the Second World War. In its first two decades of trading, despite fluctuations in

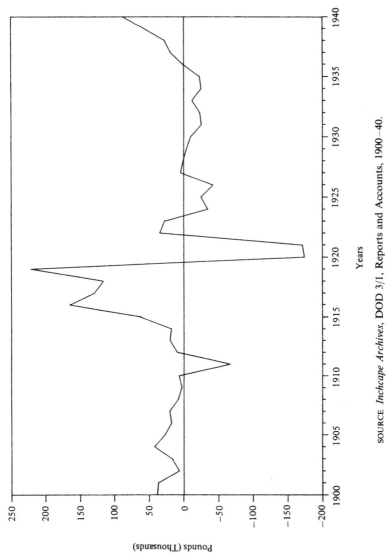

SOURCE *Inchcape Archives*, DOD 3/1, Reports and Accounts, 1900–40.

FIGURE 6.2 The performance of Dodwell & Co. Ltd, 1900–40

profits earned, the company continued to gradually increase its capital from £50 000 in 1899 to £300 000 after its record year of 1919. In the years 1908–12 the decline in tea sales at Shanghai, Hankow and Foochow resulting from the growing popularity of Indian tea, together with attempts to diversify the business of the London branch, had seriously reduced profits. The heavy loss of 1911 was caused not by a further deterioration in business but by the Colombo manager's defalcations. During the years 1910–11, prices of rubber from Ceylon had risen to fantastic heights and then collapsed. The branch manager at Colombo, with the connivance of his bookkeeper, had been speculating heavily on his own account, and used the company's cheques to meet his commitments when he found himself completely out of his depth. Dodwell, faced with the bankruptcy of this branch feared that the losses incurred could be so great as to cripple his company altogether. Such anxieties were allayed by the company's Hong Kong bankers, who pointed out that Dodwell & Co. Ltd still had large reserves and was far from ruined. In fact the money lost was almost completely recovered by 1916, through a successful action brought by the company against the firms of rubber brokers who had made the purchases of shares on behalf of the Colombo manager. Dodwell himself, nearly 60 and with failing health, made the long and onerous journey to Colombo to support his company's interests. Apparently, the original purchase orders had been signed *per pro* Dodwell & Co. Ltd. The Courts held that this meant that it was the duty of the person accepting the order to inspect the Power of Attorney. That which the company had granted specifically stated that the manager was not permitted to deal in stocks and shares on its behalf.[36]

The First World War gave a great boost to the company's performance despite the general dislocation of shipping. Then the post-war depression led to a dramatic reversal in this state of affairs, not helped by another case of the misappropriation of company funds, this time at the Buenos Aires branch in 1920–1, when a total of £88 604 was misappropriated. Recovery of excess profits taxes of £175 000 helped briefly in 1922–3, but heavy losses were resumed thereafter, as shown in Figure 6.2, which is taken from a summary of the published accounts compiled by the company's accountant. These were especially severe at Japanese ports. In the years 1920–7, the Tokyo, Yokohama and Kobe branches returned an overall loss of £184 000.[37] This was principally due to the decline of the company's import–export business as a result of the increasing popularity among the Japanese of dealing directly with overseas suppliers and customers.

In 1927 Dodwell & Co. Ltd, now headed by Carlill after the death of his founding partner in 1925, decided to act as agent only (rather than principal) in respect of its imports into Japan. Fluctuations in exchange rates with China and the overall decline in value of the Chinese dollar contributed to the substantial losses of the 1930s. These were worsened by a particularly heavy set-back – the failure of the Sanitas Mineral Water Factory, originally purchased in 1932, which occurred at a time when the Shanghai tea trade was losing heavily. The Shanghai branch recovered just before the Second World War with the gaining of agencies for Glaxo products, Aspro, Kiwi polish and Libby's canned foods.[38] Details of the background to the 'Gershevich' losses of 1931–2, referred to by the company's accountant as amounting to £31 700 have proved impossible to trace, but it would seem that Dodwell's was again suffering at the hands of an unscrupulous employee. The immediate pre-1939 recovery of most of the branches ensured that Dodwell's was well placed to face the upheavals of the early 1940s. This was especially due to the growth of Hong Kong into a modern city with its thriving consumer market. Motors were especially in demand, and this section of Dodwell's activities eventually led to a separate company. The survival of Dodwell & Co. Ltd in the 1920s and 1930s was achieved by building-up a large reserve fund of nearly £300 000 in the first two decades of the twentieth century and the reduction of the capital value of the company from £300 000 to £144 000. The failure of Dodwell & Co. Ltd to pay a dividend in all but three years (1923, 1937 and 1938) between 1920 to 1938, when they had paid 30 per cent in 1917 and 1918 appears to have been accepted by shareholders without undue opposition because the majority of them were either members of the Dodwell family (39.5 per cent) or past and present staff (24.5 per cent).

The impact of Dodwell's on British trade with the Far East from the mid-nineteenth to the mid-twentieth centuries had an importance which is not reflected in published research in this field. The company's significance in this period was largely the result of the personal contribution of Dodwell himself. Not only did he contribute to the increased profits of the shipping department of his firm, Adamson Bell & Co., but he played a prominent part in the shipping world as a whole, shown by his selection as a witness to the 1909 Royal Commission on Shipping Rings. He assisted in the expansion of his firm's trade with Japan, and one of his greatest achievements was the inauguration of a Pacific steamship service which was to lead to a vast business in passengers and freight from the Far East to American and Canadian ports on the Pacific. In assuming the direction of his firm after its bankruptcy, he continued expanding his activities, despite losing the CPR agency. His position as a shipping-agent, rather than as a shipowner or shipbuilder, enabled him to take a short-term interest in many varied commodities and services on a surprisingly small capital base: as a constant middleman he was not tied to a particular company, port or commodity, and could spread his risks widely.

V

Gibb Livingston's and Gilman's may be seen as smaller, yet similar, enterprises. Both were also substantially involved in the shipment of tea from Shanghai and Foochow in the 1870s. Statistics are hard to come by but in 1876 and 1877, for which we have figures, Gibb's exported over 12 000 chests from Foochow out of a total of over 740 000 in the former year and just over 13 000 out of a total of nearly 645 000 in the latter year. (Gilmans sent out just over 31 000 and over 18 500 respectively). In each of these years, Adamson Bell shipped about 53 000 chests, as shown in Table 6.1. From Shanghai, Gibbs exported nearly 20 000 chests out of a total of 710 000 in 1876 and just under 10 000 out of a total of 644 000 in 1877 (the comparable figures for Gilmans were 15 000 and 1000 respectively). Adamson Bell carried 81 000 and 96 000 chests in these years. Details of shipments by Butterfield and Swire from Foochow (63 000 in 1876 and 25 000 in 1877) and Shanghai (39 000 in 1876 and 3500 in 1877) show that this company was more important in this trade than Adamson Bell in only one of these years at Foochow alone. Similarly Jardine Matheson & Co. shipped only marginally more chests from Foochow in 1876 (57 000) and less in 1877 (40 600). At Shanghai, they were far eclipsed by Adamson Bell.

Richard James Gilman, A. J. H. Carlill of Adamson Bell & Co. and John Darby Gibb became members of China's circle of *chazees*, the term used for British and American tea-tasters. The new crop of teas each year was first marketed at Hankow, where the *chazees* vied for the choicest varieties at a forty-foot long tasting-counter. Close contact was maintained with the London and New York headquarters of each merchant house by cable, yet the *chazees* exercised considerable individual discretion in their deals. For example, in 1879 as the new season's crops were coming on the market, cables from London and New York reported that public taste now favoured Indian and Ceylon blends, and that the demand for China teas had fallen dramatically. These three prominent *chazees* were reluctant to believe these rumours, and Carlill particularly bought up large stocks of the choicest teas, the prices of which had fallen to a record low. When London and New York reports proved false and the market suddenly improved, they were able to make record profits, and enhance their reputations as especially shrewd buyers.[39]

Gibb Livingston's and Gilman's were also active in the import–export business and shipping-agency work. In 1872, the former was appointed Lloyd's Agent at Shanghai, and had already appeared in the pages of the *China Mail* and *North China Herald* as an agent for sailing ships and steamers.[40] In 1868, for example, it had acted as agent for the *Fusi Yama*, a 556 ton sailing ship owned by Killick Martin & Co. of London, on her arrival at Hong Kong with a general cargo of iron, other metals, cottons, yarns, beer, wine, brandy, sugar, paints, haberdashery, canvas, cordage, glassware, oilman's stores, stationery, perfumes, leather, saddlery, fabrics, furniture, guns and matches.[41] In 1883, whilst acting for the Ben Line of steamships, Gibb Livingston's was the consignee of sixteen shiploads of goods, mainly comprising coal, timber and sundries, arriving at Shanghai, from London, Sydney, New York, Japan and from other Chinese ports.[42] Unlike Dodwell's in this early period, it acquired its own tea clippers, and in 1899 purchased a fleet of steamers which subsequently sailed as the Gibb Line. Gibb Livingston's was initially employed in the Far Eastern coastal trade, but was later used in the transport of native labour to the South African diamond mines. When this trade was prohibited by the South African Government, the ships could no longer find profitable employment and were promptly sold.[43]

Gilman's achieved the distinction of representing Lloyd's on a larger scale and at an earlier date than Gibb's. In 1862 it was appointed agent at Canton, Hankow, Foochow, Hong Kong and Macau.[44] In the first three months of 1873, it handled ten consignments of goods arriving at Shanghai.[45] Like Gibb's, company tradition maintains that the company owned a number of ships, but no actual records survive. Its reputation in shipping circles in these ports, however, was considerable, especially after the famous China tea race of 1866. Gilman's chartered the *Taeping* (which was the first part of the firm's Chinese name, 'Taeping Yeung Hong', 'Great Peace Foreign Firm') which beat the rival ship *Ariel* by twenty minutes after a voyage of ninety-nine days from Foochow to London.[46]

Both firms were important local insurance company agents. Gibb's at its formation in 1836, had been a founder-member of the Union Insurance Society of Canton, and represented the Imperial Fire Insurance Co. from 1864. By the end of the nineteenth century, Gibb's had acquired agencies for no fewer than 120 marine insurance companies from all parts of the world. Gilman's was agent for the North British and Mercantile Insurance Company from 1872, and was also to extend this aspect of its business.

VI

Before the Second World War, both firms diversified their operations. Gilman's had played an important part in promoting the Hong Kong and Shanghai Banking Corporation when it was originally formed in 1864, and maintained personal representation on its Board throughout this period. Warnings from London about the growing preference for Indian and Ceylon teas were soon to prove only too valid. Gilmans' concentration on the China tea business was thus disastrous. Heavily indebted to its London agent, Ashton & Co., the firm came close to bankruptcy. It had to abandon its Shanghai and Hankow branches in the 1880s. The agency for the Australian Sandalwood Company helped in its subsequent recovery, for there was an enormous demand for the manufacture of joss sticks in Southern China. Gilman's was eventually taken over in 1917 by Duncan Paterson of Perth, Western Australia, and converted into a private limited company, incorporated in Hong Kong. Its business was again severely shaken during the Depression after the First World War, aggravated by local political unheaval, but the backing of the Hong Kong and Shanghai Banking Corporation enabled the company to prosper and expand until the Japanese occupation of December 1941. In this it was helped by the strong leadership of Geoffrey Miskin and Cedric Blaker, who had been appointed director in 1919, and who headed Gilman's until 1947 and 1958 respectively.[47]

Gibb Livingston's diversified earlier and more successfully than Gilman's. By 1908, it was widely described as 'one of the most important and best known merchant houses' of Hong Kong where, as at Shanghai, it had specialised first in shipping, then in insurance. Its new interests by the turn of the century included the Hong Kong Electric Company (from 1884) and the Shanghai Land Investment Company (from 1886). In Hong Kong it acted as agent for the Government of British North Borneo, the Shanghai Gas Co. Ltd, the Shanghai Tug and Lighter Co. Ltd and the Weihaiwei Land and Building Co. Ltd, in addition to its many traditional agencies. By the early twentieth century, it had branched out into engineering and manufacturing. Like many expatriate merchant houses, it took an active interest in municipal affairs and local institutions.[48]

Gibb's was the last of these three businesses to seek limited company status (in 1920) and, like Gilman's but unlike Dodwell's, was acquired by other concerns. In this process, Gibb's became associated with Inchcape family interests at an early date, when it was acquired by Gray Dawes & Co. in 1921. Its assured position in shipping and insurance and successful diversification into a wide range of activities gave it a solid foundation in this region to survive the abandoning of its China offices during the Second World War.[49]

VII

Caldbeck's may be seen as exceptional among Inchcape enterprises in this region through its exclusive specialisation in wines and spirits. Its reliance on this trade was justified, as its business quickly thrived. From its original base in Shanghai in 1864, Caldbeck's opened branches all along the China coast in the following decades, with early outposts at Peking and Tientsin doing particularly well. By 1882, a London office was established, Macgregor Caldbeck & Co., and before the First World War, the firm also had a booming trade at the ports of Hong Kong, Singapore, Kuala Lumpur and Penang.[50] The opening of the Hong Kong branch in 1889 was partly the result of the great popularity of horse-racing among the Taipans. Dodwell had been strongly discouraged from taking part in this sport, as we have seen, but it was not necessarily injurious to mercantile activities, because the original partners, Caldbeck and Macgregor, were able to investigate the potential of Hong Kong as a market for wines and spirits through their annual visits for racing.[51]

Before the First World War, Caldbeck's had established a reputation as 'the largest and best known [firm] in the wine and spirit trade in the East'. It quickly built up an extensive business not only with the expatriate and local communities through supplying clubs, hotels and prominent individuals, but through contracts with military and naval authorities. From the first of these in 1878, it had supplied more than 150 British men-of-war by the end of the first decade of the twentieth century, approximately fifty military messes and nearly 100 US warships in the same period.

Its popularity rested on three features of its business. First, it was prepared to supply customers on the understanding that they would be fully reimbursed for unconsumed stocks returned in good order. Second, it was able to tap the market for mineral water and 'palatable non-alcoholic beverages' through its subsidiary, the Aquarius Mineral Water Co., which produced 'Brisk' aerated water, 'Silent' still water, soda water, a sarsaparilla, ginger beer, tonic water and lemonade. Third, its representation of a wide range of top-quality wines and spirits ensured a steady demand. In champagne alone, the firm could offer a choice between Pommery & Greno, Bollinger, Duc de Montebello, Lanson, Dufaut and others. Its branch in Glasgow kept it supplied with a similarly large range of whiskies[52] – it held one of the oldest agencies in the world for Johnnie Walker Scotch.[53] Unlike Gilman's and Gibb Livingston's, this business was very much a family concern. Jack Caldbeck died in 1908 but a year earlier John Macgregor's son Jack, having learned about the wine trade in Germany and France, came out to the East to run the Hong Kong business. When John Macgregor died in 1916, Jack took over the management of the entire firm. In 1920 a private limited company was formed, eventually to 'go public' in 1929, under the Companies' Ordinance of Hong Kong. Business continued to prosper after the First World War, with Jack Macgregor's two sons, Robin and Ian, following in his footsteps, gaining experience of the wine trade in Europe before coming out to join him in the 1930s. Family control disappeared only in the late 1960s.[54]

*   *   *

These four Far Eastern enterprises, particularly Dodwell's, have a valid claim to prominence in this region at least equal to Jardine Matheson. By the Second World War, the celebrated EWO, as Jardine's was popularly known, was involved not only in shipping, tea, and the import–export trade, but in brewing, and in owning textile mills. A recently-produced commemorative history dwells much on its close relationship with the local communities but little on the level of profitability achieved.[55] The discovery of the Dodwell archives, especially concerning shipping tonnage handled and chests of tea exported, helps to establish their relative importance.

NOTES

1. These include Kwang-Ching Lui, 'British–Chinese Steamship Rivalry in China, 1873–1885', in C. D. Cowan (ed.) *The Economic Development of China and Japan* (London, 1964) pp.49–75; G. C. Allen and A. Donnithorne, *Western Enterprise in Far Eastern Economic Development* (London, 1954); S. Marriner and F. E. Hyde, *The Senior; John Samuel Swire, 1825–1898* (Liverpool, 1967); F. E. Hyde, *Blue Funnel: A History of Alfred Holt and Company of Liverpool, 1865 to 1914* (Liverpool, 1956) and *The Far Eastern Trade, 1860–1914* (London, 1973); D. R. McGregor, *The China Bird; the History of Captain Killick and One Hundred Years of Sail and Steam* (London, 1961); and M. Keswick (ed.) *The Thistle and the Jade; a Celebration of Jardine Matheson & Co.* (London, 1982).

2. Hsiao Liang-lin, *China's Foreign Trade Statistics 1864–1949* (Cambridge, Massachusetts, 1974) p.202.
3. S. Ville, 'James Kirton, Shipping Agent', *Mariner's Mirror* 67 (1981) pp.149–62.
4. *Inchcape Archives [IA]*, DOD 5/3, miscellaneous file including correspondence to and from G. B. Dodwell, 1872–1925.
5. *Royal Commission on Shipping Rings, Parliamentary Papers*, 1909, XLVIII, evidence of G. B. Dodwell, qq.18872–80.
6. Allen and Donnithorne, *Western Enterprise*, p.23. See also S. R. Brown, 'The Transfer of Technology to China in the Nineteenth Century: The Role of Direct Foreign Investment', *Journal of Economic History*, 39 (1979) pp.181–97.
7. *IA*, DOD 6/3, notebook of B. G. Dodwell, pp.104–6.
8. See Kwang-Ching Lui, 'British–Chinese Steamship rivalry', pp.49–75.
9. *IA*, DOD 6/3, notebook of G. B. Dodwell, pp.120–1.
10. Arrangements were made annually in London by Adamson Bell & Co. in conjunction with the American firm Russell & Co. (later to become Shewan Tomes & Co.) with steampship owners interested in the trade from China and Japan to New York, Dodwell's evidence, *RC on Shipping Rings*, q.18776.
11. A. S. J. Baster, 'Origins of the British Exchange Banks in China', *Economic History*, III (1934) pp.140–50.
12. See Pao Kuang Yung, 'The Compradore; His Position in the Foreign Trade of China', *Economic Journal*, 21 (1911) pp.636–41; Yen p'ing Hao, *The Compradore in Nineteenth Century China; Bridge between East and West* (Cambridge, Massachusetts, 1970); and T. Rawski, 'Chinese Dominance of Treaty Port Commerce', *Explorations in Economic History*, 7 (1969–70), which includes a revisionist view of compradores.
13. Marriner and Hyde, *The Senior*, pp.115–17.
14. This company, now known as Gellatly Hankey & Co. Ltd was acquired by the Inchcape Group in 1983.
15. McGregor, *The China Bird*, p.180.
16. Allen and Donnithorne, *Western Enterprise*, p.23.
17. *Japan Weekly Mail*, Shipping Intelligence at Yokohama, 1878.
18. *North China Herald*, Shipping Arrivals and Departures at Shanghai, 1883.
19. Allen and Donnithorne, *Western Enterprise*, p.200.
20. *Japan Mail Summary*, Shipping Intelligence at Yokohama, 1889.
21. Ibid, 1892.
22. *RC on Shipping Rings*, qq.18787–9.
23. *IA*, DOD 5/2, letters and memoirs relating to the history of the company, miscellaneous.
24. Marriner and Hyde, *The Senior*, p.123.
25. *IA*, DOD 5/3, memo written on the death of Dodwell by A. J. H. Carlill. See G. Musk, *Canadian Pacific; the Story of the Famous Shipping Line* (Newton Abbot, 1981).
26. *RC on Shipping Rings*, qq.18947–8.
27. *IA*, DOD 5/1, letters and memoirs relating to the history of the company, miscellaneous.
28. *RC on Shipping rings*, q.18944.

29. *IA*, DOD 5/1, memoirs of J. P. Dowling.
30. Ibid.
31. Ibid, memoirs of O. M. Poole.
32. *IA*, DOD 1/24 share ledger no. 1, 1899, Dodwell's personal wealth is shown by his beneficent donations and foundations – see his obituary in the *West Herts and Watford Observer*, 12 October 1925. The Probate Registry records that he left £77 860.
33. *IA*, DOD 3/1, reports and accounts, from 1899.
34. A. W. Kirkaldy, *British Shipping; its History, Organisation and Importance* (1914) pp.189–91.
35. Dodwell & Co. Ltd, *The House of Dodwell*, p.14.
36. Ibid, pp.88–9.
37. *IA*, DOD 3/1, reports and accounts, from 1899.
38. Dodwell & Co. Ltd, *The House of Dodwell*, p.49.
39. Ibid, pp.37–8.
40. See notes 17 and 18.
41. McGregor, *The China Bird*, pp.94–5.
42. *North China Herald*, Shipping Arrivals and Departures at Shanghai, 1883.
43. Simon Jensen, 'The Inchcape Group in Hong Kong', *Hong Kong Tatler*, May (1978) pp.50–1.
44. George Rawdon, 'Gilman & Co. Ltd', *Hong Kong Tatler* July (1980) p.48.
45. *China Mail*, Shipping Movements, January–March 1873.
46. Rawdon, 'Gilman & Co. Ltd', p.48.
47. P. J. Griffiths, *A History of the Inchcape Group* (London, 1977) pp.148–50.
48. A. Wright (ed.) *Twentieth Century Impressions of Hong Kong, Shanghai and other Treaty Ports, etc.* (London, 1908) pp.216, 607.
49. Griffiths, *A History of the Inchcape Group*, pp.141–2.
50. Jensen, 'The Inchcape Group in Hong Kong', p.53.
51. Colin N. Crisswell, *The Taipans: Hong Kong's Merchant Princes* (Hong Kong, 1981) pp.204–5.
52. Wright, *Twentieth Century Impressions*, pp.214, 586, 596, 646.
53. *Inchcape Magazine*, 17 (1984) pp.10–11.
54. Jensen, 'The Inchcape Group in Hong Kong', p.53.
55. Keswick, *The Thistle and the Jade*, pp.204–212.

NOTE: A version of this chapter was presented at Professor T. C. Barker's seminar in Modern Economic and Social History at the Institute of Historical Research, University of London, in the Autumn of 1984. This was subsequently published in *The Journal of Transport History*, Third Series, volume 6, number 1 (March 1985) pp.23–40. It appears again with the permission of the editor.

APPENDIX 6.1   INCHCAPE COMPANIES IN THE AMERICAN CONTINENT

Chapter 6 has shown how Dodwell's, from an early date, expanded by opening branches on the Pacific coast of the USA and Canada. The Group, since its formation, has taken much interest in this region, and it has become a source of regret that a more prominent place in American and Canadian trading networks has not been established. Nevertheless, a number of footholds have been developed, in Canada through the Borneo Company and Dodwell's, in San Francisco and the Pacific Islands with the acquisition of Atkins Kroll & Co. Ltd in 1974, and in South America with Balfour Williamson in 1981. With the acquisition of the Borneo Company in 1967, the Group gained two Canadian-based subsidiaries, the Edmonton Concrete Block Co. Ltd and its associated company, Universal Concrete Accessories Ltd. The former soon proved a liability rather than an asset, with strikes by construction workers in 1968–9 slowing down the demand for its building material products. This, together with heavy competition from larger companies, led to the decision to sell out.

The Canadian Great Lakes' transport business was seen as potentially much more profitable, so a new company, Incan Marine Ltd, was formed in 1973, jointly by Inchcape (with a 60 per cent share) and Canadian Pacific (40 per cent). Only a year later, the new firm won a valuable contract to operate rail car transport from Thunder Bay on Lake Superior to Superior, Wisconsin, USA. This and related contracts involved the construction of marine terminals and the chartering of vessels between New Brunswick and Newfoundland. Prompted by the need to build a specialist vessel in the case of one particular contract, Incan Ships Ltd was formed, with Inchcape holding a 57 per cent stake. Meanwhile, although the Edmonton Concrete Block Co. Ltd had been disposed of, Universal Concrete Accessories Ltd was still a worthwhile concern, so Inchcape Canada Ltd, the overall holding company, acquired a complementary business, Ammo Power Tools Co. Ltd. Through the acquisition of Dodwell's, shipping agency work, light engineering imports, and the retailing of business machines has been added to the Group's Canadian interests.[1]

Atkins Kroll may be seen as an especially appropriate addition to the Group. It was engaged in shipping and trading (traditional Group activities) on the west coast of the USA, in the Philippines, Guam and Micronesia (new places). Only in Singapore did both Inchcape and Atkins Kroll overlap. The original partnership of G. H. Atkins and Clifton H. Kroll set up in business in San Francisco in 1906, and shipping agents in the Pacific trade. Ship chartering led to shipowning, and by about 1920 the Atkins Kroll fleet numbered forty-nine vessels, carrying petroleum products to Australia and New Zealand and returning to San Francisco via the Philippines, Guam and the South Sea Islands with cargoes of copra. These graceful old schooners, which included the 180-foot three-masted *Palawan*, slowly gave way to regular steamer services.

Meanwhile, Atkins and Kroll had established a number of trading outposts. In Guam, where they set up a branch in 1914, it was the first company to be incorporated. This business thrived, despite the small local population, although the firm's attempt to establish a copra plantation was unsuccessful. In 1917, it formed a subsidiary company in the Philippines, and maintained interests in other South Pacific territories, including the more remote island groups acquired by the USA after the Spanish American War.

The sons of G. H. Atkins, David and Ernest, worked as mining engineers, and through them the company became well known as a supplier of tungsten and quicksilver. The company also handled copra, wood, and vegetable oils, shells and spices. Even in their most far-flung territories, the partners imported early models of Chevrolets and Model T Fords. They held one of the earliest overseas dealerships of General Motors, and certainly were the first car and truck dealers in Guam. These activities were developed during and after the First World War, when the firm also invested in a large ranch in the California Delta region which produced celery, tomatoes, potatoes and asparagus. This investment became an important insurance policy when the import–export business was drastically curtailed during the Second World War.

By the mid-1970s, when it joined the Group, Atkins Kroll employed more than 400 people in California, the Philippines, Guam, Micronesia and Singapore, dealing in imports and exports (particularly in the building trade), office equipment (including Remington typewriters) and mining tools, with annual sales making over US $30m. Subsequently the firm closed its San Francisco and Philippine offices, but its gain of the valuable Toyota franchise in Guam and Micronesia has maintained the company's prosperity.[2]

With its venture into South America in 1981, increased in scale in 1983, the Group was again branching out into a new geographical territory but, in accordance with traditional Inchcape policy, it restricted itself to the familiar activities of shipping and trading. The original partners (typically two young Scots) Alexander Balfour and Stephen Williamson, had set up in business to trade between Liverpool and South America in 1851 with a capital of only £5000. In 1853, Williamson established their first overseas branch in Valparaiso, where imports of textiles, chemicals, paint and wines were received from Liverpool in return for wool, nitrates and guano, the fertiliser derived from bird droppings. Despite the difficulties in communication between the partners imposed by such a long distance, their business expanded dramatically, especially as a result of the Californian gold rush of 1869. By the 1870s, branches had been opened in Chile and Peru, and a fleet of at least twenty ships had been acquired.

As in the case of G. B. Dodwell, who had been warned by his employers against horse-racing, the partners insisted that indulging in intoxicating liquors was strictly forbidden. This was somewhat at odds with Stephen Williamson's advice to his son Archibald, on his departure for Chile in 1882: 'as a salesman, several things are wanted . . . enthusiasm, good manners and good temper, and a high estimate of the value of the commodity you offer', because a prominent part of the firm's business was the import of sherry, port and whisky. They refused to be daunted by political upheaval, the senior Williamson advising his managers in Chile during the Revolution of 1891 that 'you may have a few riots and then all will go on again as before – only a cool head is wanted'.

By the time of Williamson's death in 1901, the firm's capital had risen from £5000 to more than £1m. The firm had established a number of nitrate mining companies, opened a new branch in Argentina, and by 1912 was developing an oil exploration business in Peru through the purchase of Milne and Company whose senior partner, Alexander Milne, had begun a search ten years earlier and discovered the first successful oil-well in Peru. An unintentional acquisition was that of Easter Island, which was taken over as a bad debt, and a local manager was installed to develop sheep-farming. It prospered by accident, too, through dealing with the German navy during the First World War, not knowing that war had broken out. Meanwhile, the partnership developed its own banking facilities, acting as a small merchant bank. As such, it was attractive to the Bank of London and South America, who took over its banking business in 1960.

Balfour Williamson's Canadian interests, which had developed after the First World War, were acquired by Dalgety, and its confirming house business went to Lonrho. Inchcape then purchased its South American trading interests which, concerned with the import–export trade, vehicle assembly and distribution, dealing in agricultural machinery, shipping, insurance and bottling, fitted in well with the Group's existing business and gave it a wider geographical spread.[3]

NOTES TO APPENDIX 6.1

1. *History of Acquisitions* [*HA*] Notes on Canada; P. J. Griffiths, *A History of the Inchcape Group* (London, 1977) pp.182–3, and *Inchcape Magazine*, 7 (1977) pp.6–7.

2. P. J. Griffiths, *History*, pp.184–6, and *Inchcape Magazine*, 3 (1975) pp.4–9, and 18 (1984) p.10.

3. *Inchcape Magazine*, 13 (1982), pp.11–12, and Wallis Hunt, *Heirs of Great Adventure: The History of Balfour Williamson and Company Limited*, vol. I 1851–1901 and vol. II 1901–1951 (London, 1951).

194

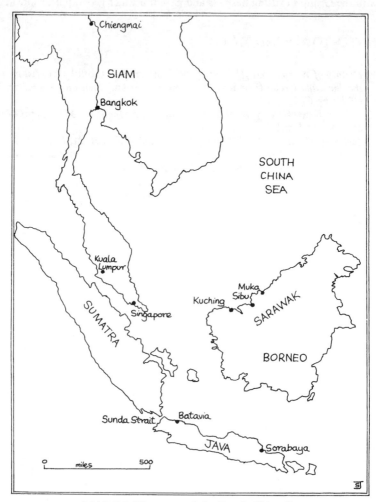

MAP 7.1 The ports of the South China Seas

7 Merchants in the South China Seas: The Borneo Company Limited and the Anglo-Thai Corporation, c.1870 to 1939

Although relatively recent acquisitions of the Inchcape Group, the Borneo Company Ltd and the Anglo-Thai Corporation, which operate principally in the areas now known as Malaysia, Indonesia and Thailand, may be seen as having much in common with the Group's founder companies in India, the Gulf and East Africa. All these businesses played a vital role in the development and expansion of the trade of these regions with the rest of the world. As general merchants and import–export agents, these companies enjoyed a prominent position among other foreign, and local, trading firms in the respective areas. Most remarkable in this context was the monopoly secured by the Borneo Company in the economic exploration of Sarawak, where the firm thrived through its unique relationship with the three generations of the English Brooke family who ruled this 'colony' as the locally-appointed Rajahs.

Table 7.1 and Figure 7.1 show the increasing – although at times fluctuating – turnover and profits of these companies. This was a result

TABLE 7.1 Performance of the Borneo Company Limited, surviving accounts
1872–1920

Year	Profit for distribution and reserves (£s)	Dividend on ord. shares (% p.a.)
1872	42 117	12½
1873	26 088	?
1874	39 803	15
1906	93 511	25
1907	71 482	25
1911	47 767	15
1912	87 093	20
1914	114 837	25
1915	89 569	20
1916	113 078	20
1917	177 415	25
1918	126 856	25
1919	167 160	30
1920	41 264	20

SOURCE *Inchcape Archives*, BCL, Reports and Accounts, 1872–4, 1906–7, 1911–20.
(Year ending 31 October.)

of the expansion of the firms' major interests: gold and other minerals in
Sarawak; teak in Siam; imports and exports of the region, together with
shipowning and shipping-agency work. How great was the overall
impact of these two companies on the economic expansion of their
respective spheres of influence, especially compared with other Western
firms?

I

The successful exploitation of the gold deposits of Sarawak was to
dominate the Borneo Company's profits from the mid-1880s to the
closing of the principal mines in the 1920s. These profits enabled them to
bear temporary losses in other activities and to expand their operations
as a whole. Ludwig Verner Helms, whose part in the early development
of this country is discussed in Chapter 1, described the extent of
Sarawak's mineral riches in a letter he wrote in 1869 to the President of
the Royal Geographical Society:

The soil in the entire limestone district is more or less impregnated
with Gold from veins which have been washed away and become

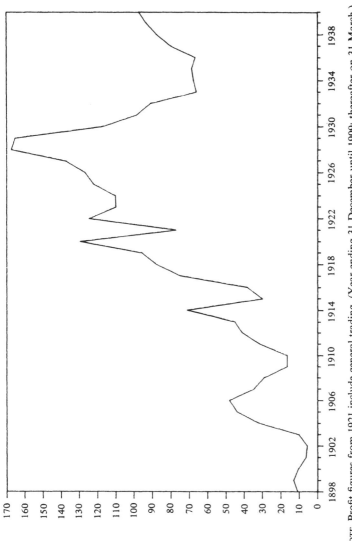

NOTE Profit figures from 1921 include general trading. (Year ending 31 December until 1909; thereafter on 31 March.)

SOURCE *Inchcape Archives*, A–T, Reports and Accounts, 1889–1940. In 1897 the company was incorporated in England.

FIGURE 7.1 The performance of the Siam Forest Co. (after 1918, the Anglo-Siam Corporation) 1898–1940

decomposed. The limestone hills, some of which are nearly a thousand feet in height, and contain grand and extensive caves, are traversed in various directions by mineral dykes of great extent, running for miles in an East and West direction. The ore is richest when still undisturbed and solid in the limestone.[1]

The main stumbling block to the Borneo Company's efforts to extract these riches was a large group of over a thousand Chinese immigrants who had settled before the arrival of the Europeans in the gold-mining district of Bau, where they laboriously washed the ores to produce the gold. They formed a totally separate community with their own culture and habits, drinking tea and *samsu* (a spirit distilled from rice), smoking tobacco and opium and frequenting their gambling dens. They worked hard and played hard, unlike the less active and enterprising Dayaks and Malays who, according to Helms, 'work little and require little'.[2]

The Rajah, anxious to develop his territory commercially and especially to recoup at least a part of his personal fortune which had been quickly expended in his early years as ruler, was reluctant to disturb the Chinese, particularly as their vices made them so easy to tax. They had been paying tax at a rate of 100 per cent on sixty balls of opium per month. When consumption fell to half this amount, the Rajah demanded the same monthly payment as before. He had gone too far. This contributed to a bloody uprising in 1857. After the murder of a young consultant metallurgist attached to the Borneo Company (whose decapitated head was suspended from the ramparts, below the Borneo Company flag, at the Rajah's wooden fort at Kuching), the company despatched a schooner, the *Waterlily* from its Singapore branch with arms, ammunition and food supplies. This helped considerably in quelling the insurrection, leaving the Borneo Company in a strong position to take over the gold workings. By 1884, the largest and last Chinese syndicate at the gold-mines, the Kongsis, had been bought out.[3]

The Borneo Company enthusiastically pioneered the development of an experimental process involving the use of cyanide in dissolving the gold from the ore. Its engineers improved the practical application of this invention, being the first in the Far East to employ it. This replaced the previous costly and time-consuming process by which the microscopic grains of gold were washed from the ores: 'crushers, steam saws, and the clatter of an engineering shop, combined with the rushing of water, made a continuous roar without a moment's cessation'.[4] Peter Duguid Thomson, sent out from the London office inspired and sustained this work,[5] vowing on his departure that he would not return home unless he made a greater success of the Company's gold-mining ventures.[6]

This and the search for further gold deposits was carried out at this time in close consultation with the Rajah who showed considerable understanding and sympathy, revealed in a letter to the local manager in 1900:

My dear Harvey, In reply to yours of today, as to securing your rights over search for gold for the rest of Sarawak, south of Baram – This if I do not make mistake is laid down in concession – viz – to work any reef or reefs after six months notice given by Govt. should gold in quantity be discovered – but I do not push so that you shall not have reasonable time to work from one place to another – I will look over terms of concession tomorrow. Yours sincerely, (signed) C. Brooke, Rajah.[7]

Such co-operation worked both ways: in 1896 the Rajah had written to the London headquarters, requesting that the brother of a friend already in Sarawak be offered 'an appointment under his brother in the work of Mining – on a salary of £12 a month' and 'if he accepts he is to be sent out 2nd. class to Singapore'.[8]

All these activities resulted in greater output and profit for the company's monopoly. Figure 7.2 shows the value of gold exported annually in Sarawak dollars (note fluctuations in its rate of exchange against the £). The impact of the Borneo Company from 1898 is clear. Annual gold production exceeded Sarawak $1m in value in the period 1901–16. Until 1921 when it was flooded and no longer workable, the Tai Parit Mine at Bau alone produced 496 225 fine ounces of gold from 2m tons of ore, estimated as worth over £2¼m.[9]

The Borneo Company's gold-mining activities in Sarawak bestowed considerable benefits on the community. Between the 1880s and the 1920s, the government received over £200 000 in royalties and workers in the gold-mines were paid more than £2m in wages. This helped to stimulate further economic activity in the region, including the extraction of other minerals, such as diamonds, antimony, silver, copper and cinnabar (mercury ore), which occurred near the gold. As Helms wrote, 'such a variety of valuable minerals within so small a district is perhaps unprecedented'.[10]

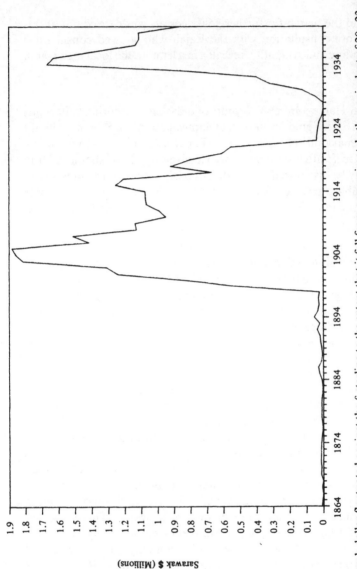

NOTE Sarawak dollar fluctuated against the £ sterling to the extent that it fell from approximately the equivalent of 20–23p in the 1860s to 1890s to the equivalent of only 8p in 1903, and was fixed at 12p in 1906.

SOURCE G. E. Wilford, 'Gold Deposits of the Bau Area, West Sarawak', reprinted from *The Geology and Mineral Resources of the Kuching – Landau Area including the Bau Mining District*, 1955, Memoirs of the Geological Survey Department, British Territories in Borneo.

FIGURE 7.2 Gold exports from Sarawak, 1864–1940

7.1 The first Rajah of
Sarawak, Sir James
Brooke, who ruled
the country from
1841 to 1868

7.2 The second Rajah, Charles Brooke,
who ruled until 1917

7.3 The last Rajah, Charles Vyner Brooke, who was deposed in 1946

II

The Company's role in the import and export trades of Kuching, Sarawak's capital, was also profitable to it and to the inhabitants as a whole. Besides the import of goods from Britain, local products were sought out and marketed by the Company. The Minute Books, kept in London, record that the firm dealt in sago, oil, pepper, tea, hides, coconut, rubber, timber and rice.[11] In developing these trades, the primitive nature of the commercial life of Sarawak in the late nineteenth and early twentieth centuries was such that backward linkages in any commodity export took place as a matter of course. These usually involved complex and time-consuming processes, as in sago manufacture, for example. From the early 1860s, after wresting control from immigrant traders as happened in the case of the gold-mines, the sago plantations of Muka Province were taken over by the Borneo Company. Sago was originally obtained from palm trees growing in salt marshes, which had to be cut down and the trunk split in two. The sago, at this stage a creamy, sticky substance, was scraped out from the heart of the tree, dropping on a wooden platform floating on top of a canoe. Water was then poured over it and it was well trodden upon, producing a thick liquid which flowed through a perforated mat covering the platform, into the canoe below, which, when full, was taken to the Company's refinery (founded by Helms). It was then purified for export to the English market, where it was used in glucose production and the traditional sago pudding.[12]

The export of oil was also an important source of income. Unfortunately, earnings from particular commodities cannot be separated in the surviving accounts, but correspondence on the subject with the Rajah suggests that local oil springs yielded large quantities of this valuable mineral. In a letter of 1903, the Rajah forwarded to the Company 'a 5 gallon drum of oil, lately discovered in the Brunei river', requesting a report on its quality and value, revealing that 'about 10 000 gallons' were available, and he intended to ship it to Kuching 'to your care for sale, and also send it to Singapore'. The Rajah helped to maintain the Borneo

7.4 Sarawak: the work of the Sea Dayaks: a row of shrunken heads

Company's monopoly in this commodity by instructing the local authorities to prevent any interested parties, native or European, from visiting the oil spring. For this, he expected to play a large part in the business, sending a copy of the way he proposed 'to manage the sale of oil in the market'. He pointed out the need to obtain extra smiths and iron to make the necessary 5- and 10-gallon drums and insisted that 'one tenth of all oil turned out belongs to the Government'.[13] The Borneo Company was subsequently to act as agent for the Royal Dutch Oil Co. in Sarawak.[14]

The Borneo Company also formed the Sarawak Planting Co. and Sarawak Rubber Estates Ltd. These ventures helped in developing the local economy not only by the marketing of products, but also by the exploration and clearing of unknown parts of the island for settlement and agriculture. Timber was donated for the new bridge built at Chiengmai at the turn of the century, a telephone network was installed and local missions received aid.[15]

The Borneo Company manager at Kuching in 1870, Helms, also acted as British consul. The other principal British inhabitants numbered only eleven – the British Resident, Mr Crookshank and his wife, the local Bishop and his wife, Oliver St John, the Government treasurer, Major Rodway, who commanded the native forces, three young men who formed the Rajah's staff, and the Rajah and Ranee themselves.[16] Of the 82 Europeans residing in Sarawak by 1872, twenty seven were connected with the Borneo company. The Rajah's benevolent rule (particularly that of the Second Rajah) and the direct access to him that was enjoyed by even his most humble subjects, created ideal circumstances for the flourishing of the Borneo Company in this region. Despite occasional differences of opinion, the Rajah maintained that this firm 'has shown a solid and stolid example to other merchants, and has formed a basis for mercantile operations; and the importance of the presence in a new state of such a large and influential body as the Borneo Company Limited cannot be overrated'.[17] The Rajah attended many company business meetings, revealing his close contact with and increasing dependence upon the firm. With the Rajah, they shared the cost of the services of a doctor brought from England,[18] and even acted as his banker. In a letter of 1895, the Rajah showed that he was trying to curb the Ranee's generosity, stating that she should only be allowed to draw on her allowance – 'no other payments to be made to her unless by my signature'.[19]

So strong was this link with the Rajahs, that the monopoly of this company managed to survive heavy outside competition until the end of

Brooke rule and the granting of independence during the Second World War. Evidence of competing companies has proved elusive. A directory of trades and professions in Sarawak in 1873 lists the company's branch officers and the employees at the cinnabar and antimony mines and the sago factory. Local merchants ran general stores, sugar, pepper and gambier estates, farms and brick kilns. The Borneo Company managed the wharves at Kuching and the coal depot. Oya was the base of the Sarawak Trading Company run by Messrs Walters, Crocker & Co, with native assistants, established in 1870, but no other record of this firm has been discovered.[20] A local firm, Tiong Bee Anne & Co. shared the Borneo Company's sago manufacturing rights from 1893.[21] However, the Company's prominence in this 'colony', compared with its other branches, was remarkable.

III

In Siam, its activities were shared with many other Western business concerns. Borneo Company activities in this country, whose opening up to Western commerce is discussed in Chapter 1, included (according to their minute books) rice milling and trading, exporting sugar, salt and tin and wharfage work. The Company represented the Ocean Marine Insurance Company, the National Bank of India, the Asiatic Petroleum Company and Nobel's explosives. The Borneo Company imported from Britain and Europe, calico, metals, marine stores, opium and Spanish dollars. Trading difficulties were encountered for a number of reasons: the absence of both a developed commercial infrastructure and accommodation for visiting merchants; the lack of a pilot service to guide vessels up the treacherous Bangkok river; and the refusal of marine insurance companies to provide cover for vessels sailing in Siamese coastal waters. By the 1870s however, the establishment of four other British commercial houses, together with two German, one French and three American firms, led to improved trading conditions. Yet the Borneo Company showed greater tenacity than their rivals. By the late 1880s, all the other British concerns had left, together with the American houses. Only the German and French firms survived. The Borneo Company has the proud boast that it is the only firm, British or otherwise, to have prospered and grown in Bangkok from the days of King Mongkut in the 1850s. Its steam rice-milling business, which used paddy husk as fuel, became a primary source of income, together with its growing number of insurance agencies (five by the 1920s) and representation of three banks: the Chartered Bank, the Oriental Banking Corporation and the Northern Bank of Scotland.[22]

As in Sarawak, where the Borneo Company enjoyed a close and beneficial relationship with the Rajah, in Siam the firm's contact with King Mongkut and his successors was to their mutual advantage. A celebrated instance of this, recalled in the film *The King and I*, was the appointment by William Adamson, the Singapore manager and Samuel Gilfillan, the Company's first representative in Bangkok,[23] of a schoolmistress to the royal children – Anna Leonowens. Even more remarkable, the company, in 1868, had advised the King on how to maintain the monarchy's stability in the event of his death while his twenty-nine sons and thirty-three daughters were still minors. The King felt a special need for experienced advice. He wrote 'our fertile country of Siam now open to eyes of many powerful foreigners whose power is increasing every day', addressing John Harvey, the managing director of the Borneo Company at this time as 'my worthy private friend'. Harvey outlined a suitable trust deed to protect his children. He also acted as stockbroker, recommending the best (British) investments for royal funds.[24] Another well-known instance of the Borneo Company's continuing harmonious relationship with the Siamese monarchy was their presentation in 1926, of a rare white elephant calf. This creature was regarded as sacred and its birth a good omen to the royal family.

IV

The greatest resource of Siam was undoubtedly its teak forests. In 1845, the Borneo Company extended its interests to Chiengmai and in 1886 opened a branch at Raheng. Louis Leonowens, the son of Anna, obtained leases to extract teak from the Chief of the Province of Lakon, and was to spend eleven years in the Company's service, not always to the firm's benefit.[25] By 1913, the Company's investment in teak exceeded £100 000.[26] A similar sum was invested by a firm which was to concentrate almost wholly in this activity in this period and, with the Borneo Company, is the joint subject of this chapter. The Anglo-Thai Corporation was originally formed in 1884, as the Siam Forest Co. Ltd of Bombay. Figure 7.3 summarises the substantial income it earned from the Siamese timber trade, which enabled them to pay dividends of up to 35 per cent.

The beginnings of the Siam Forest Company lay in the dissatisfaction of the Bombay trading house of Ewart Latham (whose background is

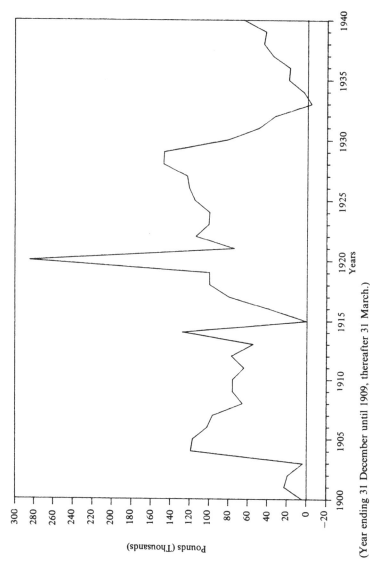

(Year ending 31 December until 1909, thereafter 31 March.)

SOURCE *Inchcape Archives*, ATC Reports and Accounts, 1889–1940. In 1897 the company was incorporated in England.

FIGURE 7.3 Anglo-Siam Corporation (before 1918 the Siam Forest Co.) timber profits, 1900–40

discussed in Chapter 1) with the high prices, poor quality, and inadequate quantity of the Burmese teak supplied to the Indian market by a British monopoly, the Bombay Burmah Trading Co. An enterprising forest surveyor, G. H. Dennis was engaged to explore the possibilities of northern Siam as an alternative source, and following in the footsteps of Leonowens, successfully obtained an extensive lease from the Chief of Lakon, to extract teak from the forests of the Me Ngow river valley.[27] A printed letter prepared by Dennis describes the nature of this lease. It was granted initially for six years and then extended to ten, under the overall authority of the King of Siam. The company agreed to pay a royalty of Rs 4 on long teak timber, Rs 1 on timber less than twelve feet in length and Rs 2 for all other types of tree felled. The full extent of this forest, located 30 miles east of Lakon and approximately 300 miles from Bangkok, was 60 by 35 miles.[28] Roughly 35 000 trees had been girdled by the end of 1885 – a process whereby suitable teak trees were identified and allowed to dry out by making cuts in the bark prior to floating them down river. This is described in the memoirs of a Company forest manager, W. O. Elder, during his first period of service in the years 1902–8:

> Deadly monotonous after a bit, as hour after hour, day after day, perhaps for months on end, soaked to the skin in the rains, or exposed to the rays of a hot weather sun, you systematically explore the countryside in the quest for TEAK. Every hillside, ridge and spur. Nothing must be left to chance, as with the aid of a few native axemen you search out and personally inspect each tree, no matter how inaccessibly placed. So easy to skimp a bit, tempting to cut out this last extra climb when limbs are beginning to weary, or fever has left you weak.[29]

The problems encountered in extracting teak included the handling of precocious elephants, attacks from Dacoits or pirates from the rivers, the difficulties of 'ounging' or keeping timber on the move as it was floated downstream to arrive eventually at Bangkok, forming the timber into rafts for storage at rafting stations, and dealing with customs officials at the forest boundaries where the cut timber was examined, the royalty assessed, and the logs marked accordingly. One of the most backbreaking of all jobs for a European forester in this region came after the floods subsided, when he would tramp up the muddy river and stream beds making a check of the logs that had become stranded. Some logs took years to reach Bangkok.

Profits, as seen in Figure 7.3, were unspectacular in the early years of the century, but the business then took off, especially thanks to the efforts of Elder, the first really successful forest manager. He negotiated additional leases, including that of Me Chune, where a tramway was subsequently constructed. 'I was paying out more than £100 000 a year', he wrote, 'spread over three up-country stations – each four days' journey from the other – before Treasury Notes came to the rescue and simplified payment considerably.'[30] Thus he was liable to armed attack, and thefts were common. Dealing with the Chief of Lakon was not always easy, to say nothing of having to explain his actions to London:

Although entirely uneducated he [the Chief of Lakon] was no fool at business, as I found out during the long negotiations which came to a climax when he and I put our signatures to a contract involving a payment on our part of not less than two hundred thousand ticals (about £20 000) in exchange for the working rights of a Forest lease (Me Tah-Camping district. Very fine timber. We got more than 40 000 logs from this contract). What a flutter there was at Head Office.

7.5 Siam: Siam Forest Company staff supervising the cutting down of teak logs in the forests in the north of Siam

210

7.6 Siam: Louis Leonowens, the son of the famous Anna, who formed a rival company in the pursuit of teak forest leases

7.7 Siam: Robert Henderson Robertson of the Borneo Company, who took
hundreds of unique photographs of Siam in the late nineteenth and early
twentieth centuries. Here, he and his servant Long examine an elephant
with a sore back

£20 000! Was the money properly secured? Were there no loopholes in
the wording of the agreement? Were our interests fully protected?
Hadn't the contract better be drawn by lawyers in Bangkok? But then
they didn't know Tan Chin Piah [Elder's half-Siamese and half-
Chinese head clerk] without whose valued advice I might never have
secured the lease at all, in face of the keen competition of the Bombay
Burmah Company and the Borneo Company.[31]

By the First World War, the Borneo Company had its own sawmill at
Bangkok, over 600 elephants, and enjoyed a steady export trade to
Europe, India and the Far East, as well as the sale of rough-cut timber
locally. The war dislocated trade, but did not adversely affect the
concessions on plant, and a quick recovery was made in the 1920s.[32] The
progress of the Siamese teak trade in the years leading up to the Second
World War may be seen in more detail in the published accounts of the

212

7.8 Siam: a Borneo Company boat approaching the rapids on the Me Ping
River on a journey from Bangkok to Chiengmai

7.9 Siam: a frequent occurrence: a log jam during the movement of the teak to
Bangkok

Siam Forest Company and the comments appended to them by the Chairman, J. M. Ryrie.[33] The poor results before the late 1890s of approximately £2000 profit per year only, were the result, he explained to anxious shareholders, of inadequate working capital, low prices of teak in London and Bombay, the heavy costs of converting the rough logs before the company had its own sawmill, and the difficulties experienced in obtaining elephants to help transport the logs. A low level in the rivers, which often occurred and was totally outside the control of the company, always reduced profits. In 1890, for example, the poor rainfall resulted in a particularly low water level, making the floating of logs almost impossible. Only 1050 logs reached Bangkok, with 9134 left in the rivers and creeks. The only fortunate result of this was that the price of teak in Bangkok and elsewhere then rose because of the diminished supply. During the 1890s, the stock of logs floating to Bangkok and held at rafting stations continued to increase, the chairman insisting that if only they could reach the capital, then profits would be assured. Ironically, an engineers' strike and temporary collapse of shipbuilding at Bangkok in 1897 put paid to these hopes, as this meant that timber cargoes had to be landed incurring extra cost rather than sold whilst floating. Two years' accounts (1897 and 1898) were then combined to present a more statisfactory figure of a profit of £41 430, but in 1898 the firm suffered another reversal when its sawmill burned down. Profits finally improved after 1903 with the reorganisation of the forest workings under Elder, the building of a new and more efficient sawmill, the acquisition of Clarke & Co (a timber business based in Bangkok) in 1908, and a series of good floating seasons and high prices for teak in Europe. Declining profits during the war, especially the dramatic drop from 1914 to 1915, were due to the interruption of trade, heavy investments in a forest tramway, and high shipping costs. Good results were achieved throughout the 1920s, especially in 1920 itself, with the tramway in full operation and large sales of rough-cut timber locally, but the 1930s' Depression hit the firm hard, causing a loss in 1933, when low prices were combined with attacks on the timber by the teredo worm. Yet the company soon recovered and, as seen in Chapter 8, Anglo-Thai (as it became in 1939–40) was to emerge stronger than ever as the twentieth century progressed.

This was partly because of the diversification of this company to encompass other activities. The acquisition of Clarke & Co. brought new sources of income -- from its agencies for mines, insurance companies and banks (as well as saving the agency fees from the Siam Forest Co. itself). Clarke's handled consignments from Europe, and orders for gunny bags from Chinese millers for whom it also chartered steamers. The firm shipped Japanese coal on behalf of Mitsui & Co, opium for the Siamese Government and consignments of sapphires and rubies to Europe; marketed Siamese produce, such as rice, pepper and hides, and imported redwood sleepers for the Siamese railways. Clarke estimated the value of his business at £4 000 per year, and was prepared to sell for shares rather than cash.[34] This acquisition was undoubtedly a bargain, as its earnings helped to maintain overall profits when income from the timber trade was low. Clarke & Co. was expanded in 1910, and when further diversification took place into mining, rubber, tobacco and the general produce trades, it provided valuable experience, which was increased with the acquisition of the Siam Forest Co.'s secretaries and founder-companies, Arbuthnot Ewart & Co, Ewart Latham & Co and Ewart Ryrie & Co. This expansion was recognised in their change of name to the Anglo-Siam Corporation in 1918. Two further developments in the commercial expansion of this firm took them to ports and regions where the Borneo Company was also active: in Singapore, and in India.

V

Singapore, where Anglo-Siam opened a branch in 1920, became another important source of profits, boosting the Corporation's income through the handling of timber exports there and the products of the Siam–Malay Rubber Co. Ltd. Singapore's general trading rose in the early 1920s and the branch did well generally.[35] It was, however, only a sideline to Anglo-Siam, but to the Borneo Company, Singapore was the foundation-stone of the business, whence it had originally branched out to Sarawak and Siam. At this important hub of trade, the Company owned wharves, docks, and a brickworks and developed one of the earliest motor distribution businesses in the East.[36] In 1925 Borneo Motors Ltd was formed from the old motor department, as a result of an enormous expansion in its trade. By the outbreak of the Second World War, this company, through branches all over Malaysia, sold a vast range of motor vehicles – Austin, Vauxhall, Chevrolet, Oldsmobile, Cadillac, Chrysler and Buick, together with trucks, trolley-buses and tractors. Borneo Company employees took a great interest in this activity, organising 'Round the Island' races in Singapore. The first managing director of Borneo Motors was the proud owner of a Styaker-

Squire, which was the first car in Malaysia to be fitted with a disappearing hood and to be sprayed with the new iridescent paint, as opposed to being painted by hand.[37]

VI

India also was a significant source of income to Anglo-Siam. Its founder partnerships were based there, and the involvement of this firm in the subcontinent was expanded through the acquisition, in 1936, of Herbertsons of Karachi, who marketed consumer goods. General trading with India kept profits high throughout the 1920s, and income from this area exceeded that from either Siam, or British Malaya, in the first half of the 1930s.[38] The Borneo Company had also maintained interests, such as the export of sugar, and investment in paper and jute mills, in India from its earliest days. Yet whereas Anglo-Siam came to rely increasingly upon India, the Borneo Company preferred to concentrate on lands further east.

British Malaya, through its importance as a source of rubber and tin, interested both the firms discussed here. In the late 1920s, they opened branches in Penang, Kuala Lumpur, Ipoh and Malacca. Income from this region contributed to Anglo-Siam's profits by as much as a third in the 1930s,[39] and similarly sustained the Borneo Company in this difficult period.[40] The latter was also well-established at the Dutch East Indies port of Batavia, handling a large part of the local import–export trade from the late 1850s. In the same letter as a description of the poor state of the rice trade and a request for more cases of Schweppes' Soda Water, W. Lorrain, the local manager, wrote to his superior, Cadell, in Singapore in 1883 that:

We have been in a dreadful state here owing to the eruption of Krakatoa, distant from this about 110 miles. It began with reports like those of heavy Cannon every one of which made the gas lamps tingle, then every five minutes or so there was a louder report which shook everything in the house. The noise was tremendous and from our verandah we could see signs of the disturbance high in the air . . . Then the natives in the office refused to stay with us any longer. Nothing being able to be done, we shut the office and made a bee line for home. We found the house, garden, and indeed every place about, covered with about an eighth of an inch of burnt sand.[41]

Fortunately, such dramatic happenings were comparatively rare, but it was generally true that the London offices of both Anglo-Siam and the Borneo Company had relatively little conception of life in the branches. Because of the difficulties and slowness of communications, local managers necessarily enjoyed a large measure of autonomy and independence of action. This changed with improvements in transport and telegraphic links throughout the twentieth century. As merchants and traders, both firms were closely involved with the owners of transport, and the Borneo Company in particular was strongly linked to the shipping industry. It was the principal shareholder, and acted as manager, of the Sarawak Steamship Company: a directory of 1870 lists the Company as the owner of the 40-h.p., 97-ton steamer *Sri Sarawak* and the 50-ton schooner *Pioneer*.[42] The Borneo Company was awarded the prestigious Lloyd's Agency at Sarawak in 1874, an honour it already held at Singapore and Bangkok. The company's Minute Books record that, by the Second World War, six shipping concerns were represented by the firm at the latter port: the P & O, BI, NYK, Straits Steamship Co., China Shippers Mutual Co. and Butterfield and Swire,[43] together with fourteen smaller shipping lines, mainly dealing in trans-shipment cargoes. The company benefited from the dramatic rise of British shipping frequenting the port of Bangkok – from only 17 500 tons in 1856 to nearly 400 000 tons by 1925. It also acted as managing agent for the Siam Steam Touring and Navigation Co. Ltd from 1881, carrying passengers to the Chartaboon sapphire mines, and shipping pepper and other coastwise goods. It represented the small Sarawak Government steamers which traded to Singapore, and owned two steamships to carry timber (especially teak) from Bangkok to Bombay, although by the 1920s it became more economical to charter Norwegian ships for this purpose.[44] The Borneo Company's contacts with shipping lines at Singapore were also considerable. In 1871, the largest ship to visit the port that year, the *William Cory*, was consigned by the firm to carry coal.[45] By 1910 they had acquired the agencies for Blue Funnel, the Glen Line, NYK and P & O.[46]

*   *   *

The activities of an informal group of merchants, based in Liverpool, Glasgow and London in the 1830s, 1840s and 1850s, had thus spread to Calcutta and Bombay, to Singapore and thence to Sarawak and Siam to seize the new commercial opportunities offered there, where thriving businesses have been developed and maintained. They survived two

World Wars, and contributed dramatically to the recent growth of the Inchcape Group of Companies. In many respects their story is similar to that of many other elements of the Group: their involvement in the import–export trades and shipping of Sarawak, Siam, Singapore, and many of the ports of India and British Malaya. That they were directed and sponsored from London makes them comparable with the shipping agencies established through Sir William Mackinnon and the BI which were held together and strengthened by the entreprenurial drive of the first Earl of Inchcape and later by his grandson. Yet, although their activities were in many ways similar, they ventured into new regions and new commodities. The overall policy or *modus vivendi* of the Inchcape Group, as outlined in the Introduction and developed in Chapter 10, is that they would venture into a new country following traditional business activities, or try a new operation in familiar surroundings. Thus, it may be seen that from early times, this hallmark of the Group was already being employed. From their original bases, Anglo-Siam and the Borneo Company struck out: the former into a new place with an old interest – teak, and the latter from an established footing, Sarawak, into a new activity – gold-mining. This specialisation in one particular commodity, and the backward and forward linkages they made to exploit to the full the commercial potential of these two valuable trading goods, marks them out from the other Inchcape Companies in the years before the Second World War. Yet the total disruption of the Far East during the years 1939–45, and the successes of the independence movements led to a reduction in the commercial autonomy of these firms. This has caused their diversification almost back to the informal 'anything considered' days of their origins.

NOTES

1. *Inchcape Archives [IA]*, BCL 7/2: L. V. Helms to Sir Roderick Murchison, president of the Royal Geographical Society, dated Sarawak, 20 January 1869.
2. Henry Longhurst, *The Borneo Story: The History of the First Hundred Years of Trading in the Far East by the Borneo Company Limited* (London, 1956) p.25.
3. Ibid, pp.26–31. A detailed description of the rebellion was written by Helms in his *Pioneering in the Far East* (London, 1882).
4. Archdeacon Arthur Sharp, *Wings of the Morning* (London, 1948) quoted by Longhurst, p.67.
5. W. H. Geikie to T. C. Martine, undated, *IA*, BCL 7/2.

6. Extraordinary General Meeting, 29 December 1916, reviewing the success of the Company's gold-mining activities from the 1880s; *IA*, BCL 1/2.
7. HH The Rajah to C. D. Harvey, dated Kuching, 28 August 1900; *IA*, BCL 7/3.
8. HH The Rajah to the Borneo Company Limited, London, dated Kuching, 1 April 1896; *IA*, BCL 7/3.
9. Longhurst, p.69.
10. See note 1. Two accounts of unsuccessful attempts to disrupt the Company's mining operations generally were privately published in the late 1890s by Archibald Allison, an independent prospector in Sarawak. They were entitled 'The Real Wreckers of British Trade and Influence in the East' and 'The Real Pirates of Borneo'.
11. Borneo Company Limited, Board Minutes, vols 1–21, 1856–1941 and file containing index to minutes; *IA*, BCL 1/1–21, 29.
12. Ranee Margaret of Sarawak, undated ms. history, 'Good Morning and Good Night', pp.120–3.
13. HH The Rajah to Borneo Company Limited, Kuching, dated Kuching, 10 April 1903; ditto, 11 April 1903; ditto, 6 April 1903 and HH The Rajah to Borneo Company Limited, London, dated Kuching, 22 July 1898; *IA*, BCL 7/3.
14. Index to minutes, 1856–1953; *IA*, BCL 1/29.
15. Ibid.
16. Ranee Margaret, 'Good Morning and Good night', p.49.
17. S. Baring Gould and C. A. Bampfylde, *A History of Sarawak Under its Two White Rajahs, 1839–1908* (London, 1909) p.426.
18. Index to minutes, 1856–1952, *IA*, BCL 1/29.
19. HH The Rajah to Borneo Company Limited, London, dated Kuching, 22 May 1895; *IA*, BCL 7/3.
20. *The Colonial Directory of the Straits Settlements, including Sarawak, Labuan, Bangkok and Saigon* (Singapore, 1873).
21. Index to minutes, 1856–1952, *IA*, BCL 1/29.
22. The Borneo Company Limited, *Sixty Years Trade in Bangkok, 1856–1926* (Bangkok, 1926) pp.1–6.
23. Longhurst, pp.40, 49–50; and photograph album and scrapbook, 1851–80, which contains copies of the letters of appointment; *IA*, BCL P/32.
24. S. P. P. M. Mongkut R. L. to John Harvey of the Borneo Company Limited, London, dated Bangkok, 3 June 1868 and John Harvey to His Majesty the Supreme King of Siam and Sovereign of Laos, dated London, 25 September 1868; *IA*, BCL 7/4.
25. Longhurst, pp.72–7, and index to minutes, 1856–1952; *IA*, BCL 1/29.
26. Borneo Company Limited, Reports and Accounts, 1913. *IA*, BCL 2/2.
27. Anthony Goodinge, ms. 'History of the Anglo-Thai Corporation Limited, 1834–1971' (1973) pp.9–11.
28. C. H. Dennis, 'Concession of Forest Rights in Siam', printed memo dated Bombay, 10 November 1885; *IA*, ATC 7/1.
29. W. O. Elder, ms. Memoirs written in 1958, p.107. *IA*, ATC 8/1.
30. Ibid, p.143.
31. Ibid, pp.139–40.

32. See note 22.
33. Siam Forest Company Limited and Anglo-Siam Corporation Limited, Reports and Accounts, 1889–1939. *IA*, ATC 2/1. The poor results of the Siamese teak trade of 1890 are also described annually in the Foreign Office annual series of Diplomatic and Consular Reports on Trade and Finance, no. 938 Siam.
34. Frederic S. Clarke to J. M. Ryrie, dated London, 9 May 1899. *IA*, ATC 7/2. See also General Minute Book, 1897–1939. *IA*, ATC 1/1.
35. See note 33.
36. Index to minutes, 1856–1952. *IA*, BCL 1/29.
37. Longhurst, pp.86–9. See also note in Centenary file, 1956–7. *IA*, BCL 8/7.
38. Chairman's printed statement, pasted in General Minute Book, 1897–1939. *IA*, ATC 1/1.
39. Ibid.
40. Longhurst, pp.83–93.
41. W. Lorrain to W. A. Cadell, dated Batavia, 28 August 1883. *IA*, BCL 7/1.
42. See note 20.
43. Index to minutes, 1856–1952. *IA*, BCL 1/29.
44. See note 22.
45. Anoh., *One Hundred Years of Singapore* (Singapore, 1921).
46. Index to minutes, 1856–1952, *IA*, BCL 1/29. Another shipping interest of the Borneo Company was their London branch's representation of the Russian Volunteer Fleet from 1909 to 1921, *IA*, BCL 7/5.

8 Conflict and Profit: The Companies in the Second World War, 1939–45

Previous chapters have concentrated on the emergence and development of several merchant partnerships which, surviving the depression of the 1930s, became established as sound commercial enterprises. Many were already linked in an embryonic 'Inchcape Group' through the prominence of the Inchcape family on their Boards of Directors and among their sharedholders[1]; others were ultimately to merge with them to form the Group in 1958 or to join it later. The process of the gradual growth of these links since then began with the Second World War. It then became clear to the Third Lord Inchcape, having recently inherited investments in a large collection of mainly Indian-based trading and agency firms and tea estates, that to protect these holdings and ensure their survival and growth a form of reorganisation and rationalisation was required. In what ways did the Second World War accelerate this process of consolidation? How did the experience of the companies in this worldwide conflict affect their future growth, especially in terms of their eventual inclusion in the Group?

I

As we have seen, the firms based in the Indian subcontinent in which the Inchcape family had maintained an interest were long-established and respected businesses. Mackinnon Mackenzie & Co. in Calcutta, Colombo, Singapore, Hong Kong, Japan and China had achieved great commercial prominence as managing and port agents for the powerful British India Steam Navigation Co. Ltd [BI]; the Macneill and Barry partnerships in India and London were well-known as managing agents and secretaries of Indian river steamers, jute mills and tea estates; Binny's had developed an important cotton and woollen textile manufacturing concern and Delmege, Forsyth & Co. had become one of the leading import–export and shipping agency houses in Colombo.

Through its large fleet of passenger and cargo ships and prominent role in the trade of the Indian Ocean, the BI was of great strategic importance to the British Government with the threatened outbreak of war: as early as 1931, the Director of Sea Transport at the Admiralty had requested that four large BI passenger vessels be 'earmarked for special service in a national emergency'. The official subsidies and contracts enjoyed by the BI stipulated that vessels were liable to requisition in wartime or when war threatened: at the Abyssinia crisis of 1935, the company rapidly responded by preparing and supplying six passenger and three cargo vessels within a week. In 1936 the BI confirmed that their entire fleet was at the disposal of the Admiralty if necessary. During the Second World War its vessels served in many parts of the world, including Greece, Crete, Madagascar, North Africa, Malta, Burma and the Straits. Over half of the BI's gross tonnage was destroyed in the process. The commandeering of BI vessels had inevitable repercussions on the agencies of Mackinnon Mackenzie & Co. in Calcutta, Gray Mackenzie & Co. Ltd in the Gulf, Smith Mackenzie & Co. Ltd on the East African coast, Macdonald Hamilton & Co. in Australia and Gray Dawes & Co. in London.[2]

Table 8.1 shows that all the countries where the embryonic Inchcape Group traded experienced an overall rise in the value of their imports and exports from and to the UK between 1940 and 1948. In the case of India, already Britain's most important trading partner and an important war base, this was dramatic. Ceylon's total trade also expanded quite impressively during the 1940s, the rise in exports being explained by the disruption in supplies of raw materials and foodstuffs from the Far East during and after the war.

The India General Navigation and Railway Company Limited and the Rivers Steam Navigation Company Limited, then known as the Joint Steamer Companies, played a vital role in the subcontinent during these years. They experienced great difficulties: a large number of key personnel had joined up by mid-1940 with the introduction of compulsory war service for Europeans, and the lack of ocean-going shipping in

Indian coastal waters severely restricted the companies' jute export business. On the other hand, the profitable employment of their steamers was boosted by several new developments. With the advance of Japanese troops into Burma, the fleets assisted in the unprecedented movement of military traffic in Assam and acted most effectively as minesweepers. Their tea shipments increased, for there was no point in employing the faster but more expensive rail service when the tea could be held up indefinitely at Calcutta docks awaiting trans-shipment overseas. Repeating its role in the First World War, the India General earned particular distinction from its work in Iraq, which necessitated the conversion of several steamers to oil-burning and to ocean-voyaging. This included transmitting cargo to Basra for export, supplying military stores to the 10th Army up the Tigris and the Russian railhead at Ahwaz, and serving the oil installations at Abadan, Kuwait and Bandar Shapour. The vessels of the Joint Steamer Companies were also responsible for the carriage of 138 000 tons of military stores from Calcutta to the Front through Assam in 1942; two years later this exceeded 1 million tons. Following the Japanese advance into Burma, the flight of 50 000 from the panic-stricken city of Calcutta alone led to an unprecedented rise in the demand for passenger space on the companies' vessels. The Quit India Movement, which resulted in the sabotage of considerable stretches of railway track, also increased steamer traffic, as troops and police had to be carried by steamer to the trouble-spots, and their earnings from cargo shipments rose at the expense of the railway companies. During the crop failure in Bengal, the Joint Steamer Companies assisted in the distribution of rice, issuing food at a discount, and the organisation of ration shops for its local employees.

Despite being subject to an excess profits tax which reached a staggering 80 per cent by 1943, the profits of these companies after tax exceeded even those of their boom years of 1927-8. In 1940, the India General recorded a profit, for dividend distribution and to carry over to the next year's balance, of nearly £67 000. By 1944, with an exchange rate of 1*s* 6*d* to the rupee, this figure exceeded £100 000. Net profit figures for the Rivers Company are not available, but their gross earnings reached nearly £900 000 in 1940 and approached £1m in 1941. After paying a generous dividend to its shareholders, the RSN carried a balance of nearly £40 000 over to 1942. These profits were announced after the deduction of heavy ship and property repair bills, depreciation, losses in the exchange of remittances and large compensation payments to workmen.[3]

Duncan Macneill & Co., the managing agent for the Rivers Company,

TABLE 8.1 Value of total trade between the UK and countries in which companies described in Chapter 8 were involved, in 1940 compared with 1948

Country	Imports from UK compared with total 1940	Exports to UK compared with total 1940	Imports from UK compared with total 1948	Exports to UK compared with total 1948
India (millions rupees)	384 / 1 697	653 / 2 063	1 535 / 6 447	1 027 / 4 587
Ceylon (millions rupees)	49 / 283	172 / 387	171 / 994	301 / 1 011
Iraq (million dinars)	1 702 / 8 700	1 066 / 4 100	19 790 / 46 000	1 294 / 8 700
Iran (million rials)	67 / 1 089	21 / 2 255	1 155 / 5 475	7 544 / 19 007
Kenya (thousand pounds)	3 420 / 10 673	2 434 / 10 298	22 915 / 44 568	9 032 / 32 486

Tanganyika (thousand pounds)	950	1707	1402	2860
Australia (million Australian pounds)	3001	4425	6736	8078
	44	76	132	156
Japan (million yen)	132	150	338	406
	11	57	—	624
	4653	5418	20265	10148
Thailand (million ticuls)	11	33	118	55
	123	183	1754	2484
Malaya (million Straits dollars)	113	163	339	235
	829	1128	1791	1764

NOTE Britain was the single most important trading partner in India, Ceylon, Iraq, Iran, Kenya, Tanganyika and Australia. All the countries experienced an overall rise in trade between 1940 and 1948, but this was uninterrupted only in the case of Ceylon.

SOURCES B. R. Mitchell, *International Historical Statistics: Africa and Asia* (London, 1982) pp.381, 384–5, 394–8, 423, 428, 453–4, 456–7, 459, 461–2, 464–5, 467 and ibid, *The Americas and Australasia* (London, 1983) pp.560, 614.

also acted as secretary for fourteen sterling tea companies, and its associated firm in India, Macneill & Co., managed ten rupee tea companies in addition to its jute mill interests. Since 1915, the first Lord Inchcape had owned the UK and Indian interests of these firms and of Barry & Co. in India and J. B. Barry & Son of London. Table 8.2, an analysis of the profits and dividends of these tea estates, comparing 1938 with 1945, shows that the majority of them achieved higher profits in the latter year. In all but one instance, a higher dividend was paid to shareholders in 1945 than they had received in 1938. The average return on investment in the estates, seen as a whole, rose from 7 per cent to 14 per cent in these years. The Upper Assam Tea Company alone declared an enormous profit for that time of £124 787 in 1945. As in the case of the river steamer companies, the shareholders were not necessarily the greatest beneficiaries of these profits: the Sterling Tea Companies' earnings were taxed at a rate of 9s 0d in the £. Although these results were to a large extent due to higher tea prices – which rose from 1s 0d per lb. in 1938 to 1s 8d by 1945 – they were achieved despite increased marine insurance payments, the requisitioning of factories, such as the Upper Assam's Nudwa factory, the higher price paid for packaging materials and transport, and the cost of providing foodstuffs for the local employees. The Indian tea industry's workers earned an increased respect in these years. The chairman of the Upper Assam Company declared in his speech at the 1945 AGM that 'many shareholders will know something of the contribution made by the Assam tea planting community, both European and Indian, to the prosecution of the campaign on the Burma front' and repeated Lord Wavell's words: 'There are few bodies of civilians who have a better record in this war than the tea planters of Assam'.[4]

Of the other companies in India which were later to form the Inchcape Group, the success of Binny & Co. Ltd in responding to the enormous wartime demand for khaki and other textiles increased their importance in this industry. The rise in the Indian defence requirements for cloth grew from a pre-war level of 4 million yards to 1400 million by 1942, which is reflected in Binny's earnings, which compares the annual profit (including the amount paid as dividends and that carried over to the next year) of five of the companies considered in this chapter, shows that Binny's distributed profits were exceptionally high. In 1944, total profits were equivalent to over £120 000 enabling them to pay a dividend of 25 per cent. Output from their mills reached unprecedented levels in these years. The Bangalore mills, for example, in the period 1942–5, produced 20 million yards of khaki cloth, together with 29 million yards of jungle

TABLE 8.2   Indian Rupee and Sterling Tea Companies, 1938, compared with
1945

Name of Co. Rupees Co's.	1938 Profit Rs	1938 Div. p.a. (as %)	1945 Profit Rs	1945 Div. p.a. (as %)
The Baghjan Tea Co. (1935) Ltd	24 626	5	87 868	15
The Barak Tea Co. Ltd	16 404	5	34 771	12½
The Bhubandhar Tea Co. Ltd	56 284	5	1 14 655	10
The Bukhail Tea Estates Ltd	21 893*	–	27 726	–
The Dirai Tea Co. Ltd	11 721	–	50 696	–
The Royapore Tea Co. Ltd	51 026	10	47 498	20
The Moraghat Tea Co. Ltd	63 103	5	2 64 124	20
The Nangd ıla Tea Co. Ltd	23 806	–	2 06 565	15
The New Assam Valley Tea Co. Ltd	38 400	7½	85 428	20
The New Monkhooshi Tea Co. Ltd	39 979	10	1 01 028	25
Sterling Co's.	(£)		(£)	
Assam Estates Ltd	7 998	7 Pref. 12½ Ord.	8 614	7 17½
The Cossipore Tea Co. Ltd	2 202	5	3 706	10
The Doodputlee Tea Co. Ltd	1 863	–	4 412	7½
Greenwood Tea Co. Ltd	7 939	5	5 368	10
Kalline Tea Co. Ltd	3 755	3	5 762	10
The Koyah Tea Co. Ltd	2 723	4	2 495	5
The Majagram Tea Co. Ltd	5 122	7½	2 387	5
The Northern Dooars Tea Co. Ltd	21 028	35	36 004	60
The Salonah Tea Co. Ltd	17 675	6	14 156	6 pref 10 ord
The Scottpore Tea Co. Ltd	4 246	5	5 080	7
The Tarapore Tea Co. Ltd	23 277	8	27 111	16
The Thanai Tea Co. Ltd	15 910	10	14 075	15
The Upper Assam Tea Co. Ltd	105 034	15	1 24 787	15
The Western Cachar Co. Ltd	3 606	5	2 045	5

*loss

NOTE Profit = Dividend + Amount carried forward and transferred to reserves
SOURCES *Inchcape Archives*, Macneill & Co., Rupee Tea Companies' Reports and
Accounts for the year to 31 December 1938, and for the year to 31 December
1945; Duncan Macneill & Co., Sterling Tea Companies' Reports and Accounts
for the year to 31 December 1938, and for the year to 31 December 1945.

green cloth, 4 million blankets, 3 million yards of greatcoat cloth, 13
million yards of flannel, 150 000 flannel puttees, 450 000 yards of
aeroplane fabric and 7 million yards of parachute cloth.
    Through difficulties in importing specialised raw materials and vital

spare parts, Binny's became more self-sufficient. Its research chemists developed their own sodium bichromate khaki dye and its engineers provided replacements for broken textile machinery, when wartime shortages could have severely disrupted production. During the war, a long overdue system of cloth quality control was introduced, whereby the price and an indication of fineness were stamped on the cloth. More importantly, in response to the wartime black-market dealings, Binny's distribution networks were rationalised into an effective pyramidal structure which ensured that retailers received regular supplies. Meanwhile, the firm gained several important new agencies. In 1947 it was paid a tribute by a member of the Viceroy's council: 'India's most important single contribution in the domain of war supplies was textiles . . . In this great effort Binny's mills played a notable part . . . (they) were unsurpassed in the matter of quality and the punctuality of their deliveries'.[5]

Ceylon suffered no interruption in the steady rise of its foreign trade during the Second World War. Delmege Forsyth & Co. Ltd, which had been acquired by the first Earl in 1918, enjoyed record growth.

II

One of the most spectacular changes in Britain's overseas commerce during these years, however, was the transformation of the economy of the Middle East. Exports from the UK to Iraq increased more than tenfold in money terms between 1940 and 1948. The even more drastic increase in the value of Iran's exports to Britain reflects the growth of the Gulf oil industry. The profits achieved by Gray Mackenzie & Co. Ltd, not yet able to take advantage of this development, stagnated in these years (as seen in Figure 8.1) but this was more than compensated by its role in the post-war oil boom. In common with other British overseas firms Gray Mackenzie suffered manpower shortages when expatriates were called up for military service. The navigation problems of the Gulf, mentioned in Chapter 3, were worsened by the huge increase in traffic. During the war, the firm employed only twelve Europeans, handling not only an expanding volume of work but, in addition to its other duties, acting as agent for the Ministry of War Transport and for the UK Commercial Corporation. The firm worked in conjunction with the inland water transport organisations of India, such as the Joint Steamer Companies, ensuring that supplies to Russia were sustained throughout the hostilities. The German vessels interned in Bandar Shapour in 1939

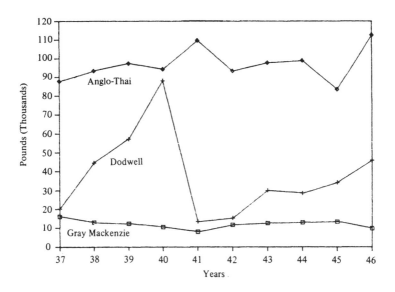

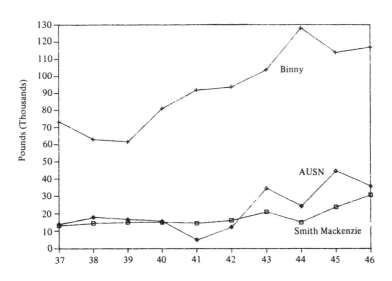

SOURCE *Inchcape Archives*, Reports and Accounts of Anglo-Thai, Dodwell, Gray Mackenzie, Smith Mackenzie, Binny and AUSN.

FIGURE 8.1 Profitability of Inchcape companies, 1937–46

remained there until captured by the Royal Navy at the end of the war. The region remained relatively free from direct enemy attacks. Gray Mackenzie's profits were reduced by the extensive damage to the firm's property by local disruption in Iraq and Iran in 1941, the requisitioning of its floating craft and property, and the commandeering of their workshops and barges in basra in 1942; the latter had made a healthy profit of £59 212 the previous year. The local authorities would agree to providing compensation only at the pre-war profit level of approximately £9 000 per year.

The 1942 AGM of Gray Mackenzie, held at the London registered office, reported that the firm had gained several new agencies, which were subsequently to fuel its post-war expansion. These included the Norwegian Shipping Board, Watts & Co., the Federal Steamship Co., the Harrison Line, the Prince Line, the Orient Line, the US Maritime Board, the New Zealand Shipping Company, Stephen Sutton & Co., the Port Line, and Cable & Wireless steamers at all ports except Basra. because of the overwhelming demand for its shipping services, Gray Mackenzie agreed to share commissions with Lynch's for the duration and offer a joint service and to pool resources with Stricks at Khorramshah, Abadan, Bushir and Bandar Shapour. This latter port enjoyed such growth that the firms were forced to seek larger premises, and were able to add to their staff with a local manager from the Tigris and Euphrates Steam Navigation Company. The firms' performance in this challenging period was valuable preparation for the later oil boom and further transformation of the economy of the Middle East in the 1950s.[6]

The British Protectorate of East Africa, which was to become Kenya and Uganda, also grew rapidly during the war years, and by 1948 the value of its imports, half of which came from the UK, had increased over sixfold since 1940. Table 8.1 shows, too, that Tanganyika, previously a German colony, doubled its trading activity. In this period, the island of Zanzibar also enjoyed comparable growth. Smith Mackenzie & Co. Ltd reaped the benefit of this increase in its import–export business, its profits increasing from over £13 000 in 1937 to over £30 000 by 1946, as seen in Figure 8.1. On the East African coast the BI had faced increasing competition from German and Japanese shipping before the war, which was then drastically reduced. Manpower shortages resulted in the closure of the Uganda office for the duration, and unlike Gray Mackenzie, the firm was unable to gain any new shipping agency contracts because of Admiralty control of all tonnage on this coast.[7]

The growing importance of British trade with Australia during the

Second World War added considerably to the activities of Macdonald, Hamilton & Co. Prompted by its large earnings during the war, it expanded its existing ventures in mining, pastoral management, and further shipping work, such as stevedoring, wool-dumping, towage, ship repairs, and cold storage of cargoes. The Australasian United Steam Navigation Company [AUSN], of which the first Lord Inchcape was chairman, and in which the family had a significant shareholding, had been declining in profitability since the mid-1920s. Suffering from the effects of waterside industrial unrest, the heavy depreciation of its ships and properties combined with the contraction of trade – especially in passengers – it incurred heavy losses. By 1937, only three of its ships carried passengers. Although six of its vessels made small profits in 1941, these were insignificant compared with the trading losses made by the remainder of the fleet. But times were to change. Requisitioned by the Australian Government and not handed back until 1947, the fleet's earnings dramatically improved to the extent that the AUSN was able to pay a 5 per cent dividend from 1943. These profits were higher than, for example, those of many typical British tramp steamers in this period. But the effect of these higher wartime profits was only to prolong artificially the company's interest in shipping. Already by 1940, the value of the AUSN's other investments, such as in property and Government Securities, exceeded that of its fleet.[8]

III

Companies operating in enemy-occupied territory suffered considerable dislocation. Table 8.1 shows that the export trade from Britain to Japan collapsed completely. The impact of the outbreak of hostilities on Dodwell's, the Borneo Company and Anglo-Thai was more far-reaching than all the companies considered hitherto combined. Trade in China had been brought to a standstill since July 1937 with the new regime, and the former's Japanese interests were already severely hampered by the import exchange restrictions in that country. Dodwell's, whose profits reached over £88 000 in 1940, found it impossible to prepare full accounts for 1941. With the sudden dislocation of trade and loss of records they were still incomplete in 1948, a result of only £13 500 being declared. The safety of their employees was at greater risk than in any other theatre of war: at least four members of Dodwell's staff died in December 1941. In India, F. G. Raddon, who rather than evacuate Rangoon when first threatened, stayed on to ensure the selling of stocks and liquidation of assets, died of malaria whilst trekking overland on foot to Calcutta. With the withdrawal of British tonnage the firm's Pacific agencies were left with a fraction of their former agency work. Dodwell's assets in enemy-occupied countries of the Far East became almost worthless. Its property and other fixed assets, valued at nearly £100 000, had to be written off, together with nearly £300 000 in working capital. Hong Kong, which had recorded unprecedented levels of trading in 1941, fell to the Japanese. Yet, with only six of its sixteen pre-war branches still in business by early 1942 – and of these, the Pacific and Indian offices under great constraint – careful management produced a healthy trading profit of £40 000. The lack of shipping was pin-pointed as the principal reason for the firm's reduction in profit, as much of its activity was traditionally based on shipping-agency work. In 1943, three more employees lost their lives in the fighting.

The following year saw the total destruction of the firm's property in Foochow. A more promising result in 1945 was achieved despite the continued lack of profits from the Far East, showing the corresponding growth in the remaining branches, and the firm's rehabilitation after the war was rapid. The Chairman's visit to the US branches resulted in the gain of a new, important agency – the Trans-Pacific Service, which it was to manage at both ends of the line. This called for a new branch at Manila.

The war in the Far East had the significant effect of demonstrating the importance of risks widely-spread. As the Chairman reported at the 1945 AGM, the London office, which used to be considered as an expensive luxury, 'is now trading with all parts of the world, and is not only a feeder for the Eastern branches, but a substantial profit-earning office. It is a great relief to me, to feel that all our eggs are no longer in the Far Eastern basket'. In seconding the speech, H. W. Lester made the point that Britain was now looking to firms like Dodwell's to rehabilitate its export trade after the war. This was especially true in the great sellers' markets of the Far East, which ensured Dodwell's rapid post-war recovery and subsequent growth. Gilman's, Gibb Livingston's and Caldbeck's, despite occupation and internment by the enemy, were also to thrive again in the post-war boom. The importance of Caldbeck's in China was such that the Shanghai branch was ordered by the new Communist administration to reopen to supply wines to the remaining diplomatic community.[9]

The Japanese occupation of Thailand in December 1941 brought total dislocation to the Anglo-Thai Corporation. Despite this, however, the overseas trade of the country was to grow in this period, especially the import of UK goods. Anglo-Thai, dealing in these and in the export of local teak and rice, made remarkable profits in the decade 1937 to 1946. The solid performance shown in Figure 8.1 was achieved despite the unsatisfactory nature of general trading in Thailand. In March 1942 a special circular was issued to shareholders describing the effects of the enemy occupation. Seven members of the Thailand staff, with their wives and children, were interned. Four of them managed to escape to Burma, where they joined the British forces. As in the case of Dodwell's, Anglo-Thai had concentrated the greater part of its business in one centre – Thailand and Malaya – and suffered the consequences. Its property, including saw mill, and other buildings in Bangkok, up-country Thailand and Malaya, were seized and destroyed. The Sedenak Rubber Estates Ltd, with stocks of timber and stores worth over £100 000, had to be written off. The Equalisation of Divided Fund and substantial reserve funds built up before the war enabled Anglo-Thai to bear these losses of stocks of general merchandise, in transit and outstanding debts from bazaars. By 1943, Anglo-Thai's foresight in purchasing a subsidiary in India – Herbertson's – paid off, when it became almost entirely dependent on Herbertson's for its trading profits. The loss of its teak leases, property and many of its staff had a similar effect on Anglo-Thai as the effects of the war in the Far East had on Dodwell's. It sought to reduce its reliance on timber and to expand its business horizons into other countries. In restarting its business Anglo-Thai was to benefit from the fact that, as in the Far East, everything was in short supply in Thailand and the company was to play an important part in the continued growth of British commerce in this region.[10]

The Borneo Company, which suffered great economic hardship and dislocation, perhaps more than any other of the firms considered here, was to demonstrate most plainly the need to diversify both regionally and in type of business activity. For three and a half years, the company was practically closed down, as it was not able to fall back on other overseas centres. Based in Sarawak, Singapore, Bangkok, Chiengmai, Batavia and Hong Kong, it did not even have holdings in India, for example, which had helped Anglo-Thai so much in the war. The surviving Borneo Company branch accounts, which had to be reconstructed from the Minute Books as published accounts could not be traced, show that from a profit of over £76 000 in 1936–7, earnings declined to a net result of only £12 886 in 1938–9. The Siam branches had declared a profit of £46 132 in 1936–7, but only £7 575 in 1938–9.

The employees of the Borneo Company suffered the greatest hardships of all the firms subsequently to be associated with the Inchcape

Group. In Singapore, the Japanese had expected to find 500 European civilians: instead, 4600 were resident in the city who were, nevertheless, incarcerated for two years in Changi prison, originally designed for only 600 inmates. In all, eighteen staff died in the conflict. No news whatever was heard of them for several years. At the 1945 AGM, the chairman, Sir Adam Ritchie, declared 'it is an extraordinary fact that an enemy, even as ruthless and efficient as the Japanese, should have been able to maintain this screen of secrecy for so long'. By 1942 all the company's branches were in enemy hands.

Yet, barely a month after Thailand had cancelled her declaration of war, the company was re-establishing its branches, beginning with the Eastern general manager's arrival in Bangkok, as head of a special British Government mission to increase rice production, and by October 1945 the branch was again in business. By the end of December the Singapore office had reopened. By early 1946, all the branches, except those in the Dutch East Indies, had been reopened.

The total losses incurred by the Borneo Company have proved impossible to calculate because of the lack of records. Its teak stocks in Thailand were expropriated, and its rubber estates in Sarawak had 'gone back', making post-war production difficult. The Bangkok office and wharves and warehouses, together with the Kuching manager's bungalow, were completely wiped out. The most grievous loss to many Borneo Company members was that of 36 000 bottles of vintage champagne, brandy, whisky and gin, on which duty had already been paid. In the company's godown in Singapore, T. C. Martine and J. Bennett poured the contents away rather than allow them to fall into the hands of the enemy. Yet the company's overall recovery was rapid despite its concentration in the worst of the war zones. By 1951, its profits exceeded £1m for the first time.[11]

Finally, the British-based retail motor business of Mann Egerton & Co. Ltd (discussed in Appendix 2.2) made a considerable contribution to the British war effort at home. Although not involved in aircraft production this time, the company played an even greater part in the Second World War than it did in the First. Its coach-building department built 4000 ambulances and as many service vehicles, such as infantry carriers. The electrical department installed equipment in over 400 naval vessels and carried out over 6000 repairs on ships in thirty-one ports, in addition to its work in degaussing ships against German mines, and helping in the development of East Anglia's first radar station. The woodworking department built ammunition boxes and, altogether, half a million pieces of furniture. One of the company's most vital contributions was the provision of training facilities for thousands of driver-mechanics and maintenance men for the armed services at its Norwich headquarters. The post-war boom in Britain was particularly demonstrated by the huge demand for private cars, which was to lead to the further expansion of Mann Egerton.[12]

Despite the appropriate of property and resources, and the exodus of their manpower into the services, Figure 8.1 generally shows that all the companies suffered some disruption but were to make a rapid recovery and considerably overall gains. Of six of the largest of these companies, only one did not show a result in 1946 which was higher than the comparable figure for 1937. The range of their activities increased. The river steamers became involved in the supply and service of Gulf oil installations; Binny's produced a whole new range of textiles; Gray Mackenzie gained several new shipping agencies and Dodwell's London office expanded dramatically with the temporary closure of its Eastern branches. As a result of the war, many firms realised the importance of widening the geographical scope of their operations. Dodwell's, with a new trans-Pacific service agency, opened a branch in Manila, and both Anglo-Thai and the Borneo Company were soon to acquire holdings in Canada.

Without exception, all the companies gained in prestige, importance and commecial standing in their respective trading areas. The BI had become even more indispensable to the British Government, the Joint Steamer Companies had made a striking contribution to the war effort, the tea planters too had played a vital role, and Binny's significance through their work in the supply of textiles cannot be exaggerated. In the Middle East, the position of Gray Mackenzie became even more assured, especially through their contribution to the support of Russia, and so did Smith Mackenzie on the East African coast. The services of the AUSN fleet when requisitioned by the Australian Government boosted their flagging morale. Dodwell's branches in the Far East and on the Pacific coasts resumed trading at the end of the occupation with a speed that suggests that their expertise was needed, however reluctantly, by ex-enemy governments. All the firms in the Far East were to play an important part in the Allied Occupation arrangements and return to normal commercial activity.

They all emerged from their experiences stronger. They had proved that they could survive; which gave them even greater incentives to return to trading and take full advantage of the post-war boom. In many ways the firms had been forced to examine their managerial structures and had improved them. The Borneo Company, Anglo-Thai, Dodwells

8.1 Binny's: a modern picture of a Ruti Jaquard Loom at the Buckingham and Carnatic Mills. During the Second World War, these mills produced the textiles to clothe millions of servicemen

and other companies had introduced Provident Funds and Pensions Schemes for their staff in these years. In addition, Binny's had developed a new distribution network, and many of the firms provided bonuses and discounts on food to their employees, which were continued after the war. To the Third Lord Inchcape, it was plain that his investments were in companies with a definite future. The firms not yet associated with the Inchcape family also faced the years ahead with new confidence, but realised the shortcomings of concentrating their activities in relatively few areas.

The post-war years saw great political changes in most of these regions. The Partition of India followed in 1947, Ceylon became independent in 1948, the transformation of the economy of the Gulf led to almost continuous political unrest, the British Colonial Government of East Africa gave way to Kenya, Uganda and Tanganyika and the Communist victories in China in 1948 made trading there impossible for many years. The Second World War, and its aftermath of post-colonialism, increased the vulnerability of these firms. It showed that their assets could be requisitioned, their trading networks destroyed, their business snatched away, with no warning and no redress. All the companies suffered incredible tax demands. For example, at the end of 1941, the Borneo Company declared a profit of £175 000; £155 000 was deducted in tax. Firms based almost solely in one region, which is true of most of these enterprises, were especially at risk due to political change, to rising nationalism, and the erosion of the old colonial structures founded in the nineteenth centuries. In facing the changes in the world economy of the post-war decades, survival became impossible without expansion and diversification.

In the decision to begin working towards the consolidation of his shareholdings into a marketable enterprise, ultimately to be launched on the London Stock Exchange, Lord Inchcape was strongly influenced by the events of the war, which had immediately preceded his succession to the active leadership of the family. The combination of the shake-up of all the companies during the war and the arrival of a new, young leader to the Inchcape family businesses inevitably favoured change. The manner of these changes was based on strengthening links between the firms, providing a UK market value for their assets and earnings, and pooling the benefits of their skills and resources. These were largely a response to lessons learned in the world conflict of 1939 to 1945.

8.2 The Second Lord Inchcape on his wedding day in 1933. His bride, his second wife, was the daughter of Rajah Brooke of Sarawak, thus linking these two families

NOTES

1. The Inchcape family holdings in this period included directorships in fourteen tea estates, in the Rivers Steam Navigation Co. Ltd, Gray Mackenzie & Co. Ltd, Smith Mackenzie & Co. Ltd, Islay Kerr & Co. Ltd, and the Mediterranean Transport Co. Ltd. Partnerships in which the third Lord Inchcape held an interest were Mackinnon Mackenzie & Co. in Calcutta, Colombo and China, Gray Dawes & Co, Macdonald Hamilton & Co, and the Macneill and Barry partnerships. The Inchcape family also held shares in the AUSN, Gibb Livingston, Binny's and Delmege, Forsyth & Co. See *Inchcape Archives [IA]* Mediterranean Transport Co. Ltd, Minute Book 1948.
2. George Blake, *BI Centenary: 1856–1956* (London, 1956) pp.93, 191–8.
3. P. J. Griffiths, *A History of the Joint Steamer Companies* (London, 1979) pp.78–88; *IA*, RSN, Balance sheet 1940–1; *IA*, IGNR, Balance sheet 1940.
4. *IA*, Duncan Macneill & Co., Sterling Tea Companies, Reports and Accounts, 1938 and 1945; *IA*, Macneill & Co., Rupee Tea Companies, Reports and Accounts, 1938 and 1945. The sterling companies were registered in London and the rupee companies in India. Lord Inchcape and other members of his family invested in many of them.
5. Binny & Co. Ltd, *The House of Binny* (Madras, 1969) pp.253–69; *IA*, Binny & Co. Ltd, Reports and Accounts, 1937–1946.
6. *IA*, Gray Mackenzie & Co. Ltd, Reports and Accounts, 1937–46; Minute Book, 1937–42; Journal, 1937–46; C. Noble, 'History of Gray Mackenzie', unpub. ms.
7. See Chapter 4.
8. See Chapter 5, and the author's 'The Decline of British Maritime Enterprise in Australia: the example of the AUSN, 1887–1961', *Business History*, vol. 27, no. 1 (March 1985) pp.59–74.
9. *IA*, Dodwell & Co. Ltd, Reports and Accounts, 1937–46; Minute Book 1932–48; the *Hong Kong Tatler*, 'The Inchcape Group in Hong Kong' (May 1978).
10. *IA*, Anglo-Thai Corporation, Reports and Accounts, 1937–46; Minute Book, 1938–45; Anthony Goodinge, 'History of the Anglo-Thai Corporation United 1834–1971', unpub. ms.
11. *IA*, Borneo Company, Minute Books 1936–48; Henry Longhurst, *The Borneo Story* (London, 1956) pp.93–108.
12. See Appendix 2.2

9 Response to a Changing World: The Formation of the Inchcape Group of Companies, 1945–58

MANU-FORTI

As the war in Europe and the Far East came to an end, the young Third Earl of Inchcape found himself at the head of a scattered and disparate network of family shareholdings. Little more than a decade later, these investments had formed the basis for the launch of a new, unique enterprise on the London Stock Exchange. This public launching of an international trading company was unprecedented, and the placing of shares with investors was to be justified by its early success and rapid expansion. Why was it thought necessary to bring the Inchcape family holdings together in this way? How was this complex legal and financial manoeuvre achieved?

Chapter 8 has shown that the majority of the companies in which the

Inchcape family held shares made large profits during the war; their earnings in the immediate post-war years were substantially higher than in the late 1930s. Still generally organised and run as partnerships rather than as limited companies, the firms operated independently of each other although enjoying some business links. Preoccupied with huge demands on their limited resources, they had been allowed to drift during the war years. Yet, in the late 1940s and early 1950s, they became increasingly vulnerable in a new world marked by the decline in power of the old colonial structures. The independence and partition of India in particular undermined the stability of the Inchcape family investments which were concentrated in that region. Two successive heads of the family businesses, the Second Earl of Inchcape and Lord Craigmyle, had died within a few years of each other, in 1939 and 1944 respectively, so that little continuity of policy and management had been possible since the death of the First Earl in 1932.

From 1939 until 1948, when the Third Earl returned from active service and his subsequent post in India to assume control of the business, it was run by a temporary caretaker administration. This, a panel of four, consisted of G. F. Hotblack, a solicitor from the firm of Waltons & Co. who had assisted in the BI – P & O merger of 1914 and who was a partner in Gray Dawes & Co; Sir William Currie, the P & O Chairman, Sir George Campbell, a partner in Mackinnon Mackenzie & Co. [MM & Co.] in Calcutta who had held many important public offices in India; and A. O. Lang the Deputy Chairman of P & O. Barings, who were to contribute significantly to the successful launching of the Group in 1958 and to its subsequent programme of expansion, offered professional advice in the person of Sir Edward Peacock.[1]

1

The Third Earl, who, after leaving the army had been learning the ropes as an assistant in the shipping agency business of MM & Co. in Calcutta, returned to London at Hotblack's request in 1948. He was now head of a series of loosely connected shareholdings, besides his own directorships and partnerships (see Appendix 9.1). In retrospect we can see that there were three options open to him, though they may not have been immediately apparent at the time. The process of the formation of the Group was not a case of the firm pursuit of a carefully designed plan, but the result of a series of pragmatic decisions based on what was possible. The first of these options was to allow the companies to continue as before; second, the overseas holdings could be sold and the capital realised and invested in UK companies to avoid the problems faced by the firms in India and elsewhere as described below; and third, the firms could be reorganised and protected by a new corporate structure which would strengthen their positions in overseas countries, by providing them with a UK market value.

The first of these possibilities was clearly no longer viable in the late 1940s. The companies had survived – and prospered – since their inception, managed and run on a relatively small capital base, but this was no longer possible. Increased death duties and other forms of taxation, heavy Indian Government restrictions on foreign trade, combined with rising operating costs because of higher rents, rates and wage bills, drastically changed their situation. The panel of four, with Lord Inchcape and the other Seniors (his cousin the Second Lord Craigmyle, Lord Inchcape's brother Alan and half-brother Simon) faced the particular problem of having to provide for the managing partners of the firms in India on their retirement, at a time of difficulty in remitting profits back to the UK. They were also concerned with the effect on the firms of liabilities for heavy death duties which in due course would inevitably be incurred. These would be calculated on the firms' separate values on a break-up basis, when the unsettled nature of the post-war market required larger cash reserves in order to maintain dividends and cover short-term losses. This would mean that the businesses were unlikely to receive the injections of capital which they needed if they remained separate and in some cases, small-scale enterprises. In this respect, they tended to operate in isolation, possibly in too narrow a way, with each management inevitably concerned only with its own particular business. Overall, if left to continue by themselves, it is likely that the value of the Inchcape family investments in these concerns would have declined more and more, possibly culminating in their eventual dissolution.

The second of the three alternatives, that of selling the overseas investments and concentrating the family's interests in the UK, could scarcely be contemplated either. The Third Earl had just returned from MM & Co, the firm which had given his grandfather his first job in the East and from which all his subsequent interests and investments had sprung. The First Earl, justly revered in his family, had built up a portfolio of a large range of businesses over many years as we have seen, and they had thrived under his direction and help. For his grandson to sell them off so soon after taking control would have been like selling his birthright, denying the value and importance of his inheritance. Not only were the family's overseas investments many and varied, but they were placed in prestigious firms, among the most respected in their localities. Moreover, during the Second World War, as seen in Chapter 8, these companies had enhanced their reputations by making essential contributions to the war effort, in the course of which they had achieved unprecedented levels of profits. To pull out of them when they faced greater difficulties, after they had recently paid such record dividends, would have looked like deserting a generous friend who was falling on hard times. Furthermore, as the value of these firms had already been undermined by their falling profits in the immediate post-war years, the price which could have been obtained for them would have been far below their true worth in the long run. At these low prices, local Indians, particularly the thriving Mahwari business community, would have been keen to buy. Lord Inchcape, however, was concerned to protect the interests of the large expatriate workforce; hundreds of young men had arrived in India since the war to work for the various firms, and many of them had brought their wives and children. There was grave doubt, subsequently justified, that these men would have been able to keep their jobs (and their pensions) in the event of sale to Indian concerns. In any case, the relatively small amount realised in such sales would not necessarily have been more profitably employed in the UK: British business was having its own difficulties. In the decision to retain these holdings, the other Seniors were prepared to take Lord Inchcape's advice. The option was open to them to realise their share of the business and retire, as Alan Mackay in fact did in course of time.

The third option, that of linking the companies more closely together and providing representation on the London Stock Exchange, may not have seemed a possibility in the late 1940s; it was rather the result of years of further thought and deliberation, the logical consequence of a series of developments aimed at adapting the structure of these companies to the modern world. Briefly, this process began with the raising of capital by sales of shares then strengthening the remaining companies and grouping them as subsidiaries of a main holding company. When the decision was made to launch this publicly-quoted holding company on the London Stock Exchange, the component businesses had to be presented in such a way as to form a package attractive to would-be investors. Thus, the reorganisation had three principal phases. First, the sale of a 48 per cent minority holding on the newly reorganised Macneill & Barry Ltd; second, increasing the family holdings in other businesses, and the purchase of the Mackinnon companies by the P & O Group; and finally, in the years 1957 and 1958, the preparation of a prospectus for the formation of the holding company, namely Inchcape & Co. Limited.

II

Phase One began in 1949. Tatas, one of the largest and most important Indian companies, had already shown considerable interest in the partnerships of Macneill & Co. and Barry & Co., who acted, *inter alia*, as agents and secretaries of tea estates, jute mills, coal mines and river steamers. Macneill & Barry Ltd had been formed in this year to take over the businesses of the two firms, together with the portfolio of The Ganges Transport and Trading Co. Ltd, which was an investment company with holdings in businesses managed by the Macneill and Barry partnerships. The Ganges company was owned by the Inchcape family and agreed to accept the relatively low price of £750 000, paid in shares, not cash, by a preference share issue in the new company of Macneill & Barry Ltd in exchange for the business interests to be transferred. Then a 48 per cent holding in this new enterprise was sold to Tatas for £500 000 in cash. This deal was negotiated personally by Lord Inchcape and Barings' representative. So began what was to be a long and complicated series of dealings with governments, other business concerns, banks, solicitors and various legal and financial advisers over the next decade. The remaining 52 per cent holding in Macneill & Barry Ltd was retained by the Seniors, who thus kept a controlling interest, but who now had £500 000 in cash with which to strengthen and sustain their investments as a whole.[2]

The second phase was marked by a series of legal and financial changes. This resulted in the partnerships in which there was an Inchcape interest being incorporated as limited liability companies. This brought considerable tax advantages, satisfied national policies in the host countries and made easier the retirement of managing partners, together with European and local staff, without the immediate disbursement of cash. For example, in the original Mackinnon Mackenzie & Co. partnership in Calcutta, an allocation of preference shares in the new limited company was made to the partners, on the understanding that the Seniors would redeem them at their face value as and when the recipients retired. This convenient device had already been used when Macneill & Barry Ltd had been formed, and had worked satisfactorily. The other Mackinnon partnerships in Pakistan, Ceylon and Hong Kong were then incorporated, as were the two UK firms of Duncan Macneill

& Co. and J. B. Barry & Son (which, after becoming Macneill, Barry & Co.) were merged to become Duncan Macneill & Co. Ltd. Gray Dawes & Co. still remained a partnership until December 1951, when incorporation in the UK on the same day as Duncan Macneill & Co. Ltd brought it in line with the other businesses. Its role in the ownership and management of Smith Mackenzie & Co. Ltd and Gray Mackenzie & Co. Ltd was thereby strengthened. Only Macdonald, Hamilton & Co. in Australia retained its partnership status for the time being, because it was still favoured by the Australian tax laws.

These early changes in the structure of the firms received a further boost with the sale of the Mackinnon companies to the P & O Group, in 1956–7. Through their links with the First Earl, they were seen as the jewel in the crown of the family investments, and for sentimental reasons had been retained in the portfolio despite the partnerships' dependence on the P & O/BI Group, for whom they acted as agents. The initial approaches were made by Sir Donald Anderson of the P & O. He had become managing director of the shipping line in the 1930s, and strongly disliked the practice, common in British shipping at the time, whereby private arrangements were made with outside managers to handle agency business at particular ports. Sir Donald had always regarded the Mackinnon companies as high on the list to become P & O subsidiaries, but in the years immediately after the war he was reluctant to pay large sums to the Inchcape family when he needed all the resources at his disposal to rebuild the P & O fleet. Although these firms were arguably the most important among the family investments, the Indian political situation was troubling, and cash from the sale was needed to consolidate the other family holdings. In retrospect, the best plan may have been to merge the Mackinnon companies with Macneill & Barry and transfer the shipping agency work to London; although possible in 1948, such a plan had become impractical by 1956.

Of the £2m sterling received from this sale, the majority came from the inclusion of the highly profitable shipping business managed by Gray Dawes & Co. Ltd. Mackinnon Mackenzie & Co. in India had been taken over by the P & O for a nominal sum for which it agreed to take responsibility for the pension liabilities of its staff. This purchase also included that of the shipping agency department of Macdonald Hamilton & Co.; the remainder in Australia was reorganised by the Seniors. The deal as a whole was again negotiated by Lord Inchcape with the help of able representation from Barings.[3] It effectively transformed the Inchcape family holdings from a group of firms predominantly concerned with shipping-agency work, especially for the

P & O/BI Group, into a less narrowly concentrated collection of businesses. The coming of long-distance aviation and the decline in the overseas passenger trade may have helped in the decision to reduce the family's involvement in shipping.

III

The completion of this sale in January 1957 ushered in the third phase. Lord Inchcape and his advisers had not only produced a modern concentration of efficient firms, protected by the fiscal and other advantages of limited liability, but now had enough capital to finance the future growth of these companies. He now had to examine each firm in turn to decide how this growth could best be achieved. A UK holding company, with shares publicly quoted on the London Stock Exchange and therefore readily marketable, through which all the firms could enjoy representation in Britain, was now essential, to act as the financial base for the whole enterprise. One of the three existing UK-based companies was first considered for this purpose. Of Gray Dawes & Co. Ltd, Duncan Macneill & Co. Ltd and St Mary Axe Securities Ltd, the foremost was the obvious choice, for it was a well-known and old-established shipping, mercantile and insurance agency of considerable repute, and it had sentimental appeal for Lord Inchcape, lying as it did at the core of the family portfolio, especially after MM & Co. had been hived-off.

Gray Dawes already held shares in a number of businesses which it was proposed should be brought into the embryonic Group, but an interest of over 50 per cent was required before these could become subsidiaries. In the case of Binny London, which had been removed from Binny (Madras) Ltd in 1920, Gray Dawes held only 3.1 per cent of the equity but St Mary Axe Securities held 43.6 per cent and its shareholders were unwilling at this stage to sell their interest in this company. An offer was therefore made to the remaining outside shareholders. It was accepted by almost all of them, and gave Gray Dawes a 55.4 per cent holding. The non-accepting 1 per cent sold out to Gray Dawes shortly after.

Gray Dawes then strengthened its holding in Smith Mackenzie & Co. Ltd and Gray Mackenzie & Co. Ltd, the merchant houses of East Africa and the Gulf respectively. Gray Dawes had previously divested itself of shares in Smith Mackenzie to avoid having to obtain UK treasury consent for any capital reorganisation, but for the launch of the Group, it increased its holding to 51.03 per cent with the purchase of 71 669 'A' or voting shares. It possessed a minority equity holding in Gray Mackenzie, but nevertheless effectively had voting control, through participating preference shares. In July 1957 a further 17 600 ordinary shares were aquired, giving a 50.42 per cent equity holding in Gray Mackenzie and its subsidiaries: the Bahrain Slipway Company Limited and the Busreh Slipway Company Limited. Meanwhile, Gray Dawes improved the geographical spread of its holdings – regarded as a vital prerequisite of the successful launching of the future Group by acquiring an interest in Macdonald Hamilton & Co. in Australia. Lord Inchcape, as President of this partnership, admitted Gray Dawes without a monetary consideration, as a partner with a 10 per cent interest in the profits or losses of the business. A firm UK base was needed by the future Group, so Gray Dawes' subsidiary, Spencer Yates & Curry Limited, which had been incorporated as a private company in England in 1924 and acted as insurance brokers and agents in Birmingham, was included.[4]

The need to avoid an undue concentration of the Group's assets in one country, India, meant that it could not absorb both Binny's and Macneill & Barry at this stage. As the former was expected to provide a good income in the Group's early years, whereas 48 per cent of the latter was now controlled by Tatas, the choice was obvious. It must be emphasised, however, that these decisions were taken to make the Group more attractive to potential investors. They were not necessarily seen as permanent arrangements.

Although Macneill & Barry Limited was excluded, the Seniors were careful to keep the best of their Indian holdings intact. These included The Ganges Transport and Trading Co. Ltd. This investment company was later acquired by Gray Dawes in the years leading up to the formation of the Group and was to play an important part in the acquisition of Binny's, in London and Madras, and its subsidiaries. An indication of the complicated and time-consuming nature of many of these involved transactions is provided by the incorporation of Binny (Madras) Ltd into the nascent Group. One of the last companies to be brought in, it was to be among its largest single constituents. 39 per cent was owned by Binny London, 24 percent by Fairlie Place Securities Ltd (the indigenous investment company through which the Seniors held their shares in Macneill & Barry Ltd), 20 per cent by The Ganges Transport & Trading Co. Ltd. and 17 per cent by various outside public investors. Donald Caswell, a chartered accountant, then Company Secretary of Gray Dawes and who became the Company Secretary on

the launch of Inchcape & Co. Limited in October 1958, and Hugh
Waters, who had had twenty years' experience as a solicitor in India
before joining the Group in 1951 at Lord Inchcape's invitation, and was
a director of Duncan Macneill & Co. Ltd from its inception, set out for
India in January 1958 with the object of acquiring control of Binny
(Madras) Ltd for Gray Dawes. Having to take into account Indian
Income and Super Tax, Capital Gains Tax, Wealth Tax, consideration
payable for shares, Companies' Act and Reserve Bank consents, they
investigated exhaustively the many alternative ways of controlling this
company. It was eventually decided to recommend that the investment
portfolios of the Ganges Company and Fairlie Place Securities be
interchanged with the minimum taxation liabilities. As a result the
Ganges Company then held 45 per cent of the Binny (Madras) capital.
Through Gray Dawes' purchase of the Ganges Company from the
Seniors and having acquired control of Binny London, Binny (Madras)
and its subsidiaries were brought into the fold.[5]

Meanwhile, it was realised that not only was a good geographical
spread of business important, but it was also necessary to exclude firms
that did not at the time present a favourable profits or assets ratio. For
this and allied reasons, Gray Dawes sold to the Seniors four companies:
Alexander Shanks and Shanks Ironfounders, the Arbroath engineers in
which the Seniors had originally taken an interest through the marriage
of the First Earl to Jenny Shanks; Gibb Livingston & Co. Ltd, the old-
established trading house in Hong Kong; and Canadian Corporate
Management Co. Ltd. (Gibb Livingston subsequently came back into
the fold in 1966 through the Borneo merger.) George Street Securities
Pty. Ltd in Australia, which, had been formed by the Seniors in 1951 to
take over the properties of Macdonald Hamilton, and China Properties
Ltd were excluded and retained by the Seniors. J. B. Westray & Co. Ltd
was sold to the New Zealand Shipping Co. Ltd (a P & O subsidiary)
because of its managing agency relationship.[6]

The minutiae of financial and legal detail which had to be investigated
and considered in bringing the companies into the Group cannot be
exaggerated. A Herculean task indeed: a financial observer at the time
said that he would have preferred to clean the Augean stables! From the
beginning, there had been real doubts that a successful public flotation
could be achieved. Gray Dawes had originally been seen as the holding
company through which the other firms could be brought together. Yet
this plan had to be abandoned when it was decided to include St Mary
Axe Securities, the Inchcape family's London-based investment com-

pany, as a separate principal subsidiary in its own right. This move gave the new Group an increased sterling content and brought it total ownership of Binny London. St Mary Axe Securities had originally been incorporated in England in 1918 as Edward Hain & Son, ship managers, and had become an investment trust for the estate of the First Earl in 1933, changing its name in 1936. Duncan Macneill & Co. Ltd, the third UK-based firm held by the Seniors, was also included in the new enterprise as a principal subsidiary, together with its own subsidiaries in Pakistan and Kenya.

IV

So the constituent parts of the future Group had been assembled, as shown in Appendix 9.2, but now a new holding company was required to link these three principal subsidiaries, a total of seventeen companies. This was necessary to avoid placing any of these subsidiaries below or above each other in the future arrangements, which could have led to a damaging reluctance to co-operate and work harmoniously together.[7]

An overall holding company was needed without delay, so on 15 August 1958, a company with a nominal capital of £2 was formed under the name of IGD Ltd, with subscribers, directors and secretary from the solicitors to the Prospectus, Slaughter and May. It was then agreed that 25 per cent of the equity should be offered to the public at 25s per share, with the company's capital structure based on £1.8m ordinary capital. In addition, £850 000 in 6½ per cent unsecured loan stock 1978/83 was issued, which was allotted entirely to the family shareholders in St Mary Axe Securities Ltd.

A full and detailed prospectus was finally signed on 23 October 1958 and published four days later, within the projected time scale. The Stock Exchange quotations were granted for the shares and loan stock and dealings began on 31 October. The issue was well received in the City and with the Press, and by 11 May 1959, the middle price of an ordinary share had risen to 31s 3d.[8]

*   *   *

The formation of a Group based upon the family investments was the only way in which the companies could survive and prosper in the second half of the twentieth century. This transformation was achieved by the careful evaluation of each holding, its attractiveness as a member of the Group, its geographical location and the changes it required for inclusion or exclusion. The rational and logical way in which the prospectus was produced, based on the criteria of what would satisfy the Stock Exchange and the investing public rather than sentiment or convenience, led to a successful flotation which was soon followed by spectacular growth. It could be argued that, in forming a Group, the investments of the Inchcape family were following the example of many large companies influenced by the waves of mergers in the 1920s and the 1950s. However, in Britain these were principally manufacturing firms, seeking greater economies of scale.[9] The Inchcape Group was formed by the timely recognition of the need for change: of the old managing agency houses of India, none now survive. The Third Earl not only preserved the value of his grandfather's assets but increased their worth several times over by grouping these previously separate businesses under the prestigious Inchcape name. This gave them status and inspired confidence. In this way, the Group became a continuing tribute to its original founder, but in a form which he could not possibly have imagined.

NOTES

1. *Inchcape Archives*, [*IA*] Internal memo, 'Group Reorganisation from 1947 Onwards', compiled by Donald Caswell, (1962) p.1.
2. Ibid pp.2–3.
3. Ibid, pp.3–7, and interview with Mr H. C. Waters, 30 July 1984.
4. Ibid, pp.7–8, internal memo 'Inchcape & Co. Limited: A Summary of Happenings during 1957 and 1958', compiled by Donald Caswell, May 1959, pp.1–2 and Prospectus, Inchcape & Co. Limited, published 27 October 1958, 'History and Business', pp.7–8.
5. Internal memo 1959, pp.7–8.
6. Ibid, pp.8–9.
7. Interview with Mr H. C. Waters, August 1983, published in 'The Times of Inchcape', Special 25th. Anniversary Supplement to the *Inchcape Magazine*, no. 16 (September 1983).
8. Internal memo 1959, pp.10–15. Ensuring that everything material was properly mentioned in the Prospectus to the satisfaction of Slaughter and May, the solicitors, involved much detailed work, including, *inter alia*, an examination of many contracts, particularly management arrangements, in which constituent companies were involved. See *History of Acquisitions* (mentioned in Chapter 10).
9. See Leslie Hannah, *The Rise of the Corporate Economy* (London, 1983) 2nd edn, chap. 9, pp.123–42.

APPENDIX 9.1 INCHCAPE FAMILY INTERESTS IN 1948

Lord Inchcape's Directorships

Cheerie Valley Tea Co. Ltd
Cossipore Tea Co. Ltd
Craigpark Tea Co. Ltd
Doodputlee Tea Co. Ltd
Gray Mackenzie Co. Ltd
Greenwood Tea Co. Ltd
Kalline Tea Co. Ltd
Koyah Tea Co. Ltd
Majagram Tea Co. Ltd
Mediterranean Transport Co. Ltd
Northern Dooars Co. Ltd
Rivers Steam Navigation Co. Ltd
Salonah Tea Co. Ltd
Scottpore Tea Co. Ltd
Smith Mackenzie & Co. Ltd
Tarrapore Tea Co. Ltd
Thanai Tea Co. Ltd
Western Cachar Tea Co. Ltd

Lord Inchcape's Partnerships

Barry & Co.
Duncan Macneill & Co.
Gray Dawes & Co.
J. B. Barry & Son
Macdonald Hamilton & Co.
Mackinnon Mackenzie & Co., Calcutta
Mackinnon Mackenzie & Co., China
Mackinnon Mackenzie & Co., Columbo
Macneill & Co.

Other firms in which the Inchcape family had interests

Alexander Shanks & Son Ltd
Australasian United Steam Navigation Company Ltd
Binny & Co. Ltd
Binny (Madras) Limited
Canadian Corporate Management Co. Ltd
China Properties Ltd

Delmege Forsyth & Co. Ltd
Ganges Transport & Trading Co. Ltd
Gibb Livingston and Company Ltd
Madura Co. Private Ltd
Shanks Ironfounders Ltd
St Mary Axe Securities Ltd

SOURCES *Inchcape Archives*, Mediterranean Transport Co. Ltd, Board Minutes, 1948, and internal memo, 'Group Reorganisation from 1947'.

APPENDIX 9.2 THE COMPOSITION OF THE INCHCAPE GROUP, 23 OCTOBER 1958

Company	Country of incorportation	Effective interest in equity (%)
Gray Dawes & Co. Limited*	England	100.00
Binny & Co. Limited	England	98.97
The Ganges Transport & Trading Company Limited	India	100.00
Binny & Co. (Madras), Limited	India	82.88
Binny's Engineering Works Private Limited	India	73.41
The Buckingham and Carnatic Company Limited	India	44.05
The Bangalore Woollen, Cotton and Silk Mills Company Limited	India	41.36
Gray Mackenzie & Co. Limited	England	50.42
Bahrein Slipway Company Limited	England	50.42
Busreh Slipway Company Limited	Iraq	50.42
Smith Mackenzie & Co. Limited	Kenya	51.03
Spencer Yates & Curry Limited	England	100.00
Duncan Macneill & Co. Limited*	England	100.00
Macneill & Kilburn Limited	Pakistan	100.00
Kilburn & Company (Pakistan), Limited	Pakistan	100.00
Karirana Estates Limited	Kenya	57.50
St Mary Axe Securities Limited*	England	100.00

*Principal subsidiary.

SOURCE *Inchcape Archives*, Prospectus, Inchcape & Co. Limited, dated 23 October 1958, 'Accountants' Report', p.3.

10 Acquisitions and Consolidation: The Inchcape Group, 1958–84

The newly-formed Group of Companies, after its successful launch in the autumn of 1958 as Inchcape & Co. Limited emerged from its first year of trading with justified confidence in the future. The Group's market capitalisation on 3 November 1958 was £2.565m, with a mid-market price of 28*s* 6*d* [142½*p*] for its 1.8m issued £1 Ordinary shares. By the accounting date of 31 March 1960, although no further shares had yet been issued, the Group's market capitalisation exceeded £4m, based on the mid-market price that day of 44*s* 6*d* (222½*p*]. In that short time the profit available for distribution to ordinary shareholders had increased from £280 000 to over £400 000 after tax, with earnings per share of 22.33*p* equivalent, an increase of 44 per cent over the previous year.

This rapid growth in a mere sixteen months was a foretaste of things to come. Group profit in 1958–9 had been £712 000. By 1976–7 it reached a staggering £73m. Despite many capitalisation issues, the price of Inchcape shares continued to rise, reaching up to 690*p* on 31 March 1973. On 30 September 1980, the Group's market capitalisation stood at nearly £400m, over 175 times the original launch value. On 14 March 1977, Inchcape was recorded as the twenty-eighth largest British

company by market value, only narrowly behind the Midland and
Lloyds Banks, the Prudential and General Accident Insurance companies, and above Bass Charrington and Hawker Siddeley.[1] By 1980,
however, the climate had changed. At the end of 1981, the median share
price had fallen from 460*p* to 270*p* and the market capitalisation was
under £225m by the end of 1982. The most recent Report and Accounts,
for 1984, suggests that the tide may have turned again, as for the year as a
whole the profit on ordinary activities before taxation was £78.9m
compared with £53.0m for the year ended 31 December 1983.

Table 10.1 and Table 10.2 quantify the spectacular transformation
which is shown dramatically in Figures 10.1 and 10.2. The prospectus
issued in 1958 shows it as a modest holding company, with seventeen
subsidiaries, their assets based mainly in the UK and in India, as
described in Chapter 9. Now the Group comprises over 700 principal
subsidiaries and associated companies, operating in over fifty countries.
How was such a dramatic rate of growth achieved, while retaining the
fundamental structure, aims and activities of its original foundations?

I

The expansion of the Group may be seen in five main phases. Each
enabled it first to survive, then to grow. Each new merger and
acquisition made the next possible. Through the purchase of the equity
of other groups, rather than just individual businesses, Inchcape & Co.
Ltd (after 1981 Inchcape PLC) increased its holdings by geometrical
progression. This was only one of the ways by which the Group
expanded. It also grew by the development of its existing companies, and
by the formation of new holding companies and new sub-groups. No
aspect of the Group stayed exactly the same over this quarter century,
except, remarkably, the overall pattern of business carried out, in
approach and type. The greater part of its income continued to be
derived from merchanting, marine services, insurance and tea estates, in
1958 as in 1984, as seen in Table 10.3, although motor distribution has
played an increasing part in the past twenty years. The development of
the member companies from their origins in the eighteenth, nineteenth
and early twentieth centuries, which have been discussed in the previous
chapters, show the establishment of their *modus vivendi*. They would
venture into a new country or set up a branch in a new district with their
traditional business activities, with familiar commodities, principals and
services, or they would try a new activity, trading and dealing with an

TABLE 10.1 Inchcape & Co. Limited, £1 ordinary shares, 1958–1984

	a Issued and fully paid	b Official quotation s d	c Median price s d	d Market capitalisation (£)
3.11.58	1 800 000	27/6–29/6	28/6	2 565 000*
31. 3.59	1 800 000	30/6–32/6	31/6	2 835 000
31. 3.60	1 800 000	43/= –46/=	44/6	4 005 000
31. 3.61	2 062 031	51/= –55/=	53/=	5 464 382
31. 3.62	2 262 031	44/6–48/6	46/6	5 259 222
31. 3.63	2 262 031	56/= –61/=	58/6	6 616 440
31. 3.64	3 393 046	45/= –49/=	47/=	7 973 658
31. 3.65	3 393 046	35/6–40/6	38/=	6 446 787
31. 3.66	3 393 046	34/= –39/=	39/6	6 361 961
31. 3.67	5 825 476	31/= –34/=	32/6	9 466 398
31. 3.68	7 281 845	38/9–40/9	39/9	14 472 666
31. 3.69	11 043 676	54/= –59/=	56/6	31 198 384
31. 3.70	14 198 130	52/6–57/6	55/=	39 044 857
		p – p	p	
31. 3.71	14 198 130	270–295	282½	37 270 091
31. 3.72	19 065 912	505–535	520	99 142 742
31. 3.73	21 147 522	640–690	665	140 631 021
31. 3.74	34 785 451	385–410	397½	138 272 167
31. 3.75	34 902 479	295–325	310	108 197 684
31. 3.76	45 517 342	400–440	420	191 172 836
31. 3.77	75 705 333	350–400	375	283 894 998
31. 3.78	79 299 438	360–410	385	305 302 836
31. 3.79	80 828 458	300–350	325	262 692 488
31. 3.80	81 113 973	335–355	365	279 843 206
30. 9.80	81 457 410	475–495	485	395 068 438
31. 3.81	81 773 170	450–470	460	376 156 580
31.12.81	84 761 107	260–280	270	228 854 980
31.12.82	84 773 959	255–275	265	224 650 990
31.12.83	84 786 055	265–285	275	233 161 651
31.12.84	84 786 055	385–405	395	334 904 917

*Price stock exchange quotation. Market capitalisation is median price multiplied by the number of shares, i.e. $d = cxa$. Column b shows the variation in the price of Inchcape shares on the particular day listed before column a, the date of the final report.

NOTE The shares were promoted by a Prospectus dated 23 October 1958 at a price of 25/-, giving a value to the Company of £2 250 000. Of the original 1 800 000 shares, 350 000 were made available to the market.

SOURCE Stock Exchange daily lists, City Business Library, Basinghall Street, London EC3.

TABLE 10.2 Inchcape & Co. Limited – dividend and earnings record

Year to 31st March	Profit before taxation (£ thousand)	Profit available to Inchcape & Co. Ltd Ordinary Shareholders (£ thousand)	Earnings in pence (p) per share	Growth in earnings per share over previous year (%)	Gross dividend in pence (p) per share
1959	712	280	15.54	—	11
1960	916	402	22.33	44	11
1961	914	471	22.86	2	11
1962	1 115	655	28.94	26	15
1963	1 209	661	29.21	1	16
1964	1 171	679	20.02	3	11.25
1965	1 110	685	20.19	1	11.25
1966	965	644	18.97	(− 6)	12.25
1967	2 853	1 459	25.05	32	12.5
1968	2 836	1 841	25.28	26	10
1969	4 704	2 391	21.65	29	7.375
1970	5 241	2 897	20.41	18	10
1971	6 544	3 437	24.20	19	12
1972	9 514	5 036	26.57	46	13
1973	14 923	7 463	35.38	33	13.65
1974	30 103	13 875	41.74	77	9.555
1975	28 096	11 466	32.94	(− 21)	10.509
1976	37 001	15 126	33.77	3	11.56
1977	73 383	32 177	42.52	89	15.528
1978	62 274	31 517	40.67	(− 4)	22.524
1979	41 052	16 282	20.19	(− 50)	23.987
1980	65 613	34 955	43.11	114	25.928
June 1981					
Dec. 1981	65 694	24 644	29.1		25.928
June 1982					
Dec. 1982	50 341	10 222	12.1		25.928
June 1983	24 506		12.3		
Dec. 1983	53 017	11 165	13.2		25.928
June 1984	35 956		16.0		
Dec. 1984	78 900	24 800	29.1		25.928

NOTES 64 original shares are equivalent to 96 shares after 1 for 2 capitalisation issue in 1963/64

120 shares after 1 for 4 capitalisation issue in 1967/68

180 shares after 1 for 2 capitalisation issue in 1968/69

225 shares after 1 for 4 capitalisation issue in 1969/70

Continued opposite

expanding range of goods, in markets which they already knew well and of which they had many years of experience.

Deviations from this pattern, either in the 1880s or 1980s, were rare and did not usually result in success. For example, in 1890 Smith Mackenzie & Co. had taken part in an early attempt to grow Arabica coffee in East Africa, a new activity. It was also in a new area. They had purchased jointly with the Imperial British East Africa Company, a plot of land at Dagoretti near Mount Ngong, the sacred mountain of the Masai, near Nairobi in mainland Kenya, far from their base at Zanzibar. The venture failed, and the investment in the land (which cost a bale of Amerikani cloth, five oxen and a string of beads) had to be written off.[2] Similarly, also in the late 1970s, the Group decided to sell its holdings in a Dutch commodity trading and broking company, Harborn, after it had suffered a series of losses. These culminated in a spectacular case of misappropriation, involving a totally bogus cargo of cocoa. As reported in the Inchcape Company Profile in the *Far Eastern Economic Review*,

In the 1977 and 1978 accounts, pre-tax profits were reduced by £6.5 million and £17.9 million respectively to cover the Harborn loss. That particular débâcle stemmed from the fact that no one in head office knew anything about commodity trading and therefore was not in any position to control what was going on. Said one director: 'We didn't have the expertise to monitor that'. Now that traditional policy had been reasserted – the company enters new businesses only in countries and regions in which it already is established or, alternatively, sets up in a new country only with a traditional Inchcape business.[3]

---

300 shares after 1 for 3 capitalisation issue in 1971/72
450 shares after 1 for 2 capitalisation issue in 1973/74
675 shares after 1 for 2 capitalisation issue in 1976/77

Earnings per share figures have not been adjusted for differences in treatment of dividends with introduction of Corporation Tax in year to 31 March, 1966, and ACT in year to 31 March, 1974. Profit available to Inchcape & Co. Limited Ordinary Shareholders includes share of results of associated companies from the year ended 31 March, 1971. Extraordinary items are not included in earnings.

4 shares @ £1.25 per share placing price in September 1958 = £80; now worth in July, 1980: 675 shares × £4.30 = £2902 (gross equivalent).

SOURCE *History of Acquisitions*, Internal Memo, November 1980, note 6; updated from published Annual Reports and Accounts year ending 31 December 1984.

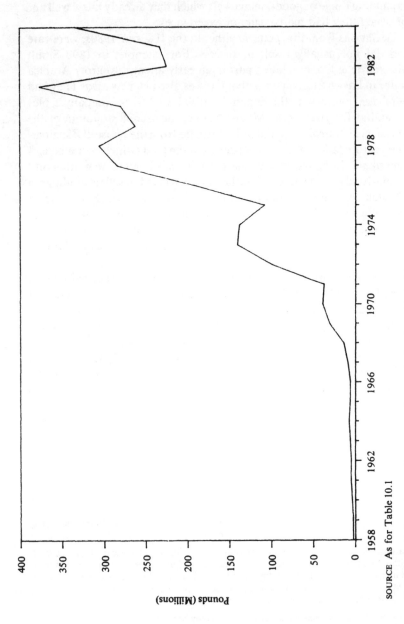

SOURCE As for Table 10.1

FIGURE 10.1 Inchcape Group, market capitalisation, 1958–84

261

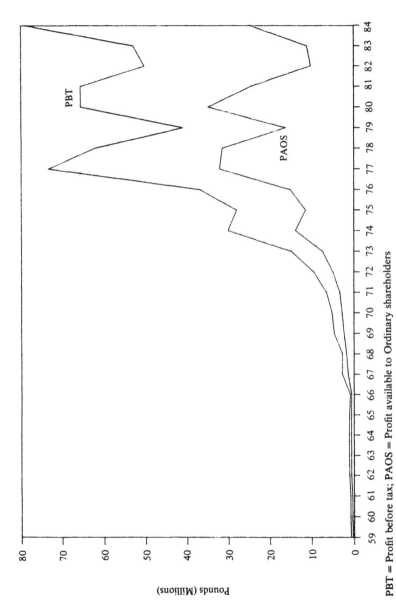

Pounds (Millions)

PBT = Profit before tax; PAOS = Profit available to Ordinary shareholders

SOURCE As for Table 10.2

FIGURE 10.2 Inchcape Group earnings, 1959–84

TABLE 10.3 Changes in the proportion of Group profits earned by different areas of business activity, sample years 1965–84, shown as % of totals

Year	General merchanting	Engineering and manufacturing	Shipping and marine services	Tea estates	Investment Trusts	Trade and other investment income	Dividend from subsidiaries in India	Timber and construction	Motor vehicle distribution	Insurance	Associated companies
1965	20.0	14.5	14.0	3.0	10.0	18.5	20.0				
1966	15.5	11.0	19.5	3.5	12.5	26.0	12.0				
1967	34.5	6.0	15.0	2.0	3.0	7.0	4.5	6.0	22.0		
1972	39.0	3.0	11.0	–**	1.0	3.0	**	4.0	39.0		
1973	45.0	1.0	8.0	–**	1.0	2.0		4.0	37.0		4.0
1076	44.0	3.0	14.0	–**	1.0	–		1.0	35.0		4.0
1978	36.0	–	17.0	–**	–	1.0		3.0	26.0	10.0	7.0
1980	28.0	–	10.0	4.0	–	1.0		6.0	40.0	6.0	7.0
1982	41.0	3.0	10.0	4.0	–	2.0		3.0	14.0	13.0	16.0
1984	21.0	*	16.0	13.0	–	*		*	21.5	7.0	*

* These headings are classified as 'others' in June 1984 Interim Report, and amount to 21.5%.

** Tea estates and dividends from India are not recorded for these years. The Group's investment in timber and motors began only with the Borneo Company, and insurance earnings were only important enough to be recorded separately after Bain Dawes was acquired.

SOURCE *Inchcape & Co. Limited/Inchcape PLC, Report and Accounts*, 1965–83 and Interim Statement, 1984.

By generally seeking expansion through these established guidelines, the merchant partnerships which formed the Group in 1958 had survived the economic vagaries of a century of overseas mercantile business. A notable success is Gray Mackenzie, for example: which had established itself as the BI agent and in the handling of imports and exports in Basra and Bushire by 1869, and ventured into new ports and new countries of the Middle East specialising in these activities.[4] Then the firm was in a position to expand its range of businesses: into the oil industry, port management, engineering maintenance, and travel, insurance and freight-forwarding agency work. Table 10.4 shows that this area constantly contributed to Group profits out of all proportion to the assets invested there. A modern example of an acquisition by Inchcape which exemplifies this policy is the merger with Specialist Services International which, among others, brought Caleb Brett into the Group. Their principal business of cargo inspection is new to Inchcape, but not its places of operation: Singapore, Malaysia and UAE are traditional Group areas, and more recently Inchcape has become established in Belgium, Holland, France, Canada and the USA, other countries where Caleb Brett is based.[5]

The policy of 'new place, old business' – 'new business, old place' coexisted with another general aim, that of allowing a large measure of local autonomy and independent operation in the running of member companies. This has had its disadvantages, when inefficient and careless local management have misused their authority – such as in the case of Radley Cotton Mills Company Limited (Toronto). The company was jointly owned, from 1966, by Inchcape (which at this stage had no other Canadian holdings) and the Wadia Group of India. Its Canadian local management was therefore supervised from a distance at London and Bombay. Some commitments were described in a subsequent Group report as 'imprudent' and 'profligate', causing initial financial embarrassment between the two Groups and the Royal Bank of Canada, which had provided loans for working capital. Such reliance on local Bank borrowings for this particular investment severely limited dealings, and was later seen as a mistake. Adequate Group finance for a project was provided in all future transactions. The Inchcape Group eventually cut its losses in this instance, handing over the business to Wadia, incurring a significant but affordable loss. The final verdict was that 'leaving the original owner to run it with no proper supervision capable of being exercised by the new owners' had "proved disastrous"'.[6] Again, the acquisition of Lighting and Leisure Ltd – an uncharacteristic mistake by Mann Egerton in 1978 – was to be

TABLE 10.4   Changes in the geographical distribution of net assets and sources of income of the Inchcape Group, sample years 1958–84, shown as % of totals

Year	UK	Australia	East Africa	Middle East	India & Pakistan	Canada	Caribbean	Hong Kong	Malaysia, Thailand Singapore, Brunei
1958 Net assets	35.8	–	12.1	12.0	37.6	2.5	–	–	–
1958 Income (before tax)	42.9	1.6	6.1	21.2	27.2	1.0	–	–	–
1965 Net assets	28.0	11.0	10.0	14.0	37.0	–	–	–	–
1965 Income (before tax)	10.0	4.0	8.0	19.0	59.0	–	–	–	–
1967 Net assets	17.0	11.0	6.0	9.0	14.0	2.0	3.0	3.0	8.0 27.0
1967 Income (after tax)	9.0 (and Europe)	8.0	8.0 (all Africa)	22.0	8.0 (investment income only)	1.0 (N. America)	1.0	6.0 (+ Far (SE Asia) East)	20.0 17.0
1973 Net assets	20.0	11.0	14.0	4.0	4.0	2.0	2.0	18.0	25.0
1973 Income (after tax)	15.0	–	11.0	20.0	1.0	(–6)	1.0	35.0	
1976 Net assets	23.0	7.0	6.0	4.0	2.0	–	1.0	23.0	34.0
1976 Income (after tax)	21.0	2.0	14.0	29.0	less than ½	(–9) (N & S America)	2.0	25.0	16.0
1980 Net assets									
1980 Profit (before tax)	18.0	6.0	1.0	11.0	1.0	2.0	2.0	29.0	31.0
1984 Net assets	30.5	1.5	2.0	7.0	12.0	–	–	28.5	17.5
1984 Profit (before tax) (6 months ended June)						–			

SOURCE Inchcape & Co. Limited/Inchcape PLC, Report and Accounts, 1959–83 and Interim Statement, 1984.

unsuccessful for the same reasons. This was due not so much to a lack of experience in a new venture but to misjudgement of its management and insufficient investigation. It was to lose at least £4m over only a few years. Similarly, the 1983 accounts revealed a loss of £30m through overtrading by the Anglo-Thai Motor Group. The Chairman, Sir David Orr, admitted that this loss was partly due to inadequate supervision from Head office, commenting that 'we should have spotted it', and that more vigorous controls had been introduced.[7]

In the vast majority of cases, however, strong local autonomy in day-to-day management and the continuance of trading under their own names has been fundamental to the success of the Group's overseas subsidiaries. This policy became a hallmark of the Inchcape Group, and effectively made it more attractive to the companies it was to take over.

II

From the launch of Inchcape & Co. Limited in 1958, a phase of further consolidation, strengthening and rationalisation of the Group's resources was needed before any large acquisitions could be contemplated. Chapter 9 showed that the formation of the Group, which offered an attractive UK-based package to would-be investors in overseas trading, was not seen as an end product in itself, but as a means of obtaining a good price for the shares and satisfying Stock Exchange requirements. The flotation, which was received well in the City, was the first move in an overall strategy which was to prepare the Group for its remarkable growth in the second half of the twentieth century,[8] as shown by the list of principal acquisitions in Table 10.5.

Phase One of this growth took place between 1958 and 1966. The newly-formed Group, unlike the previous hotchpotch of informally related partnerships and investments, enjoyed three distinct advantages. First, it was now readily identifiable by the public, especially in the City: its Stock Exchange quotation gave it immediate respectability and status. For the first time, details of the member companies, and a summary of their histories, were freely available, published in the original Prospectus. The Directors' names were also recorded, and inspired confidence.

Second, by 'going public', the Group considerably expanded its available capital resources. With a published daily share price and thus known market capitalisation, the Group had a measurable value. 25 per cent of the equity was held by the general public, and this made it easier

TABLE 10.5 Principal acquisitions by Inchcape & Co. Limited and Inchcape PLC, 1958–84

Name	Date	£1 ordinary shares	Cash	Other
Gray Dawes & Co. Ltd*	1958	1 125 000		
Duncan Macneill & Co. Ltd*	1958	218 555		£336 363 (notes and loan)
St Mary Axe Securities Ltd*	1958	120 080		
Gray Mackenzie & Co. Ltd	1960	98 884		
AUSN Co. Ltd	1960	163 147		
Macdonald, Hamilton & Co. Pty. Ltd	1961		£460 000	
Fairlie Place Securities Ltd (and interest in Macneill & Barry)	1961	200 000		
Smith Mackenzie & Co. Ltd**	1964		£337 965	
Mackenzie Dalgety Limited	1965		£536 226	
Borneo Company Limited	1967	2 432 430		£810 810 (Preference shares) £4 050 050 (Loan stock)
MOENCO Ltd	1968		£154 000	
Gilman (Holdings) Ltd	1969		£2 567 000	
G. W. Joynson & Co. Ltd	1969	120 909		
J. H. Little Group	1969		£280 000	
Mackenzie Dalgety Ltd***	1969	220 000		
VYB and Intercotra Ltd	1969	94 828		
Lusolanda Companies	1970		£534 118	
Corkhill, Hyslop Ltd	1970		£67 905	
Ocean Inchcape Ltd	1970		£4 000	
BEWAC Motor Corp. Ltd	1970			£3 254 496 (loan stock)
Dodwell Motors Ltd	1970		HK $38 541 000	
Borneo Co. Ltd preference shares	1971	346 313		
Dodwell & Co. Ltd	1972	2 000 000		£3 200 000 (loan stock)
Gray Dawes Bank, formed from Gray Dawes & Co. Ltd	1973		£2 000 000	
Mann Egerton & Co. Ltd	1973	2 979 348		£4 290 261 (loan stock)
Atkins Kroll & Co. Ltd	1974		£447 000	
Anglo-Thai Corpn. Ltd	1975	9 456 984	£101 624	
A. W. Bain Holdings Ltd	1976	3 304 417		
Gray Dawes Westray (Holdings) Ltd	1976	1 605 663		
Pride & Clarke Ltd	1978	1 076 401	£6 939 000	
Assam Company (India) Ltd	1980		£4 000 000	
Other S. American Companies	1983		£12 000 000	
SSI	1983		£35 000 000	

Other subsidiaries not listed were acquired by existing subsidiaries, e.g. Peschaud & Cie. Int. SA by Gray Mackenzie in 1975 and Lighting & Leisure Ltd by Mann Egerton in 1978.

NOTES *These were the original acquisitions in the launch of the Group in 1958 which, with two subscriber shares, equal 1.8 million. Through them, other substantial interests in Gray Mackenzie and Smith Mackenzie were acquired.
**This represents a purchase of a further 29 per cent holding.
***In 1969 a further 50 per cent was acquired.

SOURCES *Inchcape PLC, Annual Reports and Accounts*, 1959–84; *History of Acquisitions*, analysis of £1 ordinary share capital, and summary of principal changes in the Group; ledger, Inchcape PLC, and ledger, Inchcape Overseas Ltd (held by Group Consolidation).

to attract further investment when needed. The reorganisation of the member companies, which followed the Group's formation, strengthened Inchcape's capital base. The considerable assets in India and Pakistan, for instance, now had an official sterling value which could be realised. Similarly, many constituent companies which previous to 1958, were associated companies only, became subsidiaries (that is, the Group owned over 50 per cent or more of the equity). They were then included in the consolidated Group accounts rather than being recorded individually in terms of book value and dividends received. The consolidation of the Company's assets thus centralised its financial resources, revealed its true strength and prepared it for future growth.

The third benefit enjoyed by the Group after its reorganisation and flotation may be seen as a series of fiscal advantages.

One of the principal reasons for the original formation was to provide a ready-made value of assets figure for death duty purposes: otherwise, subsidiaries could be liable to a break-up valuation, company by company which, in the case of privately-owned concerns, could be crippling. In the same way, the burden of taxation on the companies in the UK, previously levied according to their status as partnerships, was considerably reduced, as they had become limited liability companies over the previous half century. When there were no taxation advantages in changing from a partnership to a limited company, firms stayed as they were, as in the case of Macdonald Hamilton in Australia.[9]

When these initial objectives had been achieved, further changes could be implemented. In 1958, the Group's Indian and Pakistani holdings did not present a satisfactory income–assets ratio. Table 10.4 shows that the greatest concentration of the Group's holdings was in these countries (37.6 per cent) but only 27.2 per cent of its overall income came from this source. Yet the future development of the Indian and Pakistani companies was seen as vital to the Group. Thus, in its early years, Binny's was further reorganised and Macneill & Barry Ltd which had previously been excluded, returned to the fold.

Binny's textile production provided essential income for the Group in 1958: nearly 11 000 000 lb of cotton and woollen goods were manufactured, valued at over £4.5m.[10] During 1959, Binny's and its subsidiaries were more closely integrated. Separate statements of the consolidated earnings and net assets of the four Binny companies were published in the Group accounts which included Macneill & Barry from 1961, showing a steady improvement and growing importance. Their taxed profits rose from £147 379 in 1959, to £191 325 in 1960, £253 738 in 1961, £295 475 in 1962, and £325 786 in 1963. This provided the Group with a sound income which contributed to its payment of a gross dividend equivalent to 11*p* in 1959, 1960 and 1961, 15*p* in 1962 and 16*p* in 1963. In 1960–1, Macneill & Barry Ltd became a Group subsidiary, together with its eleven subsidiaries. Its involvement with the Joint Steamer Companies, discussed in previous chapters, increasingly became a matter for concern, and this aspect of its activities had to be dealt with before any future acquisitions could be contemplated by the Group. Fortunately, the Indian Government was persuaded to acquire and take responsibility for the running of the Indian part of this concern, in 1965. If this problem had not been settled, the effect on the Group in 1964–5 would have been so considerable as to make the merger with the Borneo Company impossible. The emphasis placed on strengthening Group holdings in India in the early years of Inchcape, & Co. Limited was well justified: Table 10.4 shows that the proportion of net assets based in India and Pakistan in 1965 was the same as in 1958 – 37 per cent. However, Group income from this area had risen dramatically, to 59 per cent. Mr H. C. Waters, a Director of Inchcape & Co. Limited from 1960 to 1977, maintained that the Group, 'could not have come into being without the Indian connections and in its early years the company could not have consolidated itself without the assets and income from the subcontinent'. The subsequent decline of Group interests in India is summarised in Appendix 10.2.

Two further changes facilitated future Group growth. First, it strengthened its foothold in Australia through the acquisition of 100 per cent of the equity of the Australasian United Steam Navigation Company Limited [AUSN]. Previously the Group had a mere toehold in this country, with Gray Dawes' 10 per cent interest in the merchant partnership and shipping-agency business of Macdonald Hamilton & Co. With the AUSN, Inchcape not only made its first successful acquisition of a fully-quoted company, and conveniently by share issue rather than cash, but considerably increased its geographical diversity.[11] From the beginning, as discussed earlier, traditional Inchcape spheres of operation were favoured as areas for expansion, especially in the case of countries linked to the Commonwealth. In the earlier days it was felt that it was safer to expand in the Commonwealth countries and those of the Middle East, partly because the Group knew how to operate in most of them, but also because of language problems elsewhere, and the need to be reliant on local management whose ways were different from those of the Group. Although the AUSN from the early 1950s had experienced a drop in the value and earnings of its coastal fleet, its investment assets approached £800 000 and its investment earnings were nearly £50 000 in 1960. The unprofitable ships and properties of this company were then disposed of and, with the new Macdonald Hamilton partnership purchased in 1961, the Group developed the beginnings of a solid core of businesses in Australia.[12] The second development in the Group's early years was the advantageous purchase of its London Head Office which, in terms of the steady increase in its value, has been one of the most successful of Group investments. Moving into one central headquarters building also gave the staff the feeling that they had joined the Group, rather than associating solely with a particular subsidiary. The previous registered office in 122 Leadenhall Street, which was owned by the P & O, gave the Group insufficient independence and was in any case being redeveloped. Costing £810 000 in 1960, the building (bought from Spillers and originally built in 1923) is now worth an estimated £7m. To help to finance the cost of 40 St Mary Axe, the Company issued £700 000 5¾ per cent unsecured loan stock repayable in 1988, representing an especially shrewd borrowing.[13]

III

Thus, by the 1960s, the Group had improved the profitability of its Indian assets, expanded the geographical distribution of its interests and improved the co-odination of its London-based leadership with a single Head office.

Making profits of over £1m per year before taxation from 1961 to 1962, and with a market capitalisation approaching £6½m, the Group was now poised for further and unprecedented growth. The second phase of the Group's transformation was dominated by one event: the merger at the beginning of 1967 with the Borneo Company Limited. This may be seen as the single most vital transaction in the post-flotation history of the Group. Negotiations leading to the acquisition date back to 1960, when 17 per cent of the equity had been offered to Lord Inchcape personally. The Group was not then in a position to consider a substantial investment in a Group of a similar size to itself; but to keep all options open, these shares were bought by the Seniors, separately from the Group, through an Australian company called Macham Holdings Pty. Limited, an investment company in which the Seniors maintained an interest outside the Group. Inchcape & Co. Limited was to face considerable opposition from the Borneo Company Board when it made its initial merger approaches, but the holding of these shares, which had been increased to 23 per cent by 1966, considerably smoothed the path to eventual acquisition, which was achieved by an issue of 2 432 430 Inchcape shares in January 1967 (see Table 10.5).[14]

The dramatic changes brought about by this transaction may be seen in the tables: in an almost doubling of the share issue and, by including Borneo Company earnings, in the tripling of the Group's pre-tax profit, representing a 32 per cent growth in earnings per share over the previous year. The geographical distribution of assets and income of the Group changed almost completely, and there was an addition to its range of activities. Yet less tangible changes wrought by the inclusion of the Borneo Company into the Group were as, if not more, important to its subsequent programme of consolidation and expansion. This acquisition was the first major share issue by the Group, as seen in Table 10.5, and resulted in doubling the size and importance of Inchcape & Co. Limited at a stroke. Significantly, it was a good example of the Inchcape policy of 'new place, old business – new business, old place' which has been mentioned earlier in this chapter. The Borneo Company and the Inchcape Group had many activities in common, such as shipping and insurance-agency work, in representing various important British and other principals in importing goods, and in exporting local products.[15] Chapters 1 and 7 have revealed that it was very much a group in the Inchcape mould, although its constituent parts enjoyed much closer links from its mid-nineteenth century origins. Table 10.3 clearly shows that its principal business was acting as general merchants, agents, managers and secretaries: and the profits declared in this sector of Group activities increased more than fivefold after the merger. Yet the main attraction of acquiring the Borneo Company lay in its countries of operation, at a time when the Inchcape Group was especially seeking goegraphical expansion. The number of regions of operation of the Group were doubled with the inclusion of holdings in Canada, the Caribbean, Hong Kong, Malaysia, Singapore, Brunei and Thailand. In addition to this, the Borneo Company operated jointly with Inchcape in two regions – the UK and Australia – and introduced two new activities to the Group's portfolio – motor-vehicle distribution and timber and construction industries. Thus, with the merger, new businesses and new areas were combined with those already familiar to Inchcape: by their nature, the two organisations could be easily dovetailed together. By complementing each other in this way, the merged groups gained a geographical diversity and the quantity and quality of assets to enable them to survive the fluctuations of the world economy and to grow in a manner that would have been unlikely separately.

The vulnerability of the Borneo Company to takeover was strongly denied by its Board which had, after all, strengthened itself by expanding into Hong Kong, acquiring a 100 per cent stake in Gibb Livingston & Co. Ltd and its Far Eastern trading business (as discussed in Chapter 6) in 1964, after holding a majority interest in this company since 1961. The Board emphasised its viability, its opposition to joining a larger organisation, its suspicion of the prospects of Inchcape's holdings in Africa and India, and its determination to remain independent. By persisting with his offer, Lord Inchcape recognised that the Borneo Company could eventually be persuaded to see the logic of joining forces to make a stronger and more diversified group, and that the merger was therefore mutually advantageous. He also recognised his own Group's danger of having too many eggs in too few baskets.[16]

Inchcape offered particularly favourable terms to the Borneo Board, almost overstretching itself in the process; but it considered that, as a general rule, if something is worth having and is genuinely worth £100, one cannot go far wrong if one pays £105, and were even occasionally prepared to offer a figure slightly in excess of that suggested by the Group's advisers. This approach to Borneo was emphasised as a 'merger' rather than an 'acquisition', to soften the blow of being taken over in view of their initial opposition; and when the terms were agreed, the Borneo Board, finally convinced of the wisdom of the transaction, was very helpful and cordial. The entire Borneo Board then joined the Inchcape Board.[17]

The manner in which the acquisition was achieved was to be vital to the future expansion strategy of the Inchcape Group. It was to be an indication of the nature of future approaches, a test case to observers in the City and in international trading circles of Inchcape's style, as it was still largely unknown and untried among the companies quoted on the London Stock Exchange. Lord Inchcape and his advisers were thus setting a pattern, a precedent for future transactions. This was to be one of the most successful spin-offs of the merger. It also showed first that Inchcape was prepared to do its homework with an informed and fully considered approach, and was prepared to tie-up capital making purchases of equity several years in advance of an official bid, although in the case of the Borneo merger these early investments were mainly made by the Inchcape family rather than the Group. Second, it showed its persistence in continuing negotiations despite sustained opposition, and thus its confidence in its own decisions. Third, Inchcape revealed its flexibility and consideration for the shareholders of the company it approached by a willingness to provide a proportion of the puchase price in cash, as distinct from Inchcape shares. Fourth, and reflecting another principle maintained by the Group, and mentioned earlier in this chapter, Inchcape agreed that executive directors of the company acquired might become managing directors within the Group, and that the name, traditions and integrity of the business would be preserved for the benefit of both parties. Some Inchcape directors were to have justifiable misgivings that no senior management staff from Inchcape itself were to work for the Borneo Company's overseas branches until considerably later; but it was important at this stage for Inchcape to establish its reputation for retaining the individuality and autonomy of its new subsidiaries when acquired. Above all, the deal was seen as basically fair to all concerned. It received favourable reports in the Press, which helped to build up the respect which Inchcape was gaining in the City.

Subsequent events were to reinforce the Group's image in the late 1960s and in the 1970s as an expanding and dynamic international holding company with a reputation for honesty and fair dealing. The preservation of the Borneo Company's operations intact showed that Inchcape, unlike others, was not an avaricious predator, an asset stripper, buying companies and then hiving off parts which could attract a good price, short-sightedly fragmenting old established trading networks in the interests of short-term pecuniary gain.

The ramifications of this acquisition were to pervade the subsequent history of the growth of the Group to the present day. Not only did the inclusion of the Borneo Company give Inchcape the size and diversity to bear the risk of further share issues, and to enter new geographical markets and new activities (although usually careful not to combine these two features in one acquisition). The resources which Borneo brought to Inchcape led directly to specific subseqent purchases. In the third phase of the growth of the Group, Inchcape was to acquire Gilman (Holdings) Ltd, a long-established Hong Kong-based firm aided by the stake in Hong Kong which it had newly gained. This impetus to establish businesses in new areas together with a new interest in motor vehicles led to investment in motor distribution in Nigeria. The part-ownership of Alstons Ltd in Trinidad led directly from the Borneo Company's 100 per cent holding in Caribbean Investments Ltd which itself then owned 51 per cent of Charles McEnearney & Co. Ltd. In the fourth phase in the growth of the Group, another Borneo holding, Metro Cars (Hong Kong) Ltd was to play a vital part in the acquisition of Dodwell & Co. Ltd in 1972, through its earlier merger with the latter's sibsidiary, Dodwell Motors Ltd. This interest in the motor trade was then to be expanded with the purchase of Mann Egerton. Inchcape's investigations into the possible acquisition of the Anglo-Thai Corporation, achieved in 1975, had begun in 1968, when the Borneo Company first led it into Hong Kong and the trade of the South China Seas.

A further effect of the Borneo Company merger on Inchcape's subsequent programme of acquisitions was that it demonstrated the value of Barings as advisers. In some early ventures, the Group acted as its own advisers, by using Gray Dawes, but in the interests of objectivity and for an independent viewpoint, it had subsequently brought in Barings, or Kleinwort's, if a conflict of interests with Barings' other clients had intervened. Barings proved of invaluable assistance to the Group throughout this period.

IV

The third principal phase in the development of the Group may be defined as that from 1967 to 1972, from the Borneo merger to the acquisition of Dodwell's. In this period, the Group's market capitalisation increased more than tenfold, its share issue fourfold, the official quotation of its £1 Ordinary shares reaching a peak approaching 700*p* before the first oil crisis. Profit before tax tripled, with a steady annual growth in the earnings of shares over previous years. Yet, as seen in Tables 10.3 and 10.4, the range of its activities and the geographical distribution of Group assets and income (except for a rise in Far Eastern holdings and a decline in India), remained broadly the same.

The thriving mercantile business of many European firms in Hong Kong, founded on more than a century of tradition, was now seen as particularly attractive to Inchcape & Co., with their holdings in Gibb Livingston, Metro Cars and Crown Motors. Again, the Group began by making extensive investigations, and decided that because of the degree of instability in the colony at that particular time, they would need to finance the purchase of a company from within Hong Kong. Through Peter Heath, originally a director of the Borneo Company, and manager at Hong Kong, informal contacts were established with Gilman's,[18] one of Hong Kong's great groups, but which had recently suffered a decline in its business because of troubles in the colony at that time and management problems, further hindered by a lack of communication among senior Board members. Most significantly, Gilman's were actually keen to sell out but wished to avoid merging with a firm already well-established in Hong Kong, as this might result in the loss of their name, traditions and business. Aware of the growing international prowess of Inchcape & Co. Limited, who would be interested in expanding Gilman's from within to enlarge its stake in Hong Kong, the Board was receptive to the Inchcape bid; but a new problem emerged now which Inchcape had not had to face before: rival bids. If news of the approaches were to leak out, other firms might become interested, share prices would rise and Gilman's might turn out to be not such a bargain after all. Fortunately, the last-minute bid by the Hong Kong and Whampoa Dock Co. Ltd, represented by Rothschilds, did not succeed. The principal shareholders and the Directors of Gilman's honourably accepted their commitments to the original Inchcape offer agreed with them, but this offer was slightly increased for the benefit of other shareholders. In the Borneo merger, Inchcape had sufficient time to keep the principals fully informed of the changes in ownership. The greater speed required in closing the deal with Gilman's prevented similar discussions; but it is indicative of Inchcape's growing reputation that there were few agency losses caused by the change in ownership. In this case, however, Inchcape did not, as with the Borneo Company, believe that the existing management team was strong enough. Through the contribution of many Inchcape people, Gilman's soon became a far more profitable and dynamic company than it had been. Even so, the success of the Group's holdings in Hong Kong was largely due to maintaining a number of quasi-independent companies, rather than forming one large group.[19]

The motor-vehicle interests which the Borneo Company brought to the Group was to lead to an established activity in a new geographical area: Nigeria,[20] through the acquisition of British West Africa Corporation and Vivian, Younger and Bond. Inchcape already had some African interests: Smith Mackenzie & Co. Ltd, one of the founder-firms of the Group, had been trading at Zanzibar from the 1870s, and business was transacted in Tanzania, Kenya and Uganda.[21] The Group viewed its investment in Nigeria with more confidence than it did that on the east coast, a suspicion confirmed only a month after the acquisition of the Borneo Company, when the Group's trading activities in Tanzania were nationalised. Although a reasonable level of compensation was agreed and paid to the Group,[22] caution increasingly became the hallmark of Inchcape approaches in developing and potentially unstable economies. Nigeria, however, seemed much more stable: its Civil War was almost at an end, Britain was friendly with its Government, it was known that there were extensive oil resources, and the country had a relatively large population of over 50 million. The Inchcape Board, in acquiring a further interest in Nigeria, hoped that the end of the Civil War would bring a large rehabilitation programme requiring a high level of foreign imports, a trade to which it would be well suited. Nevertheless, Inchcape was already aware of the potential drawbacks: a high level of taxation, import restrictions, remittance problems, the possibility of having to accept a large element – even a majority – of Nigerian shareholding and the fact that such an undertaking would preclude them from future investment in South Africa.

Inchcape acquired its own first holding in Nigeria, paradoxically, through a failed attempt to buy John Holt & Co. (Liverpool) Ltd. This firm, significantly, had approached Inchcape seeking a merger, but the Group, worried about Holt's problems in remitting profits from West Africa, and facing higher bids from Jessels and Lonrho, pulled out, after having learned much about the region through Holts. This led them to accept an approach from a long-established Nigerian trading firm, Vivian, Younger and Bond Ltd, owned by the British Metal Corporation, which made windows, doors and flooring materials. It had a subsidiary, Intercotra Ltd, which acted as shipping and forwarding agents, so this acquisition fitted in well with the existing holdings of the Group. The relatively modest sum of £94 828 was paid in Inchcape shares saving the Group from liquidating assets or seeking further borrowings. The deal was attractive to the British Metal Corporation as it thereby avoided capital gains tax. That many companies taken over were prepared to accept Inchcape shares considerably facilitated the Group's expansion and reveals the high regard in which its shares were held in the City.

In seeking to expand its motor business in Nigeria, the Group, in early 1970, became interested in the Nigerian firm known as the BEWAC Motor Corporation Ltd, which was also a Birmingham-based vehicle distributor. It originally hesitated to become involved in the UK motor trade which, at this time, was faring badly, but negotiations showed that separating the two areas of BEWAC's business was not practicable. Mindful of the need to increase its UK assets, and justifiably confident of eventual profits from BEWAC's home distributorships, Inchcape pressed ahead. The Group then faced a new problem in its programme of acquisitions: a heavy fall in the value of shares generally on the London Stock Market had the effect of devaluing Inchcape's offer to BEWAC, necessitating an alternative offer of Convertible Loan Stock, which was fortunately within the Group's borrowing limits. Unlike the purchase of Gilman's, Inchcape was enabled to obtain in advance the agreement of British Leyland, the main principal which BEWAC represented in the UK and Nigeria.

Meanwhile, in taking further advantage of its experience of new countries through the Borneo merger, the Group increased its interests in the Caribbean.[23] Alstons Ltd, a public company in Trinidad, but also quoted in London, which had a variety of interests (in brewing, general trading, supplying materials to the building trade and in marine and general engineering) was seen as particularly attractive. The problem here was a Government Ordinance which reserved to it the right to a final veto on any takeovers of local firms by aliens, discouraging non-local bids for Alstons, a move largely the result of Jessels' acquisition, then rapid closing-down, of a Trinidad firm. Charles McEnearney's, Inchcape's local 51 per cent subsidiary trading company, was unable to finance or borrow an amount sufficient to purchase Alston's, with the additional complication of uncertainty as to whether the interest on any loan would obtain tax relief. Yet the Group was unable to expand further in the Caribbean except through McEnearney's. So they guaranteed a loan, taken out by McEnearney's, to enable them to acquire a 60 per cent stake in Alston's. The latter, impressed by the continuing independent status of McEnearney's, despite its membership of the Group, and the fact that dividends from this firm had not been remitted outside Trinidad but had been ploughed back into the company, found this bid most attractive, even though rival bidders offered higher terms. As the *Trinidad Express* put it: 'Inchcape's behaviour as an investor, unlike Jessels', has been beyond reproach'.

This third phase of growth also saw a large number of smaller acquisitions, as shown in the Appendix at the end, and ended with the breaking-off of merger talks with the P & O. In October 1972, Inchcape had made a conditional approach to the Board of P & O (of which Lord Inchcape was a director and shortly after, the Chairman) which became the leading subject of interest in the City press. The latter, however, decided that it was preferable to remain independent, and the relationship between the two Groups, which had been associated for over a century through Sir William Mackinnon and the BI, remained excellent. If the P & O had merged with Inchcape this would have resulted in the immediate diversification of the P & O's interests, a development which has subsequently taken place.

V

The next large merger, which involved a share issue almost as great as that required for the Borneo Company, ushered in a fourth phase of extensive change culminating in the record pre-tax profit achievement of £73m in 1977. The Borneo connection also aided in the acquisition of Dodwell's, another milestone in the history of the Group which brought it to Japan.[24] Yet another new problem was experienced in this case. Dodwell's, although a public company in the UK, was not officially quoted, and its Articles of Association included restrictions on share transfers which concentrated 60 per cent of the equity into only twenty-seven hands, mainly members of the Dodwell family and company employees. This initial drawback was eventually to work in Inchcape's favour, as it meant that with only a limited market for Dodwell shares, they did not command a high price. Dodwell's did not initially encourage a takeover as the firm was confident in the future profitability of its new ventures in North America, but these expectations were not fulfilled. In addition there were difficulties in trading in Japan at that time, so fearing unwelcome bids from companies less acceptable, the Company was sympathetic to Inchcape's approach and agreed to negotiations. The Chairman, J. H. Hamm, already had some contact with the Group, as, for example, he and Peter Heath were both members of the Hong Kong Association committee. He enjoyed great loyalty from the shareholders, and favoured Inchcape's offer as being more in the long-term interests of shareholders and employees than the potentially higher bids which news of the merger had prompted.[25] As he pointed out in his letter describing the offer, 'Inchcape is a company with origins as a family business very like our own . . . it would be hard to find a better partner with whom to merge'. Hamm summarised his reasons thus:

> the Inchcape offer is not only a fair and reasonable offer for the issued capital of Dodwell which takes account of future prospects, but not less importantly, it carried with it an assurance of the continuation of the firm of Dodwell under the same management and staff for the foreseeable future.

The Group's growing experience of the motor trade, from the Borneo Company and BEWAC enabled it to increase further its UK holdings without venturing into heavy industry or manufacturing which it has always aimed to avoid. Although the Stock Market and financial press looked to the Group to expand overseas, after the Borneo merger, a strengthened and enlarged UK base was seen as desirable, not only for security but also because UK tax legislation was increasingly leading this way. Resources at home were needed to provide for expansion needs and to reduce dependence on foreign remittances, which could then be restricted for taxation reasons and to leave funds for local investment. With a policy of encouraging the market share of British-made cars in the UK, it concentrated on British Leyland distributors, as Ford strictly limited the retail outlets it allowed to any one company.[26] In this context, Mann Egerton & Co. Ltd was seen as a suitable candidate for acquisition, especially as it not only had traditions in the industry going back to its earliest days but also held a prominent position in the trade by the early 1970s, with many outlets. Faced by a possible takeover bid from an unwanted source and feeling increasingly vulnerable as a result of the first wave of oil shocks, the firm was receptive to Inchcape's approaches. Persuaded of the benefits which would accrue from an association with Inchcape, Mann Egerton accepted the offer. Again the Group had to move quickly, as the rising value of its shares in a particularly buoyant market allowed it to make a share issue (the largest the Group had yet made for an acquisition) which meant that it was able to purchase the equity at a lower cost in terms of number of shares than had originally been envisaged. The Department of Trade and Industry mentioned the possibility of referring the proposed merger to the Monopolies Commission, but this did not materialise. Lord Stokes, on being approached, agreed to the increasing number of BL outlets controlled by Inchcape, declaring his pleasure at the Group's further strengthening of links. Usually, motor manufacturers prefer to avoid large groups of companies when seeking retail distributors, favouring a large number of smaller concerns, so this agreement may be seen as showing confidence in Inchcape's policy of allowing its subsidiaries considerable autonomy. No counter bids appeared, as only 72 hours elapsed between Inchcape's crucial meeting with Kleinwort Benson (representing Mann Egerton) and the announcement of the offer agreed with the Mann Egerton Board.[27] This final meeting had coincided with the Group's 1973 Annual General Meeting, at which Lord Inchcape announced that further expansion and acquisition possibilities were being considered. When, only three days later, the agreed bid of Mann Egerton was formally announced, a leading city journalist reflected that Lord Inchcape did not waste time between word and deed.

The most far-reaching and extensive acquisition achieved by the Group in the 1970s was that of the Anglo-Thai Corporation.[28] It involved the issue of nearly 9 million Inchcape £1 Ordinary shares, three times the number previously issued in any one acquisition, and resulted in an increase in Inchcape's market value by about 90 per cent. It led to an even greater concentration of Group assets in the Far East and SE

Asia, as seen in Table 10.4. The Group's pre-tax profits jumped from £37m in March 1976 to £73m a year later – a Group record – representing a staggering 89 per cent growth in earnings per share over the previous year. Yet again, the origins of the acquisition of Anglo-Thai, which go back to 1968, may be seen in the context of the Borneo merger, which established the Group's importance in the Far East and the South China Seas. Before the merger with Inchcape the Borneo Company had been interested in Caldbeck Macgregor & Co. Ltd, but on making an approach found it was already committed to Anglo-Thai, in which the Group subsequently began to take an interest, for it was a similarly growing organisation with many interests in common with Inchcape. For the first time in Inchcape's now wide experience in acquiring holdings, the intervention of one particularly uncooperative individual considerably delayed the proceedings. Sir Denys Lowson was in many ways an accomplished entrepreneur, a powerful lawyer, merchant banker and stockbroker, the head of a huge property, industrial and business empire and Lord Mayor of London to boot. Yet he was regarded in the City as not wholly above suspicion, perhaps because of his skilfully managed control of several companies through a system of interlocking shareholdings, comparable in some ways with the manner in which Lord Kylsant maintained such a position of power in the extensive Royal Mail Group.[29] Sir Denys was never brought to trial but was to some extent discredited, resigning from the Anglo-Thai Board in 1974. He had made it clear that he expected certain personal benefits in the event of a merger of the two groups, including a seat on the Inchcape Board. The possibility of Lowson controlling a large block of Inchcape shares was regarded as too distasteful – and worrying – to contemplate. So, as in the case of the Borneo Company, Inchcape continued to build up a significant holding of Anglo-Thai shares to aid it in acquiring the rest of the equity when the time was right. A problem akin to Ford's restrictions on dealerships, which led Inchcape into acquiring Mann Egerton, was to recur in these transactions. This was one of the factors which led to the abandonment of negotiations in December 1974, which had restarted after Sir Denys' resignation.

When the Estates House Investment Trust Ltd (EHIT) was formed by Hill Samuels, bringing together after his death the shares which had been controlled by Sir Denys, it effectively held 45 per cent of the voting power of Anglo-Thai. If these holdings were combined with those acquired by Inchcape, the latter would then have a majority interest in Anglo-Thai. In these circumstances and with a significant rise in Inchcape's share price, the Inchcape Board decided to announce terms

of an offer without prior consultation with Anglo-Thai. This announcement was made on 17 September 1975, the intention to do so having
been communicated to the Anglo-Thai Board and their advisers on the
previous day. The offer documents were dispatched some ten days later.
Incidentally, throughout its programme of acquisitions, the Group
never let the 'excitement of the chase' lead it into imprudent offer terms,
and did not think of suffering 'loss of face' if it was unsuccessful in a
project. So, in making a bid in this case the Inchcape Board was, of
course, aware that if some other company made a higher bid which
Inchcape would not match, the Group would make a good profit on its
10 per cent interest in the voting rights of Anglo-Thai which had already
been accumulated. In this case, a threatened problem with the Group's
debt – equity ratio made a share issue particularly preferable to loan
stock. As expected, the Anglo-Thai Board reacted strongly against the
bid, which had the welcome effect of dissuading other rival approaches,
including those from important Hong Kong groups, such as Jardines.
Once the offer had been made it was proper and possible for Baring's
and Hill Samuel's to discuss matters on behalf of Inchcape and EHIT
respectively and as a result increased terms were agreed which Hill
Samuel's considered acceptable to EHIT and fair to other Anglo-Thai
shareholders. EHIT bound itself irrevocably to accept, with the result
that with Inchcape's own holdings, Anglo-Thai would become a
subsidiary of Inchcape. Consequently opposition from the Anglo-Thai
Board became fruitless and eventually all shareholders were convinced
of the desirability of the merger, through the Inchcape Group's generous
offer and the increased value this placed on their shares, and through the
words of Lord Inchcape himself in his letter which accompanied the
increased offer:

> The great strength of the Inchcape Group lies in its geographical
> spread and diversification of interests. By joining this Group you will
> not only continue to have an investment in the existing activities and
> trading areas of Anglo-Thai, but you will also share in the Inchcape
> Group's expanding operations in many other areas, particularly the
> Middle East and Nigeria, and in a wide range of profitable activities
> into which Anglo-Thai has not ventured.

The takeover was seen by the City and by the financial press as an
excellent overseas acquisition at a reasonable price, adding even more to
the prominence and prestige of the Group as a whole.[30] This rising status
achieved a further boost with the purchase of the 75 per cent remainder

of Bain Dawes,[31] through a share issue second only to that required in the acquisition of Anglo-Thai. Although part of its origins go back to Gray Dawes' Insurance Department in the First World War, the Group had been particularly interested in this firm since 1970, when the Bain Dawes Group was formed, 50 per cent of which was held by Gray Dawes Westray (Holdings) Ltd which was jointly owned by Inchcape and the P & O. Thus the Group effectively owned 25 per cent of Bain Dawes. Neither P & O nor Inchcape would contemplate a situation in which one owned 25 per cent to the other's 75 per cent; eventually it was agreed that Inchcape should acquire all the equity. In a period of dividend restraint, Inchcape had to apply for special permission from the Treasury to almost double its ordinary dividend in the year ended March 1977. Table 10.3 shows the wisdom of this acquisition: insurance broking was to make a large contribution to Group fortunes.

VI

Thus, in 1977, the Group's profits, market capitalisation, growth in earnings of its shares and gross dividend, reached the highest point it had ever achieved. The Harborn loss of that same year, however, mentioned earlier, shook Inchcape severely, and may be seen as a significant turning-point, one of the first things to go wrong. The Group then entered what may be seen as its fifth phase which, like the first, from 1958 to 1966, was marked by processes of consolidation, strengthening, rationalisation and restructuring. The formation of the Group in 1958 brought to a head a period of great change and expansion of the Inchcape family businesses, and a period of several years was then needed to take stock and prepare for the future. In the same way, after the continuing run of major acquisitions ending in 1977 the Group needed time to assimilate its holdings, clarify its new image and define its future strategy. Significantly, the Group increasingly concentrated on developing the profitability of its UK assets, as it did in 1958, and it continued to grow, nevertheless: Gray Mackenzie, an example of a Group company which expanded dramatically from within, became an important port manager and operator in the Gulf. Further successful acquisitions made by existing subsidiaries were Poon's, an industrial and project caterer in the Middle East and Australia, and an associated company, Peschaud & Cie in France, heavy equipment transporters. The famous sailmakers Neil Pryde Ltd, and the Mazda Motor franchise – both in Hong Kong – were added to the Group's portfolio.[32] In 1978 the Group gained the valuable concession of exclusive Toyota distribution in the UK with Pride and Clarke Ltd in which it was first interested as far back as the early 1970s, occasioning the issue of over 1 million shares. This proved a most successful extension of the Group's excellent links with Toyota elsewhere, and was another example of waiting after several years of informal talks until the time was appropriate for this especially important addition to the Inchcape motor interests. It was originally a small, under-developed business which was seen as attractive to the Group because its Toyota concession could be used to offset Inchcape's concentration on BL cars in the UK. Fortunately, the partners, Pride and Clarke, had informal contacts with Dodwell's, and when approached by Inchcape, were able to obtain an independent opinion of the advantages of being a member of the Group. 80 per cent of the Marshall International Trading Co. Inc. was acquired by Inchcape Inc. in the USA. The outstanding remainder of the equity of Assam Investments Limited was added to the Group, together with a group of companies in a new area – South America.[33]

However, for the first time, the Group, by deciding to create a more streamlined image and to concentrate on its core activities, sold some of its more peripheral holdings. A conference, 'Inchcape into the 80s', helped in establishing a corporate definition of the Group, which has emerged as two distinct but related roles:

1. A professional distributor, marketer and seller of the products and technologies of our principals;
2. A skilled provider of technical services.[34]

In order to achieve this rationalisation, firms such as Harborn's in Holland (which had made such heavy losses), Gray Dawes Bank (as banking was not seen as a typical Group activity), Ocean Inchcape (its North Sea oil interests also not regarded as a core Group business) and Joynsons (commodity brokers, not seen as a typical Group interest) were sold. Further reductions in Group holdings were forced upon them by the insistence of foreign governments on larger share-holdings by locals, such as in the case of the reorganisation of Inchcape Berhad in Malaysia, BEWAC in Nigeria, McEnearney–Alston in Trinidad and Gray Mackenzie in the Gulf.

Now, in 1985, the Group is emerging from this period of retrenchment into a new, but different, phase of growth. This was heralded by the acquisition of Transcontinental Services NV, now known as Specialist Services International. At a price of £35m, it is by far the largest Inchcape acquisition to date, and well illustrates the Group's new closely-defined image, with its crude-oil cargo-inspection, loss adjusting, chemical-testing and shipping-agency subsidiaries.[35] This new phase was marked by a change in leadership: Sir David Orr came from Unilever as the new Chairman and George Turnbull arrived from Talbot UK as Group Managing Director. From the period of the Group's gradual formation, its launch into the world, and its achievement of internationally recognised status, Lord Inchcape had personified his company. The use of the single word 'Inchcape' could be used interchangeably as the Group and the man. Yet it is fitting that, typical of the fairness and honourable behaviour of the Group, and the willingness it showed to reduce family holdings when necessary when it sold 25 per cent of its equity to the public in 1958, Lord Inchcape gracefully handed over the reigns of power, by carefully providing for the Group's future prosperity with the particularly appropriate appointment of Sir David.

*   *   *

In conclusion it is clear that the Group's major acquisitions, in original selection and through successful approaches, constantly sustained its growth. No firm really wants to be taken over, if it has the choice – all would like to stay independent, and most firms which subsequently joined larger Groups look back on their independent origins with affection. Inchcape's strength lay in its reputation for being one of the most acceptable bidders possible. Rather than abruptly deliver predatory bids without warning, the Group was prepared gently to woo those companies in which it was interested, and in each case (except that of Anglo-Thai) an essential number of the shareholders concerned agreed to the proposed merger in advance of Inchcape's formal offer. The device of informal meetings with personal contacts was used many times to advantage, and several acquisitions may be seen as the result of a combination of Inchcape wanting a company, and the same company wanting Inchcape. The Group's success in acquiring other businesses is particularly seen in the fact that so many of them were willing to accept Inchcape shares rather than cash.

In the negative sense also, companies would look for a merger with Inchcape to avoid a less desirable takeover. Yet Inchcape's growth may not be seen wholly in terms of its own inner dynamics, forging ahead oblivious of the rest of the world. To a certain extent its phases of growth were influenced by changes in the world economy. The period 1958–66 was a phase of consolidation and retrenchment for the Group partly because of key problems in its areas of activity. In India, tea prices fell after a series of droughts, the India Five Year Plan and government control of the textile industry imposed many restrictions, and the Group lost the Joint Steamer Companies' business. Political uncertainty in East Africa was concomitant with problems in Iran. However, the decade of the Group's great growth which occurred from 1966–7 to 1976–7 (as seen in the tables) was considerably facilitated by boom conditions generally, fast rates of growth and the falling £ sterling. Inchcape's geographical expansion in these years enabled it to take full advantage of the favourable economic climate. Its success, however, was achieved despite continuing difficulties in India, Pakistan and East Africa, the Arab–Israeli conflicts, the uncertainty over the future of the colony of Hong Kong, losses in Ethiopia, political disturbances in Malaysia, high rates of import duty in Thailand and many other international problems. Table 10.4, showing the changing pattern of earnings of different geographical areas of Group activity, reflects these developments. Investment income only was accounted for from India and Pakistan during most of the 1970s, but the region dramatically improved in terms of its contribution to Group profits which is also shown in Table 10.4. The decline in profitability of Inchcape's African holdings, together with a reduction in profits from the Gulf, reflect not only the rise in the Far East and SE Asia as regions of importance to the Group, but internal political difficulties in the former countries. The Group has also accepted, and made the best of, changes imposed on it by foreign governments. The charge of 'exploitation' by foreign companies abroad – an accusation by host-government politicians – is rarely founded. Although the parent company does remit a measure of profits home, the greater part, especially in the case of the Inchcape companies, is always used to finance further expansion locally. It would hardly be in the interests of an international company to impoverish the local population especially if, like Inchcape, they dealt in consumer goods. Governments in host-countries were all powerful. They decided on the terms of entry of a company, the tax situation, the remittance of profits. They had the ultimate right of nationalisation and expropriation. It has been rightly said that 'a company with capital committed overseas is far more like a prisoner than an overmighty subject'.[36] That Inchcape has always been prepared to accept such reductions in its power and profitability, that it has continued its operations despite political and economic change,[37] that, being human, it has made mistakes – yet survived and prospered – is a tribute to its original master plan, and its close adhesion to its early principles and policies, the roots of which may be traced back to its pioneering merchant partnerships of the late eighteenth and nineteenth centuries.

10.1 The Inchcape Board of Directors during the Miners' Strike of 1974: from left to right, Tom Hughes, Ken Gould, Sir Michael Parsons, Peter Heath, Sir Hugh Mackay Tallack, Lord Inchcape, J. M. Sim, Hugh Waters, Bernard Greer and James Ritchie

10.3 Sir David Orr, the present Chairman

10.2 The Third Lord Inchcape

NOTES

1. Calculated from *The Times*, 14 March 1977. The share price quoted on 31 March 1975 was based on the shares of the company after further capitalisation issues, shown in the notes accompanying Table 10.2.
2. See Chapter 4.
3. *Far Eastern Economic Review*, 9 August 1984, p. 51, and *Inchcape Archives, [IA]* files on non-current holdings, Harborn Ltd.
4. See Chapter 3.
5. See Appendix of Principal Subsidiaries and Associated Companies, which also shows the year in which these businesses were acquired.
6. *History of Acquisitions (HA)* Internal Memo, November 1980, note 18.
7. See note 3.
8. See *The Times of Inchcape, 1958–1983*, 25th anniversary supplement to the *Inchcape Magazine*, no. 16 (September 1983) interview with Mr H. C. Waters, p.1.
9. Ibid.
10. Inchcape & Co. Limited, *Annual Report and Accounts*, 30 September 1959.
11. *HA*, note 8.
12. See the author's 'The Decline of British Maritime Enterprise in Australia: The Example of the Australasian United Steam Navigation Company, 1887–1961', *Business History*, vol. 27, no.1 (March 1985) pp.59–74.
13. *HA*, note 7.
14. *HA*, note 9, interview with Mr H. C. Waters, 30 July 1984, and *IA*, Borneo Company merger files.
15. With the BCL merger, the number of subsidiaries of Inchcape & Co. Limited increased from forty-one in 1966 to seventy-nine in 1967. Inchcape & Co. Limited, *Annual Report and Accounts*, September 1966, pp.2–4 and November 1967, pp.2–6. These companies, excluding those since sold, are shown in the Appendix of Principal Subsidiaries, as businesses joining the Group in 1967.
16. See note 14.
17. For every five Ordinary shares in the Borneo Company the holder received three £1 Inchcape shares each, £5 in 8 per cent unsecured loan stock 1987–90 and a 8½ per cent redeemable preference share of £1. The capital increase this represented was calculated as being nearly 34 per cent of the value of the Borneo shares; and the income increase was estimated at nearly 22 per cent. *HA*, note 9.
18. *HA*, notes 10 and 10A.
19. See the letter by Lord Inchcape explaining the nature and significance of this new subsidiary, 7 October 1968.
20. *HA*, note 11.
21. See Chapter 4.
22. Tanzanian compensation was agreed at £650 000 plus interest at 6 per cent of £167 780, making a total of £817 780 payable over five years. The first instalment was paid in June 1969 and the balance was subsequently received in full by the Group. *HA*, note 6.
23. *HA*, note 12.
24. *HA*, note 15.
25. Sime Darby, through Rothschilds, might have been prepared to offer the

equivalent of £15.25 per Dodwell share, compared with Inchcape's £12.80, but in fact this approach was too late. Of the Dodwell acquisition, *HA* note 15 records that 'in Hong Kong it was described as a *coup* and it was stated that it could only have been the speed of the transaction and the early acceptances that left other likely contenders on the sidelines'.

26. At first, Inchcape considered Ford dealers, such as Bristol Street Motors, *HA*, Note 26. Throughout the Group's programme of acquisitions, some of these companies were informally approached but confidentiality and lack of space prohibits discussion of negotiations which were not successfully pursued. Many companies, public and private and concerned with many activities in many countries were investigated, and time and trouble spent on this was never considered wasted. See *HA*, Notes 20 to 29.

27. Inchcape's offer placed a value of over £17m on the equity of Mann Egerton. Its shareholders thus enjoyed an increase in the capital value of their holdings of 60 per cent and an increase in income of just under 55 per cent. *HA*, note 16.

28. *HA*, note 17 and *IA*, Anglo-Thai merger files.

29. See Edwin Green and Michael Moss, *A Business of National Importance: The Royal Mail Group* and the author's book review in *The Journal of Transport History*.

30. In the Anglo-Thai merger, as in the case of many of its previous acquisitions, the Inchcape Group was considerably assisted by its advisers, especially Barings. Until 1977, membership of Lord Inchcape's support team in major acquisition proposals (whether successful or discontinued) included Sir Hugh Mackay Tallack, H. C. Waters and (after the Borneo merger) Peter Heath. Many others, such as Donald Caswell as Company Secretary and Oliver Brooks as Finance Director, contributed significantly.

31. *HA*, note 14.

32. Inchcape & Co. Limited, *Annual Report and Accounts*, March 1977, pp. 8–11.

33. Ibid, and 1978, 1979, 1980, 1981.

34. Inchcape PLC, *Report and Accounts*, December 1983. Chairman's Statement pp.6–8. This rationalisation has been considerably assisted by the organisation of the Group into Strategic Units, or SBUs. See letter to the board by Lord Inchcape, March 1981.

35. See Appendix.

36. W. J. Reader, *Business and Society: A Unilever Educational Booklet*, (London, 1969).

37. For example, Inchcape was one of the few international companies to continue trading in the People's Republic of China after the Cultural Revolution.

APPENDIX 10.1 Directors, past and present, of Inchcape plc, 1958–84

Date appointed	Name	Actual date of retirement, resignation, etc.
10 October 1958	The Earl of Inchcape	—
10 October 1958	*Arnold T. Orr Deas	Retired 31 March 1964
10 October 1958	Alan Mackay	Resigned 31 March 1963
10 October 1958	The Lord Craigmyle	Retired 8 July 1983

Date appointed	Name	Actual date of retirement, resignation, etc.
23 October 1958	*Sir William C. Currie	Died 3 July 1961
23 October 1958	The Viscount Simon	Retired 31 March 1973
15 January 1959	*Howard F. Morford	Died 25 December 1963
15 January 1959	Angus Mackinnon	Retired 4 September 1981
1 February 1960	Sir Gilbert Laithwaite	Retired 31 March 1969
25 August 1960	Hamilton Shedden	Retired 31 December 1967
25 August 1960	Hugh C. Waters	Retired 14 September 1977
14 September 1961	(Archibald) William Giles	Retired 31 March 1977
1 April 1962	John M. Sim	Retired 4 October 1982
1 April 1962	*Robert E. Castell	Retired 31 March 1969
1 April 1962	*Henry C. Bannerman	Retired 31 March 1965
20 December 1962	Captain (Oswald) Nigel Bailey	Resigned 31 March 1970
1 April 1963	Sir Hugh Mackay Tallack	Retired 30 September 1982
1 October 1964	*John C. Goodman	Retired 31 December 1967
1 October 1964	Neil A. Campbell	—
22 December 1966	The Lord Tanlaw	—
5 January 1967	The Earl of Ranfurly	Retired 8 July 1983
5 January 1967	Ian L. MacEwen	Retired 30 October 1970
5 January 1967	*Field Marshall Sir Gerald Templer	Retired 31 October 1969
5 January 1967	(Edward) Peter Heath	Retired 30 September 1979
5 January 1967	James A. Donald	Resigned 31 May 1968
5 January 1967	Robert A. Henderson	—
1 January 1969	Bernard R. T. Greer	Retired 30 September 1974
1 December 1970	*Charles S. Noble	Retired 31 December 1972
1 December 1970	*James M. H. Millington-Drake	Died 31 January 1983
1 December 1970	*Oliver Brooks	Resigned 30 June 1973
1 November 1971	(Harold) Peter Foxon	Retired 30 September 1984
1 November 1971	Kenneth Gould	Retired 31 December 1981
1 November 1971	Sir (John) Michael Parsons	Retired 31 March 1981
1 November 1971	James W. Ritchie	—
2 June 1972	*Jeffrey H. Hamm	Retired 30 June 1974
24 May 1973	*Sir William Luce	Died 7 July 1977
1 August 1973	Tom Hughes	Retired 30 September 1981
1 July 1974	Sir Edward F. Studd, Bt.	—
1 July 1974	*George G. D. Carter	Retired 31 December 1977
1 January 1978	Peter Baring	—
1 January 1978	Sir Eric G. Norris	—
1 January 1980	(Derek) Roy Davies	Resigned 31 January 1984
1 January 1981	Gilbert Holdsworth	—
1 April 1981	Peter J. S. Lumsden	—
15 September 1981	Sir (John) Rae McKaig	—
1 September 1982	Sir David A. Orr	—

APPENDIX 10.1—_continued_

Date appointed	Name	Actual date of retirement, resignation, etc.
1 November 1983	Peter Laister	—
1 March 1984	Alistair A. Macaskill	—
1 March 1984	(Hugh D.) Stacey Ellis	—
1 September 1984	George Henry Turnbull	—

* deceased.

NOTE The titles and decorations of the directors have been omitted on the grounds that if they were all included, this list would be excessively long and complicated. The reader is referred to _Who's Who_, _Debrett's Peerage_, _Burke's Peerage_, and the Public Relations Department at Inchcape PLC.

APPENDIX 10.2 A Note on Inchcape Group Interests in India, 1958–84

Although India was the Group's most important geographical area of activity in 1958, only one company now remains of this once large commercial empire in India. The abolition of the managing agency system in the 1960s, later followed by the stipulation that all foreign companies should sell substantial holdings to Indians, undermined these businesses considerably.

52 per cent of Binny's, the large textile firm, was sold in the mid-1960s to Indian interests. Severe labour troubles, disastrous floods and low textile prices then brought this company to near-bankruptcy, and Inchcape sold its remaining 28 per cent holding in 1983.

In 1974, Macneill & Barry Ltd was merged with Williamson Magor Ltd to become Macneill & Magor Ltd, the largest tea agency company in North East India. Inchcape retained a 27 per cent interest, but subsequently disposed of this to Williamson Tea Investments Ltd. In the meantime, however, the Group's sterling tea interests had been reconstructed to form the Assam Company (India) Ltd, and this was to become the main Group concern in India. Under local legislation, 26 per cent was then sold on the Indian market. In 1980 the Inchcape Group bought, for £4m, the remaining 61 per cent of its UK holding company, The Assam Company Ltd, a shrewd move which has subsequently paid off, especially with the recent increase in tea prices and recovery of the Indian economy. But of the traditional British managing agency houses of India, none now survive.*

* Based partly on a paper, 'Historical Notes on the Inchcape Group in India and its Future', prepared by Lord Inchcape in January 1985, and suggestions by Sir Michael Parsons in a letter to Lord Inchcape dated 17 March 1985. See Map 2 for location of these businesses.

Conclusion

All the businesses which have been considered in these pages are remarkable for one thing: they survived. In many cases for more than a century, they passed through many phases of growth and contraction, adhesion to old activities and changes to new, opening new branches and closing down old ones. They took advantage of favourable economic conditions, and suffered from adverse factors in world trade.

The element of luck in this survival has been powerful. More than anything, the companies prospered through simply being at the right place at the right time, especially in their critical early days. In this respect, they were aided by two principal developments: the aim of British politicians to establish a presence in as many parts of the world as possible, and the enormous expansion in international trade, dominated by Europe.

In extending the representation of British interests overseas, the home government was reluctant to expend large sums in setting up garrisons of soldiers and diplomatic establishments in foreign cities or in stationing fleets of naval ships at foreign ports. Instead, the establishment of independent British merchant houses, enjoying small subsidies through the award of mail contracts to British shipping companies, was seen as an inexpensive and convenient way of ensuring that British interests were represented. Mail contracts were the instruments which Sir William Mackinnon employed in founding his network of merchant and shipping-agency partnerships in India, the Gulf, East Africa and Australia, linked to their home bases in London and Glasgow.

When countries of the Far East and the South China Seas finally opened their doors to foreigners, British trading firms were to help to establish a vital footing, especially when other Western powers were equally keen to make their presence felt. A particularly good example of this process of the flag following trade rather than *vice versa* was the British commercial dominance of Sarawak. This could never have become a semi-colonial outpost through the efforts of the Rajah alone. Only the monopolistic position enjoyed by the Borneo Company in the development of the Sarawak economy consolidated and strengthened his power and influence throughout the land. In many cases the British governments were slow to show initiative in these matters; only the direct fear of other Western powers securing greater influence overseas stimulated them into financing the practical encouragement of trade. This is seen in the anxiety of British politicians over possible Russian ambitions in the Gulf, and German imperialist designs on East Africa.

These subsidies alone, especially as they were rarely generous, were insufficient to sustain these businesses for any length of time. It was the growth in world trade which provided the fuel for their subsequent expansion, for at least until the outbreak of the First World War, the continuing increase in world trade far outpaced world industrial output. The predominant feature of trading in this period was the export of manufactured goods from Europe (especially Britain) in exchange for primary products from developing countries. The large and constant demand for shipping space brought by this trade ensured a steady flow of commissions to the agents of the shipping lines, including many of the companies considered here. The dominance of British tonnage, especially with the emergence of the steamship (by 1914, Britain owned more than the rest of the world's tonnage put together), combined with her successful free trade policy, worked to the advantage of the owners of British ships and their agents, the producers of British export goods and British importers of foreign raw materials. In this sense, Britain was more successful than any other country. Her position as the most important exporter of manufactured goods to non-European primary producers, aided by the fact that for much of the nineteenth century she was also the world's largest foreign lender, gave her a vital trade surplus to stimulate growth even further.

Although the rate of expansion of world trade slowed down between the wars, these features persisted to a considerable extent. Europe's dominance had declined from almost two-thirds of world trade to just over a half, but her manufactures still found ready markets in developing countries, which still concentrated on raw material exports rather than on processed products. As we have seen, the wars disrupted trade within Europe, but they encouraged its growth between Europe and the rest of the world. The Second World War especially boosted the profits of many of these businesses. The level of world trade was the main factor behind their growth. The flourishing years of the 1960s and early 1970s were essential to the spectacular growth of the Group after it was formed in 1958. The depressed state of the world economy in the late 1970s and early 1980s was then reflected in the Group's relative stagnation. The recent recovery in world trading is similarly shown in its performance in the past year, 1984.

The help of subsidies, in the early days especially, together with a favourable economic climate, undoubtedly aided these businesses but it did not stop many others from going to the wall. Their role as middlemen rather than manufacturers and owners of transport was a further advantage. They operated on small inputs of capital, working and fixed, with few employees and expenses. Until recent times, they were able to avoid the necessity of raising capital from outside shareholders and having to pay out dividends. The fact that most of these firms were dominated by one or only a few families ensured a loyalty on the part of the partners and employees which sustained them through hard times. As representatives of a large number of British (and sometimes foreign) principals, in distributing a wide range of products, they were able to widen their risks and prevent dependence on unpredictable fluctuations in demand and supply. Most of these businesses maintained several branches in more than one country, putting their eggs in as many baskets as possible.

Flexibility in operating also helped to maintain prosperity. These businesses responded quickly to economic change. For example, the growth in demand for Far Eastern goods such as silk and tea in the USA and Canada, prompted Dodwell to initiate a trans-Pacific steamer service. When the demand for China teas fell, Gilmans, in looking for an alternative line of business, cashed in on the popularity of joss sticks in Southern China by importing sandalwood from Australia. The demand for motor cars in Malaysia in the 1920s and 1930s stimulated the Borneo Company into entering the vehicle distribution business. The same trend lay behind Dodwell's establishment of a motor subsidiary in Hong Kong. The unprecedented need for khaki to clothe troops during the Second World War was quickly recognised in Binny's textile mills. Similarly, Gray Mackenzie extended its activities in line with the opportunities offered by the oil boom. Again, the firms found themselves in the right place at the right time, but also they knew how to capitalise on their advantages.

The survival of these businesses into the 1950s and 1960s was often made possible through their determination to remain small, independent units; but the political and economic changes of the 1950s and 1960s made it unlikely that they could profitably continue in this way. By joining the Inchcape Group, whether as a founder company in 1958 or as a later acquisition, they could enjoy the best of both worlds. They had the stability and security of being members of a large group of companies, but were still able to reap the advantages of being autonomous units with their own traditions and hard-earned goodwill intact. The appreciation of their histories by Lord Inchcape and his team, and their successors, thus preserved the original businesses intact and stimulated their future growth. This awareness is also reflected, in quite a different way, in the Group's support of the study presented here.

Appendix   Principal Subsidiaries and Associated Companies of Inchcape PLC, 31 December 1984, Showing Proportion of Nominal Value of Shares Held, Interest in Equity, Activities and When Joined the Group

Shares held are ordinary or unclassified *Shares held directly by Inchcape PLC,* *or its nominees are marked**	*Country of* *incorporation*	*Proportion* *of nominal* *value of* *shares held* *%*	*Effective* *interest* *of Inchcape* *PLC in* *% equity*	*Year* *joined* *Inchcape* *Group*
Africa				
Kenya				

Mackenzie (Kenya) Limited
   Intermediate holding company
   owners of Karirana Estates Limited
   (tea producers)
	Kenya	100	100	1958

Ethiopia				
The Motor & Engineering Company of Ethiopia Limited	Ethiopia	94	94	1968
Motor vehicle distributors and general merchants				
The Americas				
United States of America				
Inchcape Inc.		100	100	1979
Intermediate holding company				
Caleb Brett USA Inc.		100	100	1984
Cargo inspection and testing	all			
Marshall Electronics Inc.	incorporated	100	99	1979
Exporters and importers/	in USA			
assemblers of medical equipment				
and hospital supplies				
Flight Accessory Services Inc.		100	100	1974
Maintenance of aircraft hydraulics and landing gear				
Canada				
Inchcape Canada Inc.	Canada	100	100	1972
Intermediate holding company, also				

Shares held are ordinary or unclassified Shares held directly by Inchcape PLC, or its nominees are marked*	Country of incorporation	Proportion of nominal value of shares held %	Effective interest of Inchcape PLC in % equity	Year joined Inchcape Group
trading in the name of Universal Fastening & Concrete Accessories as builders merchants and distributors of fasteners, concrete accessories and power tools				
Incan Ships Limited	Canada	57	57	1973
Ship owners and operators				
Chile				
Williamson Agrocomercial SA		100	100	1982
Distributors of tractors and				
industrial hardware	all			
Embotelladora (Williamson) Talca SA	incorporated	100	100	1982
Embotelladora (Williamson) SA	in Chile	96	96	1982
Bottlers of soft drinks				
Colombia				
Tracey y Compania SA	Columbia	100	100	1981
General merchants and motor vehicle distributors				
Ecuador				
Compania Ecuatoriana del Té CA		100	100	1984
Tea producers	all			
Quito Motors SA	incorporated			
Comercial e Industrial	in Ecuador	68	68	1981
Motor vehicle distributors				
SA Comercial Anglo Ecuatoriana		100	100	1981
Insurance and shipping agents and having interests in motor vehicle assembly and distribution				
Panama				
Gatun Investments SA	Panama	70	70	1981
Intermediate holding company having interests in warehousing, distribution and shipping agencies				
Peru				
Milne y Compania SA	Peru	100	100	1981
Shipping agents and distributors of motor vehicles, agricultural equipment				
Cipsa-Comercial Peruana SA	Peru	100	100	1981
Distributors of agricultural, forestry and industrial equipment				

Shares held are ordinary or unclassified Shares held directly by Inchcape PLC, or its nominees are marked*	Country of incorporation	Proportion of nominal value of shares held %	Effective interest of Inchcape PLC in % equity	Year joined Inchcape Group
Bermuda				
Inchcape (Bermuda) Limited	Bermuda	100	100	1971
Finance company				
Australasia				
Australia				
Macdonald Hamilton & Co. Pty. Limited		100	100	1962
Shipping agents, travel agents, import and export agents and marine and general engineers				
Macdonald Hamilton Services Limited		100	100	1963
General services to the mining industry in Australia				
Poon Brothers (WA) Pty. Limited		100	100	1976
Industrial and mining project caterers and administrators	all incorporated			
Caldbeck Macgregor (Australia) Limited	in Australia	100	100	1981
Intermediate holding company				
Taylor Ferguson & Co. Pty. Limited		100	100	1978
Importers and distributors of wines and spirits				
Sandalford Wines Pty. Limited		68	68	1979
Wine producers				
Bain Dawes Pacific Limited		87	87	1980
Insurance brokers and agents				
New Zealand				
Bain Dawes (NZ) Limited	New Zealand	100	100	1976
Insurance brokers and agents				
Fiji				
Marine Pacific Limited	Fiji	100	100	1970
Marine operators and salvors				
Far East				
Hong Kong				
Inchcape (Hong Kong) Limited		100	100	1963
Inchcape Enterprises Limited		65	65	1970
Caldbeck International Limited		100	100	1967
Intermediate holding companies				
Gibb Livingston & Company Limited		100	100	1967
General merchants and insurance agents				
Gilman and Company Limited		100	100	1969
General merchants, Lloyds agents, insurance agents and shipping agents				

Shares held are ordinary or unclassified *Shares held directly by Inchcape PLC, or its nominees are marked**	*Country of incorporation*	*Proportion of nominal value of shares held %*	*Effective interest of Inchcape PLC in % equity*	*Year joined Inchcape Group*
Dodwell Hong Kong Limited General merchants, shipping agents, Exporters and retailers	all incorporated in	100	100	1972
Crown Motors Limited Motor vehicle concessionaires and distributors	Hong Kong	100	100	1967
Caldbeck Macgregor (Hong Kong) Limited Importers and distributors of wines and spirits		100	100	1975
Hong Kong Reinsurance & General Insurance Company Limited Reinsurance and general insurance		100	100	1966
Malko General Agencies (Hong Kong) Limited General merchants		68	43	1977
China				
Inchcape (China) Limited Consultants	Hong Kong	100	100	1983
Japan				
Dodwell and Company Limited (Branch) General merchants, shipping agents and insurance agents	Great Britain	100*	100	1972
Caldbeck Kabushiki Kaisha Importers and distributors of wines and spirits	Japan	100	100	1975
Eurobridge Limited Shipping Agents	Hong Kong	60	60	1972
Guam				
Atkins, Kroll Inc. Motor vehicle distributors and general merchants	Guam	100	100	1974
India				
The Assam Company (India) Limited Tea Producers	India	74	74	1974
Middle East				
Gray, Mackenzie & Company Limited Intermediate holding company and managing agents	Great Britain	100	100	1958

Shares held are ordinary or unclassified Shares held directly by Inchcape PLC, or its nominees are marked*	Country of incorporation	Proportion of nominal value of shares held %	Effective interest of Inchcape PLC in % equity	Year joined Inchcape Group
Gray Mackenzie Marine Services EC Managers and operators of marine craft	Bahrain	100	100	1980
Redmack Industrial Services EC Industrial cleaning, maintenance and waste disposal services	Bahrain	100	100	1982

South East Asia
Malaysia, Singapore and Brunei

Inchcape Berhad	Singapore	63	63	1967
Inchcape (Singapore) Private Limited	Singapore	100	63	1967
Inchcape (Brunei) Sendirian Berhad	Brunei	100	63	1967
Malinch Associate Holdings Sendirian Berhad	Malaysia	100	63	1980
Kumpulan Inchcape Sendirian Berhad	Malaysia	60	38	1983

Intermediate holding companies with subsidiaries trading under the following names:

The Borneo Company 1967

Anglo French Trading Company 1977

Equatron 1978

Moutrie 1980

Optorg 1978
Borneo Motors (Singapore) 1967
Orchard Motors 1967
NBT (Brunei) 1977
B-Trak 1977

Distributors of consumer products, technical, engineering, industrial and marine products and equipment, photographic and office equipment and supplies, agricultural chemicals and fertilisers; shipping agents, freight forwarders and travel and insurance agents

Motor vehicle distributors, engineers and repairers

Industrial Resources Limited Hire purchase finance	Brunei	100	44	1984
Kontrak Manufacturing Services Sendirian Berhad	Malaysia	100	38	1977
Contract Manufacturing Services Private Limited		100	63	1977
Manufacturers of pharmaceutical products, toiletries and cosmetics				
Caldbeck Macgregor (Singapore) Private Limited		100	100	1976

Shares held are ordinary or unclassified Shares held directly by Inchcape PLC, or its nominees are marked*	Country of incorporation	Proportion of nominal value of shares held %	Effective interest of Inchcape PLC in % equity	Year joined Inchcape Group
Importers and distributors of wines, spirits and tobacco				
Heli Orient (Private) Limited	all	100	100	1979
Distributors and service agents for helicopters, fixed wing aircraft and allied equipment	incorporated in Singapore			
Intrans Distribution Services				
Private Limited		100	63	1977
Warehousemen and distributors				
Bork Singapore Private Limited		100	63	1984
Manufacturers of sliced veneers				
Thailand				
Inchcape Thailand Limited		100	100	1981
Management company				
The Borneo Company (Thailand)				
Limited		100	100	1967
General merchants, Lloyd's agents, insurance agents, shipping agents, travel agents, airport traffic handling agents, photofinishers and processors and packers of cosmetics				
Borneotech Limited		100	100	1967
Engineering merchants	all			
Jawa Manufacturing Limited	incorporated	100	100	1967
Manufacturing of pharmaceutical products and cosmetics	in Thailand			
Anglo-Thai Motors Limited		100	100	1975
Motor vehicle distributors				
Anglo-Thai (Thailand) Limited		100	100	1975
Specialists in engineering products, security and telecommunications equipment				
Caldbeck Macgregor (Thailand)				
Limited		100	100	1975
Importers and distributors of wines and spirits				
United Kingdom and Europe				
United Kingdom				
Inchcape Overseas Limited		100*	100	1978
Inchcape UK Limited		100*	100	1980
Intermediate holding companies				
Bain Dawes PLC		100	100	1976
Lloyd's insurance brokers and				

Shares held are ordinary or unclassified. Shares held directly by Inchcape PLC, or its nominees are marked*	Country of incorporation	Proportion of nominal value of shares held %	Effective interest of Inchcape PLC in % equity	Year joined Inchcape Group
underwriting agents and holding company for the Bain Dawes group				
Duncan Macneill & Company Limited		100*	100	1958
Intermediate holding company for Group investments in India, consultants on tea production and tea marketing agents				
Gray Dawes Travel Limited		100	100	1967
Travel agents				
Gray Mackenzie Overseas Limited	all	100	100	1981
Port management consultants	incorporated			
with subsidiaries providing	in			
technical engeneering services	Great			
for oilfield supply bases	Britain			
Inchcape Export Limited		100	100	1967
Export and import merchants				
Agricultural & Chemical Products Limited		100	100	1968
Export and import merchants and distributors				
Harcourt Shipping Agency Limited		100	100	1978
Freight forwarders and warehousemen				
Rucker & Slann Limited		100	100	1968
Dealers, agents and brokers in commodities and produce				
Mann Egerton and Company Limited		100*	100	1973
Motor vehicle distributors, contract hirers and manufacturers of contract furniture				
Toyota (GB) Limited		100*	100	1978
Motor vehicle concessionaires and distributors				
Specialist Services International Limited		100	100	1984
Holding company for the Specialist Services International group of companies providing cargo inspection, testing, loss adjusting and shipping services				
Caleb Brett & Son Limited		100	100	1984
Cargo inspection and testing				
Gellatly Hankey & Co. Limited		100	100	1984
Shipping services				
Graham Miller & Co. Limited		100	100	1984
Loss adjusters				

Shares held are ordinary or unclassified Shares held directly by Inchcape PLC, or its nominees are marked*	Country of incorporation	Proportion of nominal value of shares held %	Effective interest of Inchcape PLC in % equity	Year joined Inchcape Group
Belgium International Motor Company SA Motor vehicle concessionaires and distributors	Belgium	100	100	1979
Holland Caleb Brett & Son (Continental) BV Cargo inspection and testing	Holland	100	100	1984

A number of subsidiaries have been omitted on the grounds that they do not materially contribute to the profit or assets of the Group.

Principal associated companies and activities, showing proportion of equity held by the Group, effective interest in equity and particulars of capital, with activities

	Proportion of equity held by Group %	Effective interest of Inchcape PLC in equity %	Particulars of issued share and loan capital
Africa *Kenya* Mercantile Finance Co. Limited Finance Company	45	45	912 631 Ordinary Shares of Kenya shillings 20 each
Far East *China* Toyota Motor Services (China) Co. Limited Motor Vehicle Servicers	50	50	400 000 Shares of HK$1 each
The Motor Transport Company of Guang Dong and Hong Kong Limited	19	12	18 000 Shares of HK$500 each

Shares held are ordinary or unclassified Shares held directly by Inchcape PLC, or its nominees are marked*	Country of incorporation	Proportion of nominal value of shares held %	Effective interest of Inchcape PLC in % equity	Year joined Inchcape Group
Motor bus owners and operators Both incorporated in Hong Kong				
Hong Kong InchRoy Credit Corporation Limited Hire purchase finance		30	30	2 000 000 Shares of HK$10 each
Japan Dodwell Pitney Bowes Kabushiki Kaishi Distributors of business machines		50	50	200 000 Ordinary Shares of Yen 500 each
Middle East *Abu Dhabi* Gray Mackenzie & Partners (Abu Dhabi) Limited Managing agents for company operating as shipping agents and general merchants Incorporated in Hong Kong		49	49	40 000 000 Shares of HK$1 each
Redmack Industrial Services (Abu Dhabi) Limited Industrial cleaning, maintenance and waste disposal services		49	49	25 000 Ordinary Shares of dirhams 100 each
Bahrain Bahrain Maritime & Mercantile International BSC (C) Shipping and tanker agents, general merchants, Lloyd's agents, insurance brokers and agents, lightermen, travel agents and freight forwarders		48	48	5 400 000 Shares of Bahraini dinar 1 each
Dubai Gray Mackenzie & Partners (Central Emirates) Private Limited Managing agents for company operating as shipping agents and general merchants in Dubai, Ajman, Sharjah and Umm-Al-Qwain		49	49	25 000 Ordinary shares of dirhams 1000 each
Kuwait Kuwait Maritime & Mercantile Co.		49	49	200 000 Ordinary

Shares held are ordinary or unclassified Shares held directly by Inchcape PLC, or its nominees are marked*	Country of incorporation	Proportion of nominal value of shares held %	Effective interest of Inchcape PLC in % equity	Year joined Inchcape Group
KSC Shipping agents and general merchants				shares of Kuwaiti dinar 1 each
Oman Oman United Agencies LC General merchants, lightermen and travel agents		49	49	60 000 Ordinary shares of Omani rials 10 each
Ras Al Khaimah Ras Al Khaimah Port Services Private Limited Port operators		49	49	20 000 Ordinary shares of dirhams 100 each
Saudi Arabia Marine and Transportation Services (Saudia) Limited Port and marine operators		50	50	2000 Shares of Saudi ryals 1000 each
South East Asia *Malaysia* Sebor (Sabah) Sendirian Berhad General merchants		40	25	6 150 000 Ordinary shares of M$1 each
Sebor (Sarawak) Sendirian Berhad General merchants		40	25	6 133 333 Ordinary shares of M$1 each
Kuching Hotels Sendirian Berhad Hotel owners		49	31	11 500 000 Ordinary shares of M$1 each
Timuran Holdings Berhad Holding company for Eastern Agencies (Malaysia) Sendirian Berhad, general merchants and Caldbeck Macgregor (Malaysia) Sendirian Berhad, importers and distributors of wines and spirits		49	49	30 000 000 Ordinary shares of M$1 each
SK Timber Corporation Sendirian Berhad Timber extractors		45	29	16 000 000 Ordinary shares of M$1 each
Singapore Rolex Singapore Private Limited Distributors and service agents for watches		49	31	5 000 000 Ordinary shares of S$1 each

Companies listed above have been treated in the Accounts as 'associated companies' for the purpose of the statement of standard accounting practice no. 1 (revised) issued by the Accounting Standards Committee of The Institute of Chartered Accountants in England and Wales – see *Report and Accounts*. A number of companies in which the Group has not less than 20 per cent of the equity have been omitted from the above list on the grounds that to include them would produce particulars of excessive length in relation to their importance. This appendix lists only the principal subsidiaries and associated companies. the complete list includes 823 businesses, operating in sixty-seven countries. Those countries not mentioned above are: Angola, Austria, the Bahamas, Bangladesh, Brazil, Cameroun, Channel Islands, Caribbean, Denmark, Djibouti, France, Gabon, Germany, Greece, Iran, Italy, Ivory coast, Lebanon, Liechtenstein, Luxembourg, Macau, Malta, Mexico, Netherlands Antilles, New Caledonia, New Hebrides, Nigeria, Norway, Philippines, Papua New Guinea, Portugal, South Africa, Spain, Sudan, Switzerland, Taiwan, Tanzania, Uganda, UAE and Zimbabwe.

SOURCE Inchcape PLC, Report and Accounts, 31 December 1984, pp. 45–53.

Companies owned by the Group and subsequently sold

The Aquacultural Insurance Services Ltd	1981
Affin Credit (Malaysia) Sdn Bhd	1979
American Hardwood Co. Ltd	1981
Assembly Services Sdn Bhd	1982
Assistance International Ltd	1984
PT Austral Byna	1979
Automotive Industries Sdn Bhd	1982
Aviation Finance Ltd	1980
BAII Leasing Service Ltd	1984
Bahrain Slipway Co. Ltd	1980
Bain Dawes (East Anglia) Ltd	1982
Bain Dawes Sagese SA	1979
JK Bayne Ltd	1983
Binny (London) Ltd	1982
Bishopsgate Businesscare Ltd	1984
Bishopsgate Holidaycare Ltd	1984
Bishopsgate Insurance PLC	1984
Bishopsgate Services Ltd	1984
Bishopsgate Travel Ltd	1984
Bishopsgate Travel Care Ltd	1984
Borneo Motors (Malaysia) Sdn Bhd	1982
Boyup Brook Sawmills Pty Ltd	1983
Cappers Finance Pty Ltd	1979
Caribbean Investments Ltd	1983
Comprehensive International Freight Forwarders Ltd	1983

Companies owned by the Group and subsequently sold—*continued*

Crown Motors Services China Co. Ltd	1980
Dolfra Services Ltd	1981
Estate Care Property Management Ltd	1984
Freudenberg Export GmbH	1980
Garsia Investments Ltd	1981
PT Garsia Sumatra Timber	1981
Gladesville Holdings Pty Ltd	1983
Gray Dawes Bank Gp	1983
Harborn Group	1983
Harborn (Rotterdam) BV	1980
Harvey Trinder (Victoria) Pty Ltd	1979
Hughes Ltd	1982
Inchcape Chemco Ltd	1980
Joynson Group	1983
Jurong Alloys Pte Ltd	1979
PT Kahajan Timber	1981
Leadenhall Insurance PLC	1984
Management Computer Services Sdn Bhd	1978
Mann Egerton Electrical Ltd	1982
Manufacturing Associates Pte Ltd	1980
D. J. Millars Pty Ltd	1983
Millars (W.A.) Pty Ltd	1983
MISC Agencies KK	1983
Motor Imports Co. Ltd	1983
Moutrie & Co. (Hong Kong) Ltd	1979
NBT (Malaysia) Sdn Bhd	1982
NBT (Sarawak) Sdn Bhd	1982
Neil Pryde USA	1979
Pacific Hardwood Products Ltd	1984
Photoluxe Industries Ltd	1982
Peschaud Compania del Paraguay SA	1979
Ras-al-Khaimah Port Services	1981
Recter en van der Veere BV	1980
Richmond Packaging Pte Ltd	1980
St Louis Car Inc	1978
Sarawak Properties Sdn Bhd	1982
Shaw & Co. (Life Pension) Ltd	1984
Territory Timber and Hardware Pty Ltd	1983
Trinder Investment (NG) Pty Ltd	1978
Tung Tai Trading Ltd	1983
Vernat Eastern Agencies Ltd	1981
Young Nichol & Co. Ltd	1979

Companies owned by the Group and subsequently liquidated

Aedon Ltd	1979
The African Mercantile Company (Overseas) Ltd	1980
Ammo Power Tool & Drilling Co. (1975) Ltd	1980
Aronstead (Batley) Ltd	1979
AUSN (Australia) Pty Ltd	1982
A. W. Bain (Insurance Brokers) Ltd	1982
Bain Dawes & Gomez Castelazo SA	1980
Bain Dawes (Aviation Reinsurance Brokers) Ltd	1982
Bain Dawes (Construction Insurance Brokers) Ltd	1982
Bain Dawes (Energy Insurance Brokers) Ltd	1982
Bain Dawes Italia SRL	1982
Bain Dawes Tasmania Pty Ltd	1983
Bain Dawes S.A. Pty Ltd	1983
Bain Dawes W.A. Pty Ltd	1983
W. S. Bate Ltd	1983
BEWAC (Mansfield) Ltd	1983
BMR (Malaysia) Sdn Bhd	1981
Borderline Navigation Co. Ltd	1979
Borneo Berhad	1980
The Borneo Company (Malaysia) Sdn Bhd	1983
Borneo Motors (Brunei) Ltd	1981
Botswoods Ltd	1979
Bristol-Saunders Sales Ltd	1978
Bristol Tractors Ltd	1978
Frank Bull's Garage (Successors) Ltd	1978
Butler & Webster Ltd	1983
Champion Motors (Malaysia) Sdn Bhd	1983
Chemco International Ltd	1980
Columbia Wood Products Co. Ltd	1979
Cresswell Pomeroy Ltd	1982
Daihatsu Belgium SA	1982
Diploma International Ltd	1982
DTC (Macau) Ltd	1980
Duncan Roberts (Malaysia) Sdn Bhd	1981
Eastern Automobiles (Colchester) Ltd	1980
Edie Alluvials Ltd	1980
Ekholm Wood Products (Sweden) Ltd	1979
Engineering Supplies (Asia) Ltd	1979
Equatron (Malaysia) Sdn Bhd	1981
Export Traders Ltd	1981
Fartex Ltd	1979
Forcast Foundries Ltd	1978
Forest Management Consultant Ltd	1978
Forest Marketing Services (1976) Ltd	1983
Franchet et Vasel SA	1981
Garsin Timber Industries (France) Ltd	1979

Companies owned by the Group and subsequently liquidated—*continued*

Greyfriars Vehicle Contracts Ltd	1979
Goldsash Sales Ltd	1979
Haadyai Bowling Co. Ltd	1982
Hamshaws of Lincolnshire Ltd	1978
H. A. Hamshaw Ltd	1980
Harborn Commodities SARL	1981
Harvey Trinder (NSW) Pty Ltd	1979
Heli Orient Bahrein	1980
I. B. Nominees Ltd	1980
Inchcape Malaysia Sdn Bhd	1983
Inchcape Management (Services) Pte Ltd	1981
Indonesian Industrial Services Ltd	1981
G. W. Joynson & Co. (Ireland) Ltd	1979
Kanga Timber (Australia) Ltd	1978
Kenya Livestock & Estates Ltd	1980
Klaus Tropical Timber (Germany) Ltd	1980
Labtest Taiwan Ltd	1981
Lachenal Timber Development (Switzerland) Ltd	1978
Limoon Far East Ltd	1983
J. H. Little Engineering Ltd	1982
Lighting & Leisure Industries Ltd	1982
Mann Egerton (Finance) Ltd	1980
Marianas Agencies Inc.	1982
Melinga Mining & Finance Co. Pty Ltd	1981
Metal Castings Exp. Pty Ltd	1983
Michigan Timber Co. Ltd	1979
F. Mitchell (Nottingham) Ltd	1979
Molson Ltd	1979
Montor Pte. Ltd	1978
Morkell & Carnhill Ltd	1979
F. H. Moss (Garages) Ltd	1980
Motor Associates Pte Ltd	1980
Motor Investments Bhd	1983
Muang Rare Ruamtoon Co Ltd	1982
The North Borneo Trading Co. (Borneo) Ltd	1983
H. E. Nunn & Co. Ltd	1980
H. E. Nunn (Bury St. Edmunds) Ltd	1978
H. E. Nunn (Manchester) Ltd	1978
H. E. Nunn (Norwich) Ltd	1978
Nunns Finance Ltd	1978
G. Oberdan & Co. Pty Ltd	1983
Okura Investments Co. Ltd	1978
Pacific and Atlantic Investment Co. Ltd	1983
Pacific Biomed Supplies Inc.	1981
Padstow Holdings Pty Ltd	1980
Pan United Agencies Pte Ltd	1979
Pedroni Hardwood Timber	1978

Philippine Lumber Products Co. Ltd	1980
Plus Lighting Ltd	1979
Poon Brothers Pty Ltd	1978
Poon (Singapore) Pty Ltd	1980
Property Associates Pte Ltd	1981
Rejang Transport Co. Sdn Bhd	1980
RMA Ltd	1982
Royal Motor Company SA	1982
Samols Latimer (Sales) Ltd	1979
Sheerlite Engineering Ltd	1979
Sheerlite Trident Ltd	1979
M. Singer Hardware Ltd	1979
F. G. Smith (Motors) Ltd	1980
Smithco Saipan Inc.	1981
Smiths Hotel & Restaurant Supply co. Ltd	1981
Steel & Cripps Ltd	1982
Trafalgar Wood Products Ltd	1979
Triumph Wood Products Ltd	1979
The Warden Finance Co. Ltd	1978
Universal Concrete Accessories (1975) Ltd	1980
Westbound Timber Co. Ltd	1979
Wroughton Carding Co. Ltd	1984

Select Bibliography

I PRIMARY SOURCES

The Inchcape Archives, at the time of writing located at the Group's London
Head Office at 40 St Mary Axe, London EC3A 8EU, were the principal primary
source for this study. The vast majority of these records have never previously
been consulted by historians. In addition to the corporate and financial material
usually preserved as a matter of course by most companies, these archives, which
relate to over 100 separate businesses, include a particularly rich collection of
notebooks, correspondence, contemporary memoirs and photographs.

The inevitable gaps due to the inconsistent survival of documentation and the
imbalance between the different companies in this respect was partially made
good from a variety of other sources. The BI–P&O Collection held by the
National Maritime Museum at Greenwich and Woolwich includes much
informative correspondence relating to the firms who acted as agents for these
lines. The Zanzibar National Archives, which were consulted with the kind
permission of the Ministry of Education, Culture and Sport, added significantly
to the story of Smith Mackenzie & Co. in Chapter 4.

Other primary material to which reference has been made includes commercial directories and almanacs, many of which are preserved in the British Library
and the Institute of Historical Research of the University of London. The
Lloyd's Collection at the Guildhall Library, London, provided vital quan-
titative detail about shipping entrances and clearances. Contemporary newspapers, such as the *North China Herald* and the *China Mail*, were consulted at
the British Library's Newspaper Library at Colindale. Reports on the economies
of many of the countries discussed here, together with correspondence relating
to the granting of mail contracts, were found among the Parliamentary Papers.
The Foreign and Commonwealth Offices' series at the Public Record Office at
Kew provided background material to aspects of British trading overseas,
particularly relating to the Persian Gulf and East Africa. The India Office
Library also yielded similar information. For the modern period, details of
current businesses were investigated at the City Business Library in Basinghall
Street.

II SECONDARY SOURCES

These have been divided into two sections: books and mss relating directly to
Inchcape companies, and more general works on the subject of international

trading, pertaining to particular countries or the world as a whole. The latter section is intended as a general guide only and does not attempt to list all the secondary sources used in the writing of the present work. The notes to each chapter contain full references, including place and date of publication, at the first mention of each book or article to which reference is made in that chapter.

On Inchcape Companies

Antrobus, H. A., *A History of the Assam Company, 1839–1953* (Edinburgh, 1957)

Binny & Co. Ltd, *The House of Binny* (London, 1969).

Blake, George, *Gellatly's 1862–1962* (London, 1962).

Bolitho, Hector, *James Lyle Mackay: First Earl of Inchcape* (London, 1936).

Borneo Company Limited, The, *Sixty Years Trade in Bangkok, 1856–1926* (Bangkok, 1926).

Brame, Alfred, *The India General Steam Navigation Company Limited* (London, 1900).

Dodwell & Co. Ltd, *The House of Dodwell: A Century of Achievement, 1858–1958* (London, 1958).

Griffiths, P. J., *A History of the Inchcape Group* (London, 1977).

Griffiths, P. J., *The Joint Steamer Companies* (London, 1979)

Hunt, Wallis, *Heirs of Great Adventure: The History of Balfour Williamson & Co. Ltd.* vol. I, 1851–1901 and vol. II 1901–51 (London, 1951).

Jones, Stephanie, 'British India Steamers and the Trade of the Persian Gulf, 1862–1914' in *The Great Circle, the Journal of the Australian Association for Maritime History*, 7, 1 (1985).

Jones, Stephanie, 'The Decline of British Maritime Enterprise in Australia: The Example of the Australasian United Steam Navigation Company Limited, 1887–1961', *Business History*, XXVII, 1 (1985).

Jones, Stephanie, 'George Benjamin Dodwell: A Shipping Agent in the Far East, 1872–1909', *The Journal of Transport History*, 6, 1 (1985).

Laxon, W. A., 'The Eastern Mails: The Story of the Eastern and Australian Steamship Co. Ltd', *Sea Breezes* (1963).

Longhurst, Henry., *The Borneo Story: the First Hundred Years of the Borneo Company Limited* (Londo, 1956).

McKellar, N. L., *From Derby Round to Burketown: the AUSN Story* (Queensland, 1977).

Smith Mackenzie & Co. Ltd, *The History of Smith Mackenzie & Co. Ltd* (London, 1937).

Mss. histories of Inchcape Companies include those by George Blake on Mackinnon Mackenzie & Co.; W. O. Elder and Anthony Goodinge on the Anglo-Thai Corporation, Edward Hopkins on Gray Mackenzie & Co., C. Johnson on the India General and Charles Noble on Gray Mackenzie & Co.

General Works

Allen, G. C. and Donnithorne, Audrey., *Western Enterprise in Far Eastern Economic Development* (London, 1954).

Bach, John, *A Maritime History of Australia* (Melbourne, 1976).

Blake, George, *The Ben Line: The History of a Merchant Fleet, 1825–1955* (London, 1956).

Blake, George, *BI Centenary: 1856–1956* (London, 1956).

Broeze, Frank, 'Underdevelopment and Dependency: Maritime India During the Raj', *Modern Asian Studies* 18, 3 (1984).

Bruce, C. A., 'Report on the Manufacture of Tea, and the Extent and Produce of Tea Plantations in Assam', *Asiatic Society of Bengal Journal*, 8 (1839).

Cain, P. J., *Economic Foundations of British Overseas Trade, 1815–1914* (London, 1980).

Case, Margaret H., *South Asian History, 1750–1950: A Guide to Periodicals, Dissertations and Newspapers* (Princeton, 1968).

Checkland, S. G., *The Gladstones: a Family Biography, 1764–1851* (Cambridge, 1971).

Chirol, Valentine, *The Middle Eastern Question, or Some Problems of Indian Defence* (London, 1903).

Cowan, C. D., *The Economic Development of China and Japan* (London, 1964).

Crisswell, Colin N., *The Taipans: Hong Kong's Merchant Princes* (Hong Kong, 1981).

Curzon, George, *Persia and the Persia Question* (London, 1892).

Farnie, D. A., *The English Cotton Industry and the World Market, 1815–1896* (Oxford, 1979)

Foreman-Peck, James, *A History of the World Economy* (Brighton, 1983).

Galbraith, J. S., *Mackinnon and East Africa, 1878–1892: A Study in the 'New Imperialism'* (Cambridge, 1972).

Gibson, J. F., *Brocklebanks 1700–1950* (Liverpool, 1953)

Griffiths, P. J., *The British Impact on India* (London, 1952)

Griffiths, P. J., *A History of the Indian Tea Industry* (London, 1967)

Hannah, Leslie, *The Rise of the Corporate Economy* (London, 1983) 2nd edn.

Harcourt, Freda, 'The P & O Company: Flagships of Imperialism', in Sarah Palmer and Glyndwr Williams (eds) *Charted and Uncharted Waters: Proceedings of a Conference on the Study of Maritime History* (London, 1982).

Hopkins, A. G., 'Imperial Business in Africa: Part I, Sources' and 'Part II, Interpretations', *Journal of African History*, XVII, 1 (1976) and XVII, 2 (1976).

Jones, Geoffrey, *The State and the Emergence of the British Oil Industry* (London, 1981).

Kelly, J. B., *Britain and the Persian Gulf, 1795–1880* (Oxford, 1969).

Kenwood, A. G. and Lougheed, A. I., *The Growth of the International Economy, 1820–1960* (London, 1971).

Keswick, M. (ed.), *The Thistle and the Jade: A Celebration of Jardine, Matheson & Co.* (London, 1982)

Landen, Robert Goran, *Oman Since 1856* (Princeton, 1967)

Lorimer, J. G., *Gazetteer of the Persian Gulf, Oman and Central Arabia* (Calcutta, 1908–15).

MacGregor, D. R., *The China Bird: The History of Captain Killick and One Hundred Years of Sail and Steam* (London, 1961).

Marriner, Sheila. and Hyde, Francis. E., *The Senior: John Samuel Swire, 1825–1898* (Liverpool, 1967).

Mathias, Peter, *The First Industrial Nation: An Economic History of Britain, 1700–1914* (London, 1969).

Mitchell, B. R., *International Historical Statistics: Africa and Asia* (London, 1982).

Munro, J. F., *Africa and the International Economy, 1800–1960* (London, 1976).

Munro, J. Forbes, 'Scottish Business Imperialism: Sir William Mackinnon and the Development of Trade and Shipping in the Indian Ocean', *ESRC Report* B00/23/0049 (1984).

Munro, J. Forbes, 'Sir William Mackinnon', in *Dictionary of Scottish Business Biography* (Aberdeen, forthcoming).

Musk, G., *Canadian Pacific: The Story of the Famous Shipping Line* (Newton Abbot, 1984).

Nicholas, Stephen J., 'The Overseas Marketing Performance of British Industry, 1870–1914', *Economic History Review*, XXXVII (1984).

Thurston, Anne, 'Kenya and East Africa: Sources in British Official Records', unpublished ms. (1982).

Tuson, Penelope, *A Brief Guide to Sources for Middle East Studies in the India Office Records* (London, 1982).

Wright, A. (ed.) *Southern India: its History, Peoples, Commerce and Resources* (London, 1914–15).

Wright, A. (ed.) *Twentieth Century Impressions of Hong Kong, Shanghai and Other Treaty Ports* (London, 1908).

Index

NOTE: where relevant, sub-entries are in chronological order